A More Perfect Union

A More Perfect Union

DOCUMENTS IN U.S. HISTORY

FIFTH EDITION

Volume 2: Since 1865

Paul F. Boller, Jr.

Professor Emeritus, Texas Christian University

Ronald Story

University of Massachusetts, Amherst

HOUGHTON MIFFLIN COMPANY

Boston New York

To Martin and Eliza

Sponsoring Editor: Colleen Kyle
Associate Editor: Leah Strauss
Senior Project Editor: Christina M. Horn
Senior Production/Design Coordinator: Carol Merrigan
Assistant Manufacturing Coordinator: Andrea Wagner
Senior Cover Design Coordinator: Deborah Azerrad Savona
Senior Marketing Manager: Sandra McGuire

Cover Design: Wing Ngan/Stoltze Design
Cover Image: © Michael Nevros/© FOLIO, Inc.

Copyright © 2000 by Houghton Mifflin Company. All rights reserved.

No part of this work may be reproduced or transmitted in any form or by any means, electronic or mechanical, including photocopying and recording, or by any information storage or retrieval system without the prior written permission of the copyright owner unless such copying is expressly permitted by federal copyright law. With the exception of nonprofit transcription in Braille, Houghton Mifflin is not authorized to grant permission for further uses of copyrighted selections reprinted in this text without the permission of their owners. Permission must be obtained from the individual copyright owners as identified herein. Address requests for permission to make copies of Houghton Mifflin material to College Permissions, Houghton Mifflin Company, 222 Berkeley Street, Boston, MA 02116-3764.

Printed in the U.S.A.

Library of Congress Catalog Card Number: 99-72019

ISBN: 0-395-95959-4

23456789-CS-03 02 01 00

Contents

Chapter Three

Industry, Expansion, and Reform

Chapter Seven

Contemporary Times

Preface

Our two-volume reader, *A More Perfect Union: Documents in U.S. History,* presents students with the original words of speeches and testimony, political and legal writings, and literature that have reflected, precipitated, and implemented pivotal events of the past four centuries. The readings in Volume I cover the era from Columbus's voyage of discovery to Reconstruction. Volume II begins with the post–Civil War period and concludes with selections that relate to recent history. We are pleased with the reception that *A More Perfect Union* has received, and we have worked toward refining the contents of this new edition.

Nearly a third of the material is new to this edition. New selections in Volume I include, for example, the rules and regulations of seventeenth-century Harvard, a description of the Great Awakening by Jonathan Edwards, addresses by labor organizer Ely Moore and Transcendentalist poet and essayist Ralph Waldo Emerson, and a freshly edited version of Roger B. Taney's *Dred Scott* decision of 1857. Among the new selections in Volume II are a suffragist Declaration of Principles and statements by Theodore Roosevelt on taxation, George C. Marshall on rebuilding postwar Europe, and Representative Barbara Jordan on the impeachment of Richard Nixon.

The readings in these volumes represent a blend of social and political history, along with some cultural and economic trends, suitable for introductory courses in American history. We made our selections with three thoughts in mind. First, we looked for famous documents with a lustrous place in the American tradition—or the Gettysburg Address, for example, or Franklin D. Roosevelt's First Inaugural Address. These we chose for their great mythic quality, as expressions of fundamental sentiments with which students should be familiar. Second, we looked for writings that caused something to happen or had an impact when they appeared. Examples include the Virginia slave statutes, Thomas Paine's *The Crisis,* the Emancipation Proclamation, and Earl Warren's opinion in *Brown* v. *Board of Education of Topeka*—all of them influential pieces, some of them famous as well. Third, we looked for documents that seem to reflect important attitudes or developments. Into this group fall the writings of Upton Sinclair on industrial Chicago and of Martin Luther King, Jr., on Vietnam. In this category, where the need for careful selection from a wide field was most apparent, we looked especially for thoughtful pieces with a measure of fame and influence. Horace Mann's statement on schools reflected common attitudes; it also caused something to happen and is a well-known reform statement. We have also tried to mix a few unusual items into the stew, as with the "Report of the Joint Committee on Reconstruction" and a letter from a Catholic nun in early Colorado.

We have edited severely in places, mostly when the document is long or contains extraneous material or obscure references. We have also, in some cases, modernized spelling and punctuation.

Each document has a lengthy headnote that summarizes the relevant trends of the era, provides a specific setting for the document, and sketches the life of the author. In addition, "Questions to Consider" guide students through the prose and suggest ways of thinking about the selections.

We would like to thank the following people who reviewed the fifth edition manuscript for one or both volumes: Kurk Dorsey, University of New Hampshire; Paul G. Faler, University of Massachusetts at Boston; Richard H. Peterson, San Diego State University.

We would also like to thank the following people who reviewed the manuscript in prior editions: John K. Alexander, University of Cincinnati; June G. Alexander, University of Cincinnati; Judith L. Demark, Northern Michigan University; Harvey Green, Northeastern University; Ben Rader, University of Nebraska at Lincoln; C. Elizabeth Raymond, University of Nevada–Reno; Thomas Templeton Taylor, Wittenberg University; and John Scott Wilson, University of South Carolina.

We owe a debt of gratitude to Laura Ricard, our editorial assistant for this edition. We also wish to express our appreciation to the editorial staff of Houghton Mifflin Company for their hard and conscientious work in producing these volumes.

P. F. B.
R. S.

A More Perfect Union

A girl teaches her mother to read in the postwar South. (Division of Political History, Smithsonian Institution, Washington, D.C.)

CHAPTER ONE

Reconstructing the Union

1. Klansmen of the Carolinas

   Report of the Joint Committee on Reconstruction (1872)

2. A Kind of Unity

   What the Centennial Ought to Accomplish (1875)
   SCRIBNER'S MONTHLY

3. Aftermath

   Address to the Louisville Convention (1883)
   FREDERICK DOUGLASS

1

Klansmen of the Carolinas

Reconstruction developed in a series of moves and countermoves. In a white Southern backlash to Union victory and emancipation came the "black codes" for coercing black laborers and President Andrew Johnson's pardon of Confederate landowners. Then in a Northern backlash to these codes and pardons came the Civil Rights bills, the sweeping Reconstruction Acts of 1867, and the Fourteenth and Fifteenth Amendments, all designed to guarantee black political rights. White Southerners reacted to these impositions in turn with secret night-time terrorist or "night rider" organizations designed to shatter Republican political power. Congress tried to protect Republican voters and the freedmen with the Force Acts of 1870 allowing the use of the army to prevent physical assaults, but Northern willingness to commit troops and resources to the struggle was waning. By the mid-1870s only three states remained in Republican hands, and within three years racist Democrats controlled these, too. The night riders had turned the tide.

Although numerous secret societies for whites appeared in the Reconstruction South—including the Order of the White Camelia (Louisiana), the Pale Faces (Tennessee), the White Brotherhood (North Carolina), and the Invisible Circle (South Carolina)—the largest and most influential society, and the one that spawned these imitators, was the Ku Klux Klan, the so-called Invisible Empire. The Klan began in Tennessee in 1866 as a young men's social club with secret costumes and rituals similar to those of the Masons, the Odd-Fellows, and other popular societies. In 1867, however, following passage of the Reconstruction Acts, anti-Republican racists began to see the usefulness of such a spookily secret order, and the Klan was reorganized to provide for "dens," "provinces" (counties), and "realms" (states), all under the authority of a "Grand Wizard," who in 1867 was believed to have been Nathan B. Forrest, a former slave trader and Confederate general.

The Klan structure was probably never fully established because of the disorganized conditions of the postwar South. Other societies with different names emerged, and the Reconstruction-era "Ku-Klux" may have disbanded as a formal entity in the early 1870s. But it clearly survived in spirit and in loosely formed groups, continuing to terrorize Republicans and their allies among the newly enfranchised freedmen into the 1870s and sowing fear among the black families who composed, after all, the labor force on which the white planters still depended. The excerpt reprinted below includes congressional testimony by David Schenck, a member of the North Carolina Klan seeking to portray it in the best possible light, followed by testimony from Elias Hill, a South Carolina black man victimized by a local "den" of the Klan. Schenck and Hill were testifying before a joint Senate-House committee concerned with antiblack terrorism.

Questions to Consider. The oath taken by David Schenck emphasizes the Klan's religious, constitutional, and benevolent qualities, whereas Elias Hill's story reveals its terrorist features. Are there elements in the Klan oath that seem to hint at or justify the use of violence? Why does the oath contain the phrases "original purity," "pecuniary embarrassments," and "traitor's doom"? What "secrets of this order" could deserve death? Klansmen later claimed that because they could terrorize the superstitious freedmen simply by using masks, odd voices, and ghostly sheets, no real violence was necessary. Opponents have claimed, on the other hand, that Klansmen were basically sadists acting out sexual phobias and deep paranoia. What light does Elias Hill's testimony shed on these conflicting claims? What position did Hill hold in the black community? Did the Klansmen seem to be assaulting him because of his condition or because of his position in the black community? Why did they ask Hill to pray for them? Would it be fair or accurate to call the Ku Klux Klan a terrorist organization that succeeded?

Report of the Joint Committee on Reconstruction (1872)

A select committee of the Senate, upon the 10th of March, 1871, made a report of the result of their investigation into the security of person and property in the State of North Carolina. . . . A sub-committee of their number proceeded to the State of South Carolina, and examined witnesses in that State until July 29. . . .

From *Report of the Joint Select Committee to Inquire into the Condition of Affairs in the Late Insurrectionary States* (Government Printing Office, Washington, D.C., 1872), 25–27, 44–47.

A North Carolina Ku Klux Klan meeting to plan the murder of a black Republican, from an 1871 engraving in a New York publication. Although the artist imagined the scene, he managed to convey both the bizarre and spooky garb of the Klan members and the defenselessness and terror of the lone kneeling freedman. The Klan victimized not only former slaves suspected of supporting the Republican party but also freedmen who managed to obtain land or learn to read and write. (Library of Congress)

David Schenck, esq., a member of the bar of Lincoln County, North Carolina . . . was initiated in October, 1868, as a member of the Invisible Empire. . . . In his own words: "We were in favor of constitutional liberty as handed down to us by our forefathers. I think the idea incorporated was that we were opposed to the [fourteenth and fifteenth] amendments to the Constitution. I desire to explain in regard to that that it was not to be—at least, I did not intend by that that it should be—forcible resistance, but a political principle."

The oath itself is as follows:

> I, (name,) before the great immaculate Judge of heaven and earth, and upon the Holy Evangelist of Almighty God, do, of my own free will and accord, subscribe to the following sacred, binding obligation:
>
> I. I am on the side of justice and humanity and constitutional liberty, as bequeathed to us by our forefathers in its original purity.
>
> II. I reject and oppose the principles of the radical [Republican] party.
>
> III. I pledge aid to a brother of the Ku-Klux Klan in sickness, distress, or pecuniary embarrassments. Females, friends, widows, and their households shall be the special objects of my care and protection.
>
> IV. Should I ever divulge, or cause to be divulged, any of the secrets of this order, or any of the foregoing obligations, I must meet with the fearful punishment of death and traitor's doom, which is death, death, death, at the hands of the brethren. . . .

Elias Hill of York County, South Carolina, is a remarkable character. He is crippled in both legs and arms, which are shriveled by rheumatism; he cannot walk, cannot help himself . . .; was in early life a slave, whose freedom was purchased by his father. . . . He learned his letters and to read by calling the school children into the cabin as they passed, and also learned to write. He became a Baptist preacher, and after the war engaged in teaching colored children, and conducted the business correspondence of many of his colored neighbors. . . . We put the story of his wrongs in his own language:

"On the night of the 5th of May, after I had heard a great deal of what they had done in that neighborhood, they came . . . to my brother's door, which is in the same yard, and broke open the door and attacked his wife, and I heard her screaming and mourning. I could not understand what they said, for they were talking in an outlandish and unnatural tone, which I had heard they generally used at a negro's house. They said, 'Where's Elias?' She said, 'He doesn't stay here; yon is his house.' I had heard them strike her five or six licks. Someone then hit my door. . . .

"They carried me into the yard between the houses, my brother's and mine, and put me on the ground. . . . 'Who did that burning? Who burned our houses?' I told them it was not me. I could not burn houses. Then they hit me with their fists, and said I did it, I ordered it. They went on asking me didn't I tell the black men to ravish all the white women. No, I answered them. They struck me again. . . . 'Haven't you been preaching and praying about the Ku-Klux? Haven't you been preaching political sermons? Doesn't a [Republican Party newspaper] come to your house? Haven't you written letters?' Generally one asked me all the questions, but the rest were squatting over me—some six men I counted as I lay there. . . . I told them if they would take me back into the house, and lay me in the bed, which was close adjoining my books and papers, I would try and get it. They said I would never go back to that bed, for they were going to kill me. . . . They caught my leg and pulled me over the yard, and then left me there, knowing I could not walk nor crawl. . . .

"After they had stayed in the house for a considerable time, they came back to where I lay and asked if I wasn't afraid at all. They pointed pistols at me all around my head once or twice, as if they were going to shoot me. . . . One caught me by the leg and hurt me, for my leg for forty years has been drawn each year, more and more, and I made moan when it hurt so. One said, 'G–d d—n it, hush!' He had a horsewhip, [and] I reckon he struck me eight cuts right on the hip bone; it was almost the only place he could hit my body, my legs are so short. They all had disguises. . . . One of them then took a strap, and buckled it around my neck and said, 'Let's take him to the river and drown him.' . . .

"Then they said, 'Look here! Will you put a card in the paper to renounce all republicanism? Will you quit preaching?' I told them I did not know. I said that to save my life. . . . They said if I did not they would come back the next week and kill me. [After more licks with the strap] one of them went into the house where my brother and sister-and-law lived, and brought her to pick me up. As she stooped down to pick me up one of them struck her, and as she was carrying me into the house another struck her with a strap. . . . They said, 'Don't you pray against Ku-Klux, but pray that God may forgive Ku-Klux. Pray that God may bless and save us.' I was so chilled with cold lying out of doors so long and in such pain I could not speak to pray, but I tried to, and they said that would do very well, and all went out of the house. . . ."

Satisfied that he could no longer live in that community, Hill wrote to make inquiry about the means of going to Liberia. Hearing this, many of his neighbors desired to go also. . . . Others are still hoping for relief, through the means of this sub-committee.

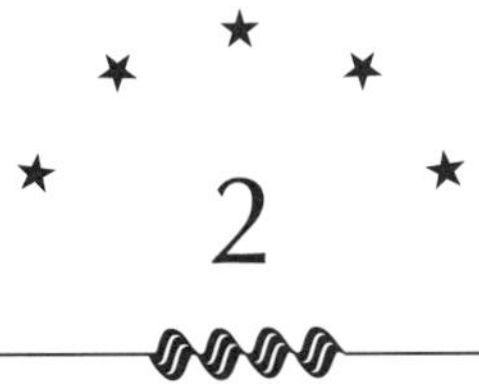

A Kind of Unity

Despite Congress's seizure of control over Reconstruction policy and Ulysses S. Grant's defeat of Andrew Johnson for the presidency in 1868, Radical Reconstruction—the garrisoning of the South, the disfranchisement of former rebels, and the control of Southern state governments by Republican votes—did not last long in most places. During President Grant's first term of office, the white-dominated Democratic Party gained control of North Carolina, Tennessee, and Virginia, the three ex-Confederate states with the lowest percentage of black population. During Grant's second term, Democrats seized control of Alabama, Arkansas, Georgia, Mississippi, and Texas. That left Republican governments (and federal troops) in Florida, Louisiana, and South Carolina, three states with large black populations.

Those states mattered greatly in national politics. During the election of 1876 both parties resorted to fraud. Two sets of electoral returns came in from the three states, and it was necessary for Congress to set up an electoral commission to decide whether Rutherford B. Hayes, the Republican candidate, or Samuel J. Tilden, the Democratic standard bearer, had won. By a strict party vote of 8 to 7, the commission awarded all 20 disputed electoral votes to the Republicans. Hayes became president, with 185 votes to Tilden's 184. In the end, Southern Democrats reached a compromise with Northern Republicans. The Democrats agreed to accept the commission's decision and the Republicans promised to withdraw the remaining federal troops from the South. In April 1877, the last federal soldiers left the South. Solid Democratic control—and stepped-up measures to disfranchise black voters—quickly followed.

Although political maneuvering was important in finally killing Republican Reconstruction, the underlying reason it died was simply that Northerners were losing the will to suppress an increasingly violent white South. The nation's approaching centennial celebration in 1876 triggered an especially strong outpouring of sentiment in favor of improving sectional feelings by withdrawing the troops, even if withdrawal meant the resurgence of the Democratic Party. That, in turn, would permit an overdue rebonding of the century-old republic.

The following unsigned editorial ran in the August 1875 issue of *Scribner's Monthly,* an influential, generally Republican, New York magazine. It expressed, with unusual eloquence, this emotional yearning for peace.

Questions to Consider. What was the occasion of the *Scribner's* editorial? Was this a natural time to consider troop withdrawals? What, in the view of the editor, was the major accomplishment of the Civil War? What specific political theory had been tested and defeated? When addressing the "men of the South," was the editor speaking to all Southern men? What did the phrase "brotherly sympathy" mean? Was it naive or was it realistic for the writer to think that the upcoming centennial could "heal all the old wounds" and "reconcile all the old differences"? Would Abraham Lincoln have agreed with the spirit of this editorial?

What the Centennial Ought to Accomplish (1875)

SCRIBNER'S MONTHLY

We are to have grand doings next year. There is to be an Exposition. There are to be speeches, and songs, and processions, and elaborate ceremonies and general rejoicings. Cannon are to be fired, flags are to be floated, and the eagle is expected to scream while he dips the tip of either pinion in the Atlantic and the Pacific, and sprinkles the land with a new baptism of freedom. The national oratory will exhaust the figures of speech in patriotic glorification, while the effete civilizations of the Old World, and the despots of the East, tottering upon their tumbling thrones, will rub their eyes and sleepily inquire, "What's the row?" The Centennial is expected to celebrate in a fitting way—somewhat dimly apprehended, it is true—the birth of a nation.

Well, the object is a good one. When the old colonies declared themselves free, they took a grand step in the march of progress; but now, before we begin our celebration of this event, would it not be well for us to inquire whether we have a nation? In a large number of the States of this country there exists not only a belief that the United States do not constitute a nation, but a theory of State rights which forbids that they ever shall become one. We hear about the perturbed condition of the Southern mind. We hear it said that multitudes there are just as disloyal as they were during the civil war. This, we believe, we are justified in denying. Before the war they had a theory of State rights. They fought to establish that theory, and they now speak

From *Scribner's Monthly* 10 (August 1875), 509–510.

Miss Liberty's torch. A display at the great 1876 Centennial Exposition, Philadelphia. (Samuel Castner Collection/Free Library of Philadelphia)

of the result as "the lost cause." They are not actively in rebellion, and they do not propose to be. They do not hope for the re-establishment of slavery. They fought bravely and well to establish their theory, but the majority was against them; and if the result of the war emphasized any fact, it was that *en masse* the people of the United States constitute a nation—indivisible in constituents, in interest, in destiny. The result of the war was without significance, if it did not mean that the United States constitute a nation which cannot be divided; which will not permit itself to be divided; which is integral, indissoluble, indestructible. We do not care what theories of State rights are entertained outside of this. State rights, in all the States, should be jealously guarded, and, by all legitimate means, defended. New York should be as jealous of her State prerogatives as South Carolina or Louisiana; but this theory which makes of the Union a rope of sand, and of the States a collection of petty nationalities that can at liberty drop the bands which hold them together, is forever exploded. It has been tested at the point of the bayonet. It went down in blood, and went down for all time. Its adherents may mourn over the fact, as we can never cease to mourn over the events which accompanied it, over the sad, incalculable cost to them and to those who opposed them. The great point with them is to recognize the fact that, for richer or poorer, in sickness and health, until death do us part, these United States constitute a nation; that we are to live, grow, prosper, and suffer together, united by bands that cannot be sundered.

Unless this fact is fully recognized throughout the Union, our Centennial will be but a hollow mockery. If we are to celebrate anything worth celebrating, it is the birth of a nation. If we are to celebrate anything worth celebrating, it should be by the whole heart and united voice of the nation. If we can make the Centennial an occasion for emphasizing the great lesson of the war, and universally assenting to the results of the war, it will, indeed, be worth all the money expended upon and the time devoted to it. If around the old Altars of Liberty we cannot rejoin our hands in brotherly affection and national loyalty, let us spike the cannon that will only proclaim our weakness, put our flags at half-mast, smother our eagles, eat our ashes, and wait for our American aloe to give us a better blossoming.

A few weeks ago, Mr. Jefferson Davis, the ex-President of the Confederacy, was reported to have exhorted an audience to which he was speaking to be as loyal to the old flag of the Union now as they were during the Mexican War. If the South could know what music there was in these words to Northern ears—how grateful we were to their old chief for them—it would appreciate the strength of our longing for a complete restoration of the national feeling that existed when Northern and Southern blood mingled in common sacrifice on Mexican soil. This national feeling, this national pride, this brotherly sympathy *must be restored;* and accursed be any Northern or Southern man, whether in power or out of power, whether politician, theorizer, carpet-bagger, president-maker or plunderer, who puts obstacles in the way of such a restoration. Men of the South, we want you. Men of the South, we long for the restoration of your peace and your prosperity. We would see your cities thriving, your homes happy, your plantations teeming with plenteous harvests, your schools overflowing, your wisest statesmen leading you, and all causes and all memories of discord wiped out forever. You do not believe this? Then you do not know the heart of the North. Have you cause of complaint against the politicians? Alas! so have we. Help us, as loving and loyal American citizens, to make our politicians better. Only remember and believe that there is nothing that the North wants so much today, as your recognition of the fact that the old relations between you and us are forever restored—that your hope, your pride, your policy, and your destiny are one with ours. Our children will grow up to despise our childishness, if we cannot do away with our personal hates so far, that in the cause of an established nationality we may join hands under the old flag.

To bring about this reunion of the two sections of the country in the old fellowship, should be the leading object of the approaching Centennial. A celebration of the national birth, begun, carried on, and finished by a section, would be a mockery and a shame. The nations of the world might well point at it the finger of scorn. The money expended upon it were better sunk in the sea, or devoted to repairing the waste places of the war. Men of the South, it is for you to say whether your magnanimity is equal to your valor—whether you are as reasonable as you are brave, and whether, like your old chief, you accept that definite and irreversible result of the war which makes you and yours forever members of the great American nation with us. Let us see to it, North and South, that the Centennial heals all the old wounds, reconciles all the old differences, and furnishes the occasion for such a reunion of the great American nationality, as shall make our celebration an expression of fraternal good-will among all sections and all States, and a corner-stone over which shall be reared a new temple to national freedom, concord, peace, and prosperity.

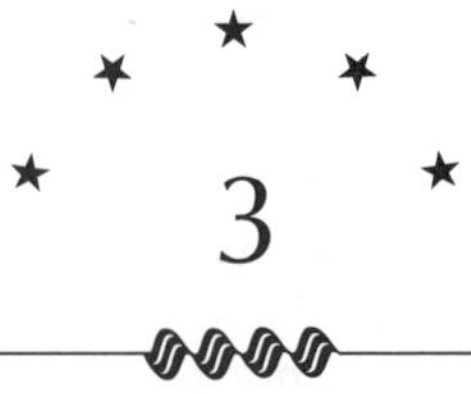

AFTERMATH

Fredrick Douglass regarded the Declaration of Independence as a "watchword of freedom." But he was tempted to turn it to the wall, he said, because its human rights principles were so shamelessly violated. A former slave himself, Douglass knew what he was talking about. Douglass thought that enslaving blacks fettered whites as well and that the United States would never be truly free until it ended chattel slavery. During the Civil War, he had several conversations with Lincoln, urging him to make emancipation his major aim. He also put unremitting pressure on the Union army to accept black volunteers, and after resistance to admitting blacks into the army gave way, he toured the country encouraging blacks to enlist and imploring the government to treat black and white soldiers equally in matters of pay and promotion.

Douglass had great hopes for his fellow blacks after the Civil War. He demanded they be given full rights—political, legal, educational, and economic—as citizens. He also wanted to see the wall of separation between the races crumble and see "the colored people of this country, enjoying the same freedom [as whites], voting at the same ballot-box, using the same cartridge-box, going to the same schools, attending the same churches, travelling in the same street cars, in the same railroad cars, on the same steam-boats, proud of the same country, fighting the same war, and enjoying the same peace and all its advantages." He regarded the Republican party as the "party of progress, justice and freedom" and at election time took to the stump and rallied black votes for the party. He was rewarded for these services by appointment as marshal of the District of Columbia in 1877, as recorder of deeds for the District in 1881, and as minister to Haiti in 1889. But he was also asked by Republican leaders to keep a low profile, was omitted from White House guest lists, and was excluded from presidential receptions even though one duty of the District marshal was to introduce the guests at White House state occasions.

Douglass was puzzled and then upset by the increasing indifference of Republican leaders to conditions among blacks after the Civil War. In 1883 he attended a convention of blacks in Louisville, Kentucky, which met to discuss their plight and reaffirm their demand for full civil rights. In his keynote address, which is reprinted here, Douglass vividly portrayed the discrimination and persecution his people encountered, but he continued to believe that "prejudice, with all its malign accomplishments, may yet be removed by peaceful means."

Born into slavery in Maryland in 1817, Frederick Augustus Washington Bailey learned to read and write despite efforts to keep him illiterate. In 1838 he managed to escape to freedom and adopted the name Frederick Douglass. Shortly afterward he became associated with William Lloyd Garrison and developed into such an articulate spokesman for the antislavery cause that people doubted he had ever been a slave. In 1845 he published his *Narrative of the Life of Frederick Douglass, an American Slave,* naming names, places, dates, and precise events to convince people he had been born in bondage. Douglass continued to be an articulate spokesman for the black cause throughout his life. Shortly before his death in 1895 a college student asked him what a young black could do to help the cause. "Agitate! Agitate! Agitate!" Douglass is supposed to have told him.

Questions to Consider. In the following address Douglass was speaking to a convention of blacks in Louisville, but his appeal was primarily to American whites. How did he try to convince them that blacks deserved the same rights and opportunities as all Americans? How powerful did he think the color line was? What outrages against his people did he report? What was his attitude toward the Republican party, which he had so faithfully served? Were the grievances he cited largely economic or were they social and political in nature?

Address to the Louisville Convention (1883)

FREDERICK DOUGLASS

Born on American soil in common with yourselves, deriving our bodies and our minds from its dust, centuries having passed away since our ancestors were torn from the shores of Africa, we, like yourselves, hold ourselves to be in every sense Americans, and that we may, therefore, venture to speak to you in a tone not lower than that which becomes earnest men and American citizens. Having watered your soil with our tears, enriched it with our blood, performed its roughest labor in time of peace, defended it against en-

From Philip Foner, ed., *The Life and Writings of Frederick Douglass* (4 v., International Publishers, New York, 1955), IV: 373–392. Reprinted by permission.

Frederick Douglass. Douglass's greatest work came before and during the Civil War. One of the most eloquent and magnetic of all the abolitionist leaders, he contributed enormously to the antislavery cause. During the Civil War he pressed hard for the enlistment of blacks to fight in the Union armies on an equal footing with whites. After the war he continued his efforts for civil rights, including black suffrage. For his services to the Republican party he received appointments as secretary to the Santo Domingo commission, marshal and recorder deeps for the District of Columbia, and U.S. minister to Haiti. (National Portrait Gallery, Smithsonian Institution/Washington, D.C.)

emies in time of war, and at all times been loyal and true to its best interests, we deem it no arrogance or presumption to manifest now a common concern with you for its welfare, prosperity, honor and glory. . . .

It is our lot to live among a people whose laws, traditions, and prejudices have been against us for centuries, and from these they are not yet free. To assume that they are free from these evils simply because they have changed their laws is to assume what is utterly unreasonable and contrary to facts. Large bodies move slowly. Individuals may be converted on the instant and change their whole course of life. Nations never. Time and events are required for the conversion of nations. Not even the character of a great political organization can be changed by a new platform. It will be the same old snake though in a new skin. Though we have had war, reconstruction and abolition as a nation, we still linger in the shadow and blight of an extinct institution. Though the colored man is no longer subject to be bought and sold, he is still surrounded by an adverse sentiment which fetters all his movements. In his downward course he meets with no resistance, but his course upward is resented and resisted at every step of his progress. If he comes in ignorance, rags, and wretchedness, he conforms to the popular belief of his character, and in that character he is welcome. But if he shall come as a gentleman, a scholar, and a statesman, he is hailed as a contradiction to the national faith concerning his race, and his coming is resented as impudence. In the one case he may provoke contempt and derision, but in the other he is an affront to pride, and provokes malice. Let him do what he will, there is at present, therefore, no escape for him. The color line meets him everywhere, and in a measure shuts him out from all respectable and profitable trades and callings. In spite of all your religion and laws he is a rejected man.

He is rejected by trade unions, of every trade, and refused work while he lives, and burial when he dies, and yet he is asked to forget his color, and forget that which everybody else remembers. If he offers himself to a builder as a mechanic, to a client as a lawyer, to a patient as a physician, to a college as a professor, to a firm as a clerk, to a Government Department as an agent, or an officer, he is sternly met on the color line, and his claim to consideration in some way is disputed on the ground of color.

Not even our churches, whose members profess to follow the despised Nazarene, whose home, when on earth, was among the lowly and despised, have yet conquered this feeling of color madness, and what is true of our churches is also true of our courts of law. Neither is free from this all-pervading atmosphere of color hate. The one describes the Deity as impartial, no respecter of persons, and the other the Goddess of Justice as blindfolded, with sword by her side and scales in her hand held evenly between high and low, rich and low, white and black, but both are the images of American imagination, rather than American practices.

Taking advantage of the general disposition in this country to impute crime to color, white men *color* their faces to commit crime and wash off the hated color to escape punishment. In many places where the commission of crime is alleged against one of our color, the ordinary processes of law are set aside as too slow for the impetuous justice of the infuriated populace. They take the law into their own bloody hands and proceed to whip, stab, shoot, hang, or burn the alleged culprit, without the intervention of courts, counsel, judges, juries, or witnesses. In such cases it is not the business of the accusers to prove guilt, but it is for the accused to prove his innocence, a thing hard for him to do in these infernal Lynch courts. A man accused, surprised, frightened, and captured by a motley crowd, dragged with a rope about his neck in midnight-darkness to the nearest tree, and told in the coarsest terms of profanity to prepare for death, would be more than human if he did not, in his terror-stricken appearance, more confirm suspicion of guilt than the contrary. Worse still, in the presence of such hell-black outrages, the pulpit is usually dumb, and the press in the neighborhood is silent or openly takes side with the mob. There are occasional cases in which white men are lynched, but one sparrow does not make a summer. Every one knows that what is called Lynch law is peculiarly the law for colored people and for nobody else. If there were no other grievance than this horrible and barbarous Lynch law custom, we should be justified in assembling, as we have now done, to expose and denounce it. But this is not all. Even now, after twenty years of so-called emancipation, we are subject to lawless raids of midnight riders, who, with blackened faces, invade our homes and perpetrate the foulest of crimes upon us and our families. This condition of things is too flagrant and notorious to require specifications or proof. Thus in all the relations of life and death we are met by the color line.

While we recognize the color line as a hurtful force, a mountain barrier to our progress, wounding our bleeding feet with its flinty rocks at every step, we do not despair. We are a hopeful people. This convention is a proof of our faith in you, in reason, in truth and justice—our belief that prejudice, with all its malign accomplishments, may yet be removed by peaceful means; that, assisted by time and events and the growing enlightenment of both races, the color line will ultimately become harmless. When this shall come it will then only be used, as it should be, to distinguish one variety of the human family from another. It will cease to have any civil, political, or moral significance, and colored conventions will then be dispensed with as anachronisms, wholly out of place, but not till then. Do not marvel that we are discouraged. The faith within us has a rational basis, and is confirmed by facts. When we consider how deep-seated this feeling against us is; the long centuries it has been forming; the forces of avarice which have been marshaled to sustain it; how the language and literature of the country have been pervaded with it; how the church, the press, the play-house, and other influences of the country have been arrayed in its support, the progress toward its extinction must be considered vast and wonderful. . . .

We do not believe, as we are often told, that the Negro is the ugly child of the national family, and the more he is kept out of sight the better it will be for him. You know that liberty given is never so precious as liberty sought for and fought for. The man outraged is the man to make the outcry. Depend upon it, men will not care much for a people who do not care for themselves. Our meeting here was opposed by some of our members, because it would disturb the peace of the Republican party. The suggestion came from coward lips and misapprehended the character of that party. If the Republican party cannot stand a demand for justice and fair play, it ought to go down. We were men before that party was born, and our manhood is more sacred than any party can be. Parties were made for men, not men for parties.

The colored people of the South are the laboring people of the South. The labor of a country is the source of its wealth; without the colored laborer to-day the South would be a howling wilderness, given up to bats, owls, wolves, and bears. He was the source of its wealth before the war, and has been the source of its prosperity since the war. He almost alone is visible in her fields, with implements of toil in his hands, and laboriously using them to-day.

Let us look candidly at the matter. While we see and hear that the South is more prosperous than it ever was before and rapidly recovering from the waste of war, while we read that it raises more cotton, sugar, rice, tobacco, corn, and other valuable products than it ever produced before, how happens it, we sternly ask, that the houses of its laborers are miserable huts, that their clothes are rags, and their food the coarsest and scantiest? How happens it that the land-owner is becoming richer and the laborer poorer?

The implication is irresistible—that where the landlord is prosperous the laborer ought to share his prosperity, and whenever and wherever we find this is not the case there is manifestly wrong somewhere. . . .

Flagrant as have been the outrages committed upon colored citizens in respect to their civil rights, more flagrant, shocking, and scandalous still have been the outrages committed upon our political rights by means of bull-dozing and Kukluxing, Mississippi plans, fraudulent courts, tissue ballots, and the like devices. Three States in which the colored people outnumber the white population are without colored representation and their political voice suppressed. The colored citizens in those States are virtually disfranchised, the Constitution held in utter contempt and its provisions nullified. This has been done in the face of the Republican party and successive Republican administrations. . . .

This is no question of party. It is a question of law and government. It is a question whether men shall be protected by law, or be left to the mercy of cyclones of anarchy and bloodshed. It is whether the Government or the mob shall rule this land; whether the promises solemnly made to us in the constitution be manfully kept or meanly and flagrantly broken. Upon this vital point we ask the whole people of the United States to take notice that whatever of political power we have shall be exerted for no man of any party who will not, in advance of election, promise to use every power given him by the Government, State or National, to make the black man's path to the ballot-box as straight, smooth and safe as that of any other American citizen. . . .

We hold it to be self-evident that no class or color should be the exclusive rulers of this country. If there is such a ruling class, there must of course be a subject class, and when this condition is once established this Government of the people, by the people, and for the people, will have perished from the earth.

Miss Liberty welcoming a family of Jewish immigrants. (YIVO Institute for Jewish Research)

CHAPTER TWO

Minorities

A Sister on the Frontier

Roman Catholics found a niche in predominantly Protestant North America when Charles I granted Lord Baltimore a charter to establish the colony of Maryland. But prejudice compelled even Lord Baltimore to enjoin Catholics to worship "as privately as may be" and to avoid public discussion of their beliefs. Elsewhere in the colonies, Catholics often faced hostility, and they persevered by keeping their religious convictions to themselves. With the Revolution and the religious freedom it promised, Catholics expected their position to improve—after all, they had fought enthusiastically for the cause, and the Catholic Count Pulaski, the top cavalry commander in the southern campaign, had died a hero of the Revolution.

Things did get better. With greater numbers of European Catholic immigrants arriving, churches and dioceses multiplied, missionaries went west, and schools were founded. As the Catholic population increased, however, so again did nativist suspicions. By the 1830s anti-Catholicism was so virulent that in Boston a mob burned the Ursuline convent school. The huge influx of Irish Catholics in the 1840s and 1850s further aroused American prejudices, which lessened only somewhat during the Civil War and its bitter aftermath.

Yet Catholics remained intent on spreading their faith. And in contrast to their reception in some urban areas, they were often welcome on the frontier. Of Catholic schools in the Ohio and Indiana wilderness one observer reported:

> Everywhere in America, in the best society, the most accomplished and influential ladies have been educated in convents, and though they may never go over to Rome they love and respect their teachers. . . . Education is removing prejudices, and the chaotic condition of the Protestant community, divided into warring sects, increases the power of a Church whose characteristic is unity, and whose claim is infallibility.

Sister Blandina Segale was a Catholic missionary and teacher who found herself in the rough cowboy country of the Colorado Territory in the 1870s. Sent by the Sisters of Charity to the town of

Trinidad, she labored in the Southwest (in what is today Colorado and New Mexico) among the predominantly Mexican population for twenty-one years. Hers was hardly a monastic existence; Sister Blandina's experiences included an encounter with Billy the Kid, whom she charmed into inviting her to call on him should she ever need assistance, and the rescue of a man about to be lynched by a mob. Her indomitable spirit, shrewd insight, and quick-wittedness are illustrated in the document below, a fragment from a journal she kept in the form of letters to her sister, Sister Justina, in Cincinnati. Here she records how she was able to get a new school built, a tale that reflects both her resourcefulness as an individual and the self-sufficient fashion in which the Catholic church established itself on the frontier.

Following her days in the territory, Sister Blandina returned to Cincinnati, where she and her sister established the Santa Maria Institute, the oldest aid society for Italian immigrants. There she labored for thirty-five years, personally instructing nearly 80 percent of the Italian population in the Catholic faith.

Questions to Consider. What qualities made Sister Blandina particularly well suited to life in a frontier situation? What kind of relationship did she have with the people she served? To what extent did she respect local wisdom and customs? How would you describe the relationship between local people and women?

Letter from Colorado (1876)

BLANDINA SEGALE

Dear Sister Justina:

To-day I asked Sister Eulalia if, in her opinion, we did not need a new school building, which would contain a hall and stage for all school purposes. She said: "Just what we need, Sister. Do you want to build it?" I answered, "Yes, I do." She added, "We have not enough cash to pay interest on our indebtedness. Have you a plan by which you can build without money? If so, I say build."

"Here is my plan, Sister. Borrow a crowbar, get on the roof of the schoolhouse and begin to detach the adobes. The first good Mexican who sees me will ask, "What are you doing, Sister?" I will answer, "Tumbling down this structure to rebuild it before the opening of the fall term of school."

From Sister Blandina Segale, *At the End of the Santa Fe Trail* (Milwaukee, 1948), 62–65.

You should have seen Sister Eulalia laugh! It did me good. After three days' pondering how to get rid of low ceilings, poor ventilation, acrobats from log-rafters introducing themselves without notice, and now here is an opportunity to carry out a test on the good in human nature, so I took it. I borrowed a crowbar and went on the roof, detached some adobes and began throwing them down. The school building is only one story high.

The first person who came towards the schoolhouse was Doña Juanita Simpson, wife of the noted hero of Simpson's Rest. When she saw me at work, she exclaimed, *"Por amor de Dios, Hermana, qué, está Vd. haciendo?"* (For the love of God, Sister, what are you doing?)

I answered, "We need a schoolhouse that will a little resemble those we have in the United States, so I am demolishing this one in order to rebuild."

"How many men do you need, Sister?"

"We need not only men, but also straw, moulds, hods, shovels—everything it takes to build a house with a shingle roof. Our assets are good-will and energy."

Earnestly Mrs. Simpson said: "I go to get what you need."

The crowbar was kept at its work. In less than an hour, Mrs. Simpson returned with six men. One carried a mould, another straw, etc. The mould carrier informed me at once that women only know how to *encalar* (whitewash), the men had the trades and they would continue what I began. In a few days the old building was thrown down, the adobes made and sunburnt. In two weeks all the rubbish was hauled away. The trouble began when we were ready for the foundation. Keep in mind it was only by condescension I was permitted to look on. At this juncture I remarked to the moulder:

"Of course, we will have a stone foundation."

"Oh, no!" he answered, "we use adobes laid in mud."

"Do you think if we laid a foundation with stone laid in mortar, the combination would resist the rainy season better than adobes laid in mud?"

"No, no, Sister we never use stone for any of our houses," he replied.

I was at the mercy of the good natives and my best move was to let them have their way. Moreover, I recalled the fact that in the Far East there are mud structures centuries old in a good state of preservation. No mistake would be made by not changing their mode of building in that one point. We got the necessary lumber, sashes and shingles from Chené's mill, sixty miles from Trinidad. Wagons hauled the material. As the Chené, family has a daughter at our boarding school, there will be no difficulty in meeting our bill. Mr. Hermann's daughter is a resident student, and Mr. Hermann is a carpenter and will pay his bill by work.

When the schoolhouse was ready for roofing, a number of the town carpenters offered to help. The merchants gave nails, paints, brushes, lime, hair, etc.

But now came the big obstacle. There is but one man who calls himself a plasterer, and his method is to plaster with mud. It is impossible to get a smooth surface with mud. I remarked to the plasterer: "You will use lime, sand and hair to plaster the schoolrooms."

His look plainly said: "What do women know of men's work?" Yet he condescended to explain: "I am the plasterer of this part of the country; if I should use any material but mud, my reputation would be lost."

I said to him, "But if lime, sand and hair made a better job, your reputation would gain."

He made answer, "Sister, I'll make a bargain with you. I will do as you suggest, but I will tell my people I carried out your American idea of plastering."

We both agreed to this. Meanwhile, the other men had shouldered their implements and were on their way home. The plasterer had to mix the sand, lime and hair following my directions. All that was done satisfactorily to me, at least. But there was not a man to carry the mortar to the plasterer, so I got the bucket and supplied a man's place. The comedy follows:

Rev. Charles Pinto, S.J., pastor, took pleasure in telling his co-religionists that the study of human nature, combined with good will and tactfulness, were building a schoolhouse.

On this day of my hod-carrying, the Rt. Rev. Bishop Machebeuf of Denver, Colorado, arrived on his visitation. The first place to which he was taken was the schoolhouse being built without money. Bishop and Pastor had just turned the kitchen corner when the three of us came face to face. Both gentlemen stood amazed. I rested my hod-bucket. Father Pinto looked puzzled. The Bishop remarked:

"I see how you manage to build without money." I laughed and explained the situation.

They took the bucket, and the three of us went to where the plasterer was working. After the welcome to the Bishop, the plasterer said:

"Your Reverence, look at me, the only Mexican plasterer, and I am putting aside my knowledge to follow American ways of doing my trade; but I told Sister the failure will not be pointed at me." The Rt. Rev. Bishop analyzed the material at a glance, then said: "Juan, if this method of plastering is better than yours, come again to help Sister when she needs you. If it fails, report to me and between us we shall give her the biggest penance she ever received."

The schoolroom walls turned out smooth, the plaster adhesive, and the plasterer will now make a lucrative living at his American method of plastering.

5

Indian Autumn

Conflict between whites and Native Americans began with the first colonial landings and continued undiminished into the late nineteenth century. At that time, the United States finally completed its conquest of the continent and extended its authority over all the lands formerly held by the indigenous peoples. After the Civil War, whites began moving in large numbers along the new rail lines west of the Mississippi River. As part of this movement, the U.S. Army fought continuous wars against the larger and more combative Native American nations—notably the Comanche, Apache, Kiowa, Cheyenne, and Sioux. The army also harassed most of the smaller nations. Native Americans won occasional victories, for example, the Sioux victory over former Civil War General George A. Custer at the Little Bighorn in 1876. Most of the time, however, the tribespeople fell victim to the U.S. Army's superior organization, supplies, and firepower. Whites' slaughter of the vast buffalo herds on which the Native Americans had based their lives—thirteen million buffalo had been killed by 1883—virtually ensured that the tribes would be crushed. The last major military clash between the government and the Native Americans came with the slaughter of scores of Sioux families in 1890 at Wounded Knee, South Dakota.

The Plains peoples were confined almost entirely to reservations. These large tracts of land had been set aside by the U.S. government as places where, with the protection and economic aid of the Indian Office, the Plains peoples might continue their nomadic communal ways. But this policy was a failure. Tribal ranks, already severely depleted by the Plains wars, were further thinned by the growing scarcity of buffalo. Moreover, large tribes were often widely divided on scattered reservations, where resident U.S. government agents usually proved unwilling or unable to prevent looting by white settlers and theft of funds earmarked for tribal assistance.

"Chief Joseph's Story," excerpted below, is a commentary on events during the 1870s. It describes both the encounters—peaceful and otherwise—of the Nez Percés[1] of the Oregon and Idaho country with U.S. settlers and authorities and the betrayals that accompanied those encounters. Born about 1840, "Young Joseph" was the son of a chief of a major Nez Percé band, who had also been christened Joseph by white missionaries. The father had refused to cede tribal lands to the U.S. government following the discovery of gold in the Oregon country, and he passively resisted white efforts to settle the area. When his father died in 1873, "Young Joseph"—named Hinmatonyalatkit, or Thunder Traveling Over The Mountains, in his native tongue—continued the policy of noncooperation. In early 1877 General O. O. Howard ordered the Nez Percés off the land, promising them a reservation elsewhere in the Oregon region. "Young Joseph," seeking to protect his people, agreed to leave, but other Nez Percés did not. A skirmish quickly escalated into a series of pitched battles that decimated the tribe. After armed resistance and a masterly retreat of 1,500 miles, "Young Joseph" surrendered in October 1877. He and his band were sent to Indian Territory, then in 1885 to Washington state. Chief "Young Joseph," by now a figure of legendary proportions to Native Americans and whites alike, died in 1904.

Questions to Consider. What were the key features in the history of relations between Native Americans and whites, as "Young Joseph" told it? In "Young Joseph's" eyes, was the U.S. Army merely an arm of westward expansion or was it an autonomous agent? Given the Nez Percé beliefs (as the chief summarized them), do you think the Americans' westward advance could have occurred without wrecking the tribal nations? In his policy proposals at the end of the passage, was "Young Joseph" advocating a policy of assimilation, separate but equal status, ethnic autonomy, or simple justice? Was his vision practical at that time? Can you see any alternative that might have suited both sides?

Chief Joseph's Story (1879)

YOUNG JOSEPH

My friends, I have been asked to show you my heart. I am glad to have a chance to do so. I want the white people to understand my people. Some of you think an Indian is like a wild animal. This is a great mistake. I will tell

1. **Nez Percé,** like "Joseph," was a European-American name imposed by American explorers in place of the tribal name.

From "Chief Joseph's Own Story," *North American Review* (April 1879), 415–433.

Young Joseph. A late-nineteenth-century Nez Percé chief. (Division of Political History, Smithsonian Institution, Washington, D.C.)

you about our people, and then you can judge whether an Indian is a man or not. I believe much trouble and blood would be saved if we opened our hearts more. I will tell you in my way how the Indian sees things. The white man has more words to tell you how they look to him, but it does not require many words to speak the truth. What I have to say will come from my heart, and I will speak with a straight tongue. Ah-cum-kin-i-ma-me-hut (the Great Spirit) is looking at me, and will hear me.

My name is In-mut-too-yah-lat-lat (Thunder-traveling-over-the-mountains). I am chief of the Wal-lam-wat-kin band of Chute-pa-lu, or Nez Percés (nose-pierced Indians). I was born in eastern Oregon, thirty-eight winters ago. My father was chief before me. When a young man he was called Joseph by Mr. Spalding, a missionary. He died a few years ago. There was no stain on his hands of the blood of a white man. He left a good name on the earth. He advised me well for my people.

Our fathers gave us many laws, which they had learned from their fathers. These laws were good. They told us to treat all men as they treated us; that we should never be the first to break a bargain; that it was a disgrace to tell a lie; that we should speak only the truth; that it was a shame for one man to take from another his wife, or his property, without paying for it. We were taught to believe that the Great Spirit sees and hears everything, and that He never forgets; that hereafter He will give every man a spirit-home according to his deserts; if he has been a good man, he will have a good home; if he has been a bad man, he will have a bad home. This I believe, and all my people believe the same.

The first white men of your people who came to our country were named Lewis and Clarke. They also brought many things that our people had never seen. They talked straight, and our people gave them a great feast, as a proof that their hearts were friendly. These men were very kind. They made presents to our chiefs and our people made presents to them. We had a great many horses of which we gave them what they needed, and they gave us guns and tobacco in return. All the Nez Percés made friends with Lewis and Clarke, and agreed to let them pass through their country, and never to make war on white men. This promise the Nez Percés have never broken. . . .

Next there came a white officer who invited all the Nez Percés to a treaty council. After the council was opened he made known his heart. He said there were a great many white people in the country, and many more would come; that he wanted the land marked out so that the Indians and white men could be separated. If they were to live in peace it was necessary, he said, that the Indians should have a country set apart for them, and in that country they must stay. My father, who represented his band, refused to have anything to do with the council, because he wished to be a free man. He claimed that no man owned any part of the earth, and a man could not sell what was not his own. . . .

For a short time we lived quietly. But this could not last. White men had found gold in the mountains around the land of the winding water. They stole a great many horses from us, and we could not get them back because we were Indians. . . . We could have avenged our wrongs many times, but we did not. Whenever the Government has asked us to help them against other Indians we have never refused. When the white men were few and we were strong we could have killed them off, but the Nez Percés wished to live at peace. . . .

Year after year we have been threatened, but no war was made upon my people until General Howard came to our country two years ago and told us that he was the white war-chief of all that country. He said: "I have a great many soldiers at my back. I am going to bring them up here, and then I will talk to you again. I will not let white men laugh at me the next time I come. The country belongs to the Government, and I intend to make you go upon the reservation."

I remonstrated with him against bringing more soldiers to the Nez Percé country. He had one house full of troops all the time at Fort Lapwei. . . .

When the party arrived there General Howard sent out runners and called all the Indians to a grand council. In the council General Howard informed us in a haughty spirit that he would give my people thirty days to go back home, collect all their stock, and move on to the reservation, saying, "If you are not here in that time, I shall consider that you want to fight, and will send my soldiers to drive you on." . . .

When I returned to Wallowa I found my people very much excited upon discovering that the soldiers were already in the Wallowa Valley. We held a council, and decided to move immediately to avoid bloodshed. . . .

We gathered all the stock we could find, and made an attempt to move. We left many of our horses and cattle in Wallowa, and we lost several hundred in crossing the river. All my people succeeded in getting across in safety. Many of the Nez Percés came together in Rocky Cañon to hold a grand council. . . .

Again I counseled peace, and I thought the danger was past. We had not complied with General Howard's order because we could not, but we intended to do so as soon as possible. I was leaving the council to kill beef for my family when news came that a young man whose father had been killed had gone out with several hot-blooded young braves and killed four white men. He rode up to the council and shouted: "Why do you sit here like women? The war has begun already." [Following many battles] I went to General [Colonel Nelson] Miles and gave up my gun, and said, "Tell General Howard I know his heart. What he told me before, I have it in my heart. I am tired of fighting. Our chiefs are killed; Looking-Glass is dead, Ta-Hool-Hool-Shute is dead. The old men are all dead. It is the young men who say yes or no. He who led on the young men is dead. It is cold, and we have no blankets: the little children are freezing to death. My people, some of them, have run away to the hills, and have no blankets, no food. No one knows where they are—perhaps freezing to death. I want to have time to look for my children, and see how many of them I can find. Maybe I shall find them among the dead. Hear me, my chiefs! I am tired; my heart is sick and sad. From where the sun now stands I will fight no more forever."

Words do not pay for my dead people. They do not pay for my country, now overrun by white men. They do not protect my father's grave. They do not pay for my horses and cattle. Good words will not give me back my children. Good words will not make good the promise of your War Chief, General Miles, [of reservation land in Idaho]. Good words will not give my people good health and stop them from dying. Good words will not get my people a home where they can live in peace and take care of themselves. I am tired of talk that comes to nothing. . . .

I know that my race must change. We cannot hold our own with the white men as we are. We only ask an even chance to live as other men live. We ask to be recognized as men. We ask that the same law shall work alike on all men. If the Indian breaks the law, punish him by the law. If the white man breaks the law, punish him also.

Let me be a free man—free to travel, free to stop, free to work, free to trade where I choose, free to choose my own teachers, free to follow the religion of my fathers, free to think and talk and act for myself—and I will obey every law, or submit to the penalty.

Whenever the white man treats the Indian as they treat each other, then we shall have no more wars. We shall be all alike—brothers of one father and one mother, with one sky above us and one country around us, and one government for all. Then the Great Spirit Chief who rules above will smile upon this land, and send rain to wash out the bloody spots made by brothers' hands upon the face of the earth. For this time the Indian race are waiting and praying. I hope that no more groans of wounded men and women will ever go to the ear of the Great Spirit Chief above, and that all people may be one people.

In-mut-too-yah-lat-lat has spoken for his people.

Young Joseph

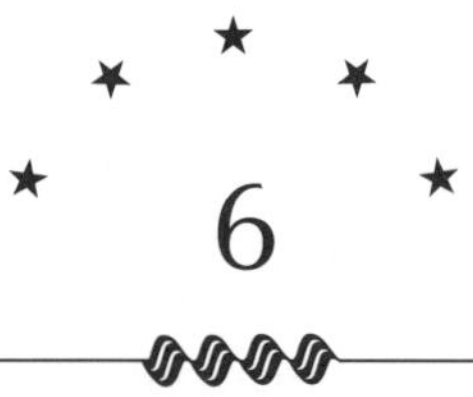

6

NEWCOMERS

The sprawling city was as fundamental a fact of life as the great West or the bitter South in the late nineteenth century, and most Americans found it simultaneously exciting and unsettling. Cities were exciting because they symbolized prosperity and progress, cardinal virtues of the country for decades if not centuries. These urban centers were full of good and novel things to buy and do in a land lusting to do both. But cities were also unsettling—seething (so it seemed) with greedy landlords, corrupt politicians, and radical workers. Most unsettling of all, they were populated by foreigners, not "real" Americans—immigrants from a dozen lands, speaking as many languages and exhibiting as many objectionable habits. These newcomers spilled out from the waterfronts of New York, Baltimore, or Chicago into vast impoverished tenement districts that strained not only public morality but also public order and public health. They may have been lovers of liberty "yearning to be free," as it said on the Statue of Liberty, but they were also "huddled masses."

For most Americans, New York City—the country's largest city and chief port of European debarkation—was the epitome of the immigrant city. No U.S. city could claim more foreign-born inhabitants or more crowded housing conditions. Relatively little open space remained for new residential or business construction. But New York was more than an immigrant center; it was also the publishing and literary capital of the United States. By 1890, hundreds of reporters and writers lived in the city, working for dozens of newspapers and magazines, not counting the foreign-language press. When the United States developed an appetite for urban coverage, New York had a thriving industry to supply it.

Jacob Riis, a Danish immigrant, was a pioneer in the field of urban exposé journalism. Riis, who arrived in New York in 1870, wandered in semipoverty for several years before becoming a city police reporter, first for the *New York Tribune,* then for the *Evening Sun*. His beat was the lower East Side, a teeming immigrant district. For twenty-two years, until 1899, his office was directly across from police headquarters. Here, he wrote, "I was to find my lifework." But Riis was more than a reporter; he became a reformer, determined not only to describe slum life but to improve it. His goal was partly to establish better building codes, but chiefly to ensure that all immigrants learned English and were assimilated thoroughly into American life. This path, after all, was the one that Jacob Riis himself had followed. *How the Other Half Lives,* which first appeared as a series of newspaper essays (one of which is excerpted below), was a weapon in Riis's crusade.

Jacob Riis, born in Ribe, Denmark, in 1849, was educated by his father and became an apprentice carpenter before emigrating to the United States in 1870. By 1890 he had become one of the best-known, most colorful newspapermen in New York. *How the Other Half Lives,* which Riis illustrated with startling photographs of slum conditions, made him a byword in the nation as well. Among its readers was another budding reformer and member of the New York City police board—Theodore Roosevelt, who befriended Riis, accompanied him on forays into the slums, and supported his reform efforts. Riis carried on his crusade in later books, including several on immigrant children, and saw significant improvements in slum schools and recreational facilities. He died in Barre, Massachusetts, in 1914.

Questions to Consider. Modern readers will instantly notice Riis's constant use of stereotypes in discussing various immigrant groups. Why might an intelligent, sympathetic reporter of the 1890s resort to such stereotypes? How could such an author be seen (as Riis was) as a champion of liberal social reform? Riis was a reporter, not a social scientist. Are his descriptions and explanations of group social mobility persuasive? When he explains why immigrant groups tend to form separate enclaves, is he persuasive? Would a writer about homelessness in the 1990s approach the task as Riis did?

How the Other Half Lives (1890)

JACOB RIIS

When once I asked the agent of a notorious Fourth Ward alley how many people might be living in it I was told: One hundred and forty families, one hundred Irish, thirty-eight Italian, and two that spoke the German tongue. Barring the agent herself there was not a native-born individual in the court. The answer was characteristic of the cosmopolitan character of lower New

From Jacob Riis, *How the Other Half Lives* (Scribner's, New York, 1907), 14–21.

Bandit's Roost, Mulberry Street, Manhattan. Jacob Riis took this photograph of the toughest, most dangerous denizens of the Lower East Side in 1890, about the time he enlisted the assistance of Theodore Roosevelt, then chairman of the New York Police Commission. (Museum of the City of New York)

York, very nearly so of the whole of it, wherever it runs to alleys and courts. One may find for the asking an Italian, a German, a French, African, Spanish, Bohemian, Russian, Scandinavian, Jewish, and Chinese colony. Even the Arab, who peddles "holy earth" from the Battery as a direct importation from Jerusalem, has his exclusive preserves at the lower end of Washington Street. The one thing you shall vainly ask for in the chief city of America is a distinctively American community. . . .

They are not here. In their place has come this queer conglomerate mass of heterogeneous elements, ever striving and working like whiskey and water in one glass, and with the like result: final union and a prevailing taint of whiskey. The once unwelcome Irishman has been followed in his turn by the Italian, the Russian Jew, and the Chinaman, and has himself taken a hand at opposition, quite as bitter and quite as ineffectual, against these later hordes. Wherever these have gone they have crowded him out, possessing the block, the street, the ward with their denser swarms. But the Irishman's revenge is complete. Victorious in defeat over his recent as over his more ancient foe, the one who opposed his coming no less than the one who drove him out, he dictates to both their politics, and, secure in possession of the offices, returns the native his greeting with interest, while collecting the rents of the Italian whose house he has bought with the profits of his saloon. . . .

In justice to the Irish landlord it must be said that like an apt pupil he was merely showing forth the result of the schooling he had received, reenacting, in his own way, the scheme of the tenements. It is only his frankness that shocks. The Irishman does not naturally take kindly to tenement life, though with characteristic versatility he adapts himself to its conditions at once. It does violence, nevertheless, to the best that is in him, and for that very reason of all who come within its sphere soonest corrupts him. The result is a sediment, the product of more than a generation in the city's slums, that, as distinguished from the larger body of his class, justly ranks at the foot of tenement dwellers, the so-called "low Irish." . . .

An impulse toward better things there certainly is. The German ragpicker of thirty years ago, quite as low in the scale as his Italian successor, is the thrifty tradesman or prosperous farmer of today.

The Italian scavenger of our time is fast graduating into exclusive control of the corner fruit-stands,while his black-eyed boy monopolizes the bootblacking industry in which a few years ago he was an intruder. The Irish hod-carrier in the second generation has become a bricklayer, if not the Alderman of his ward, while the Chinese coolie is in almost exclusive possession of the laundry business. The reason is obvious. The poorest immigrant comes here with the purpose and ambition to better himself and, given half a chance, might be reasonably expected to make the most of it. To the false plea that he prefers the squalid homes in which his kind are housed there could be no better answer. . . .

As emigration from east to west follows the latitude, so does the foreign influx in New York distribute itself along certain well-defined lines that waver and break only under the stronger pressure of a more gregarious race or the encroachments of inexorable business. A feeling of dependence upon mutual effort, natural to strangers in a strange land, unacquainted with its language and customs, sufficiently accounts for this.

The Irishman is the true cosmopolitan immigrant. All-pervading, he shares his lodging with perfect impartiality with the Italian, the Greek, and the "Dutchman," yielding only to sheer force of numbers, and objects equally to them all. A map of the city, colored to designate nationalities, would show more stripes than on the skin of a zebra, and more colors than any rainbow. The city on such a map would fall into two great halves, green for the Irish prevailing in the West Side tenement districts, and blue for the Germans on the East Side. But intermingled with these ground colors would be an odd variety of tints that would give the whole the appearance of an extraordinary crazy-quilt. From down in the Sixth Ward, upon the site of the old Collect Pond that in the days of the fathers drained the hills which are no more, the red of the Italian would be seen forcing its way northward along the line of Mulberry Street to the quarter of the French purple on Bleecker Street and South Fifth Avenue, to lose itself and reappear, after a lapse of miles, in the "Little Italy" of Harlem, east of Second Avenue. Dashes of red, sharply defined, would be seen strung through the Annexed District, northward to the city line. On the West Side the red would be seen overrunning the old Africa of Thompson Street, pushing the black of the negro rapidly uptown, against querulous but unavailing protests, occupying his home, his church, his trade, and all with merciless impartiality.

Hardly less aggressive than the Italian, the Russian and Polish Jew, having overrun the district between Rivington and Division Streets, east of the Bowery, to the point of suffocation, is filling the tenements of the old Seventh Ward to the river front, and disputing with the Italian every foot of available space in the back alleys of Mulberry Street. The two races, differing hopelessly in much, have this in common: they carry their slums with them wherever they go, if allowed to do it. Little Italy already rivals its parent, the "Bend," in foulness. Other nationalities that begin at the bottom make a fresh start when crowded up the ladder. Happily both are manageable, the one by rabbinical, the other by the civil law. Between the dull gray of the Jew, his favorite color, and the Italian red, would be seen squeezed in on the map a sharp streak of yellow, marking the narrow boundaries of Chinatown. Dovetailed in with the German population, the poor but thrifty Bohemian might be picked out by the sombre hue of his life as of his philosophy, struggling against heavy odds in the big human bee-hives of the East Side. Colonies of his people extend northward, with long lapses of space, from below the Cooper Institute more than three miles. The Bohemian is the only foreigner with any considerable representation in the city who counts no wealthy man of his race, none who has not to work hard for a living, or has got beyond the reach of the tenement.

Down near the Battery the West Side emerald would be soiled by a dirty stain, spreading rapidly like a splash of ink on a sheet of blotting paper, headquarters of the Arab tribe, that in a single year has swelled from the original dozen to twelve hundred, intent, every mother's son, on trade and barter. Dots and dashes of color here and there would show where the Finnish sailors worship their djumala (God), the Greek pedlars the ancient name of their race, and the Swiss the goddess of thrift. And so on to the end of the long register, all toiling together in the galling fetters of the tenement. Were the question raised who makes the most of life thus mortgaged, who resists most stubbornly its levelling tendency—knows how to drag even the barracks upward a part of the way at least toward the ideal plane of the home—the palm must be unhesitatingly awarded the Teuton. The Italian and the poor Jew rise only by compulsion. The Chinaman does not rise at all; here, as at home, he simply remains stationary. The Irishman's genius runs to public affairs rather than domestic life; wherever he is mustered in force the saloon is the gorgeous centre of political activity. The German struggles vainly to learn his trick; his Teutonic wit is too heavy, and the political ladder he raises from his saloon usually too short or too clumsy to reach the desired goal. The best part of his life is lived at home, and he makes himself a home independent of the surroundings, giving the lie to the saying, unhappily become a maxim of social truth, that pauperism and drunkenness naturally grow in the tenements. He makes the most of his tenement, and it should be added that whenever and as soon as he can save up money enough, he gets out and never crosses the threshold of one again.

7

FROM ANOTHER SHORE

In 1882, Congress passed the Chinese Exclusion Act, prohibiting Chinese workers from entering this country for a period of ten years. As the date of expiration approached, however, pressure from powerful sources mounted for renewing the law. Leading the fight was the Immigration Committee of the House of Representatives, under the chairmanship of Representative Herman Stump of Maryland, who produced a stream of witnesses describing how the Chinese used drugs, committed crimes, and lusted after American women. Stump distilled the most important parts of this testimony in the report, reprinted below, that accompanied the committee's recommendation that the exclusion act be renewed.

The committee and its witnesses were persuasive. Not only did Congress extend the law for another ten years, but in 1893 President Grover Cleveland named Representative Stump superintendent of immigration. The exclusion act and Stump's appointment in turn set the stage for a treaty between the United States and China, signed in 1894, barring the immigration of Chinese laborers for ten years from the date of the exchange of ratifications. Those who had left the United States were permitted to return, provided they had wives, children, parents, or property worth $1,000 in this country. The treaty gave China the right to exclude American workers (of which there were none in China), but not American merchants and officials (who were numerous and important there). Chinese were thus all but barred from American soil, even as the Statue of Liberty (a gift of France) was unveiled in 1886 to welcome immigrants from Europe.

By 1900, Japanese workers, too, were entering the United States in sizable numbers; outcries against the "yellow peril" were again raised in the West. The so-called Gentleman's Agreement of 1907 between Washington and Tokyo instantly reduced the flow of unskilled Japanese laborers into the United States.

Questions to Consider. The congressional report of 1892 argued that the Chinese presence in the United States was a threat to American "institutions." What institutions did the Immigration Committee seem most concerned about? Why does the report mention the "vegetable" diets of the Chinese? One aim of the committee was evidently to reduce the "smuggling" of Chinese aliens into the country. Why might such smuggling have taken place, and why did immigration officers seem unable to prevent it? The committee based much of its argument on the idea that the Chinese either could not or would not assimilate. Assuming that this lack of assimilation was a genuine problem, what alternatives might the committee have explored besides exclusion?

Congressional Report on Chinese Immigration (1892)

There is urgent necessity for prompt legislation on the subject of Chinese immigration. The exclusion act approved May 6, 1882, and its supplement expires by limitation of time on May 6, 1892, and after that time there will be no law to prevent the Chinese hordes from invading our country in number so vast, as soon to outnumber the present population of our flourishing States on the Pacific slope. . . .

The popular demand for legislation excluding the Chinese from this country is urgent and imperative and almost universal. Their presence here is inimical to our institutions and is deemed injurious and a source of danger. They are a distinct race, saving from their earnings a few hundred dollars and returning to China. This they succeed in doing in from five to ten years by living in the most miserable manner, when in cities and towns in crowded tenement houses, surrounded by dirt, filth, corruption, pollution, and prostitution; and gambling houses and opium joints abound. When used as cooks, farm-hands, servants, and gardeners, they are more cleanly in habits and manners. They, as a rule, have no families here; all are men, save a few women, usually prostitutes. They have no attachment to our country, its laws or its institutions, nor are they interested in its prosperity. They never assimilate with our people, our manners, tastes, religion, or ideas. With us they have nothing in common.

Living on the cheapest diet (mostly vegetable), wearing the poorest clothing, with no family to support, they enter the field of labor in competition with the American workman. In San Francisco, and in fact throughout the whole Pacific slope, we learn from the testimony heretofore alluded to, that the Chinamen have invaded almost every branch of industry; manufacturers of cigars, cigar boxes, brooms, tailors, laundrymen, cooks, servants, farmhands, fishermen, miners and all departments of manual labor, for wages and prices at which white men and women could not support themselves and those dependent

From *Congressional Record,* October 1892.

Chinese-American merchant. A late-nineteenth-century Chinese-American dry goods store, San Francisco. (University of California at Berkeley, Bancroft Library)

upon them. Recently this was a new country, and the Chinese may have been a necessity at one time, but now our own people are fast filling up and developing this rich and highly favored land, and American citizens will not and can not afford to stand idly by and see this undesirable race carry away the fruits of the labor which justly belongs to them. A war of races would soon be inaugurated; several times it has broken out, and bloodshed has followed. The town of Tacoma, in 1887, banished some 3,000 Chinamen on twenty-four hours' notice, and no Chinaman has ever been permitted to return.

Our people are willing, however, that those now here may remain, protected by the laws which they do not appreciate or obey, provided strong provision be made that no more shall be allowed to come, and that the smuggling of Chinese across the frontiers be scrupulously guarded against, so that gradually, by voluntary departures, death by sickness, accident, or old age, this race may be eliminated from this country, and the white race fill their places without inconvenience to our own people or to the Chinese, and thus a desirable change be happily and peacefully accomplished. It was thought that the exclusion act of 1882 would bring about this result; but it now appears that although at San Francisco the departures largely exceed the arrivals, yet the business of smuggling Chinese persons across the lines from the British Possessions and Mexico has so greatly increased that the number of arrivals now exceed the departures. This must be effectually stopped.

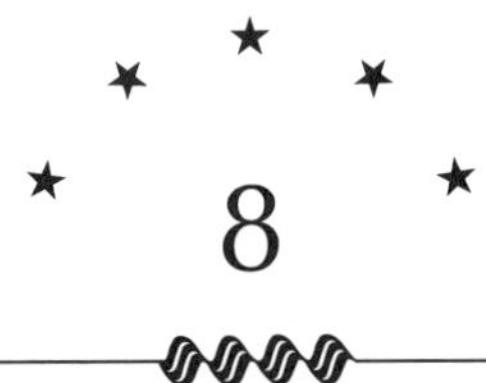

New South, Old South

Following the Civil War, the South suffered two ordeals: racism and poverty. The problem of race touched all Southerners, from oppressed former slaves to anxious white farmers and city dwellers. Poverty, especially the bleak agricultural poverty characteristic of the South, intensified the already severe problem of race. These twin cauldrons finally boiled over in the 1890s, when more than one hundred and fifty blacks were lynched per year, and collapsing farm prices drove many thousands of families—black and white—into bankruptcy.

The Cotton States Exposition of Industry and the Arts, held in Atlanta in 1895, was designed to address the problem of poverty. Mainly the brainchild of Atlanta publishers and bankers, the exposition made much of the prospects for railroad expansion, iron and textile manufacturing, and lumber and tobacco processing. It was hoped their success would reduce the South's unhappy dependence on agriculture and tie the region to the rest of industrial America. But the explosive issue of race also loomed. To address it, the exposition organizers, almost as an afterthought, invited Booker T. Washington, head of the Tuskegee Institute, a black vocational school in Tuskegee, Alabama, to speak to the mostly white exposition gathering. The exposition produced only a slight effect on Southern industrialization—manufacturing did not become widespread there until the 1920s and industrial prosperity has barely arrived even today. Washington's speech, however, was of major importance. His moderate message, accommodating tone, and stress on business and hard work generally pleased his listeners, who marked him as a worthy spokesman for his race. His reputation soon spread to the white North and to blacks as well. Thus, almost overnight, Washington became a prominent figure whose message mattered to everyone, especially in the South.

Not everyone agreed with Washington's approach. Black intellectuals and reformers still found their inspiration in Frederick Douglass, the great abolitionist and stalwart of Radical Reconstruction and equal rights. In their eyes, Washington's acceptance of disfranchisement and segregation seemed a betrayal. They thought his refusal to condemn lynching was a surrender and viewed his influence as mostly negative. One of the most forceful of these critics was Ida B. Wells, a Chicago woman born to Mississippi slaves. Wells's *A Red Record,* excerpted below, told the gruesome story of antiblack violence in the South in persuasive, compelling terms. It thus formed an important counterpoint to Washington's conservative views.

Booker T. Washington was born a slave in Virginia in 1856, and he worked from the age of nine in West Virginia salt furnaces and coal mines. He later worked his way through Hampton Institute, a black school in Virginia, established by philanthropists following the Civil War. After graduating in 1875, he briefly attended a theological seminary in Washington, D.C. In 1881, he accepted the headship of Tuskegee Institute, which he built up from two small buildings and 40 pupils to one hundred buildings, 1,500 students, and a $1 million endowment a quarter-century later. Washington was successful at attracting funds from Northern tycoons and was at least tolerated by Southern politicians. His years of greatest fame came after the Atlanta speech and especially after President Theodore Roosevelt's invitation to dine at the White House in 1901. It was in these years that Washington developed what detractors called a "Tuskegee machine," based on the support of Tuskegee graduates and black businessmen and the willingness of Northern charities and politicians to seek his advice on donations and appointments. His well-known autobiography, *Up From Slavery,* appeared in 1901. He died, exhausted from overwork, in Tuskegee, Alabama, in 1915.

Ida B. Wells was born a slave in Holly Springs, Mississippi, in 1862. She was educated in a freedmen's school, became a teacher herself, and eventually moved to Memphis, Tennessee, where she taught school and attended Fisk University. She turned to journalism in 1891 after losing her teaching post for refusing to give up her seat in a "whites-only" railroad car. When she wrote against antiblack violence, whites retaliated by burning her newspaper office. She left the South in 1892, in time marrying Ferdinand Barnett, a prominent black Chicagoan. A tireless writer and speaker for both women's and black rights, Wells encouraged the Niagara Movement, a 1909 initiative of W. E. B. Du Bois and other militants opposed to the Tuskegee Machine. She refused to support its successor organization, the National Association for the Advancement of Colored People (NAACP), on the grounds that it was too moderate. She died in Chicago in 1931.

Questions to Consider. In reading Washington's Atlanta speech, consider especially the time in which it was delivered. Was Washington, as Wells and others accused, trading black rights for black work? Or was he attempting to use the leverage of black labor to achieve something even more precious—black safety—in the turbulent 1890s? Why might 1895 have seemed an especially good time to move whites in this way? When Washington said, "Cast down your bucket where you are," was he speaking mainly to whites or to blacks? Were there population movements in the 1890s that might have prompted him to address both groups?

Why did Ida B. Wells go to such enormous pains in *A Red Record* to establish the record, from white sources, of antiblack atrocities in the post–Civil War South? For whom does she appear to have been writing? Were there models elsewhere in American society for this kind of "exposé" journalism? In this excerpt, she also takes care to refute the arguments given by white Southerners to justify the violence. Do these passages constitute an attack on paternalism—male chauvinism—as well as on racism? If Wells wrote, as she said, "in no spirit of vindictiveness," why did whites burn her newspaper office for printing similar stories? Was vindictiveness inherent in the material, bound inevitably to provoke outrage and assault? What strategies did Wells devise to avoid this?

Atlanta Exposition Address (1895)

BOOKER T. WASHINGTON

Mr. President and Gentlemen of the Board of Directors and Citizens: One-third of the population of the South is of the Negro race. No enterprise seeking the material, civil, or moral welfare of this section can disregard this element of our population and reach the highest success. I but convey to you, Mr. President and Directors, the sentiment of the masses of my race when I say that in no way have the value and manhood of the American Negro been more fittingly and generously recognized than by the managers of this magnificent Exposition at every stage of its progress. It is a recognition that will do more to cement the friendship of the two races than any occurrence since the dawn of our freedom.

Not only this, but the opportunity here afforded will awaken among us a new era of industrial progress. Ignorant and inexperienced, it is not strange that in the first years of our new life we began at the top instead of at the bottom; that a seat in Congress or the state legislature was more sought than real estate or industrial skill; that the political convention or stump speaking had more attractions than starting a dairy farm or truck garden.

From Booker T. Washington, *Up from Slavery: A Biography* (Doubleday, Page and Co., New York, 1901), 218–225.

A ship lost at sea for many days suddenly sighted a friendly vessel. From the mast of the unfortunate vessel was seen a signal, "Water, water; we die of thirst!" The answer from the friendly vessel at once came back, "Cast down your bucket where you are." A second time the signal, "Water, water; send us water!" ran up from the distressed vessel, and was answered, "Cast down your bucket where you are." And a third and fourth signal for water was answered, "Cast down your bucket where you are." The captain of the distressed vessel, at last heeding the injunction, cast down his bucket, and it came up full of fresh, sparkling water from the mouth of the Amazon River. To those of my race who depend on bettering their condition in a foreign land or who underestimate the importance of cultivating friendly relations with the Southern white man, who is their next-door neighbour, I would say: "Cast down your bucket where you are"—cast it down in making friends in every manly way of the people of all races by whom we are surrounded.

Cast it down in agriculture, mechanics, in commerce, in domestic service, and in the professions. And in this connection it is well to bear in mind that whatever other sins the South may be called to bear, when it comes to business, pure and simple, it is in the South that the Negro is given a man's chance in the commercial world, and in nothing is this Exposition more eloquent than in emphasizing this chance. Our greatest danger is that in the great leap from slavery to freedom we may overlook the fact that the masses of us are to live by the productions of our hands, and fail to keep in mind that we shall prosper in proportion as we learn to dignify and glorify common labour, and put brains and skill into the common occupations of life; shall prosper in proportion as we learn to draw the line between the superficial and the substantial, the ornamental gewgaws of life and the useful. No race can prosper till it learns that there is as much dignity in tilling a field as in writing a poem. It is at the bottom of life we must begin, and not at the top. Nor should we permit our grievances to overshadow our opportunities.

To those of the white race who look to the incoming of those of foreign birth and strange tongue and habits for the prosperity of the South, were I permitted I would repeat what I say to my own race, "Cast down your bucket where you are." Cast it down among the eight millions of Negroes whose habits you know, whose fidelity and love you have tested in days when to have proved treacherous meant the ruin of your firesides. Cast down your bucket among these people who have, without strikes and labour wars, tilled your fields, cleared your forests, builded your railroads and cities, and brought forth treasures from the bowels of the earth, and helped make possible this magnificent representation of the progress of the South. Casting down your bucket among my people, helping and encouraging them as you are doing on these grounds, and to education of head, hand, and heart, you will find that they will buy your surplus land, make blossom the waste places in your fields, and run your factories. While doing this, you can be sure in the future, as in the past, that you and your families will be surrounded by the most patient, faithful, law-abiding, and unresentful people that the world has seen. As we have proved our loyalty to you in the past, in nursing your children, watching by the sick-bed of your mothers and fathers, and often following them with tear-dimmed eyes to their graves, so in the future, in our humble way, we shall stand by you with a devotion that no foreigner can approach, ready to lay down our lives, if need be, in defense of yours, interlacing our industrial, commercial, civil, and religious life with yours in a way that shall make the interests of both races one. In all things that are purely social we can be as separate as the fingers, yet one as the hand in all things essential to mutual progress.

There is no defense or security for any of us except in the highest intelligence and development of all. If anywhere there are efforts tending to curtail the fullest growth of the Negro, let these efforts be turned into stimulating, encouraging, and making him the most useful and intelligent citizen. Effort or means so invested will pay a thousand per cent interest. These efforts will be twice blessed—"blessing him that gives and him that takes."

There is no escape through law of man or God from the inevitable:—

> *"The laws of changeless justice bind*
> *Oppressor with oppressed;*
> *And close as sin and suffering joined*
> *We march to fate abreast."*

Nearly sixteen millions of hands will aid you in pulling the load upward, or they will pull against you the load downward. We shall constitute one-third and more of the ignorance and crime of the South, or one-third its intelligence and progress; we shall contribute one-third to the business and industrial prosperity of the South, or we shall prove a veritable body of death, stagnating, depressing, retarding every effort to advance the body politic.

Gentlemen of the Exposition, as we present to you our humble effort at an exhibition of our progress, you must not expect overmuch. Starting thirty years ago with ownership here and there in a few quilts and pumpkins and chickens (gathered from miscellaneous sources), remember the path that has led from these to the inventions and production of agricultural implements, buggies, steam-engines, newspapers, books, statuary, carving, paintings, the management of drug stores and banks, has not been trodden without contact with thorns and thistles. While we take pride in what we exhibit as a result of our independent efforts, we do not for a moment forget that our part in this exhibition would fall far short of your expectations but for the constant help that has come to our educational life, not only from the Southern states, but especially from Northern philanthropists, who have made their gifts a constant stream of blessing and encouragement.

The wisest among my race understand that the agitation of questions of social equality is the extremest folly, and that progress in the enjoyment of all the privileges that will come to us must be the result of severe and constant struggle rather than of artificial forcing. No race that has anything to contribute to the markets of the world is long in any degree ostracized. It is important and right that all privileges of the law be ours, but it is vastly more important that we be prepared for the exercise of these privileges. The opportunity to earn a dollar in a factory just now is worth infinitely more than the opportunity to spend a dollar in an opera-house.

In conclusion, may I repeat that nothing in thirty years has given us more hope and encouragement, and drawn us so near to you of the white race, as this opportunity offered by the Exposition; and here bending, as it were, over the altar that represents the results of the struggles of your race and mine, both starting practically empty-handed three decades ago, I pledge that in your effort to work out the great and intricate problem which God has laid at the doors of the South, you shall have at all times the patient, sympathetic help of my race; only let this be constantly in mind, that, while from representations in these buildings of the product of field, of forest, of mine, of factory, letters, and art, much good will come, yet far above and beyond material benefits will be that higher good, that, let us pray God, will come, in a blotting out of sectional differences and racial animosities and suspicions, in a determination to administer absolute justice, in a willing obedience among all classes to the mandates of law. This, coupled with our material prosperity, will bring into our beloved South a new heaven and a new earth.

A Red Record (1895)

IDA B. WELLS

Not all nor nearly all of the murders done by white men, during the past thirty years in the South, have come to light, but the statistics as gathered and preserved by white men, and which have not been questioned, show that during these years more than ten thousand Negroes have been killed in cold blood, without the formality of judicial trial and legal execution. And yet, as evidence of the absolute impunity with which the white man dares to kill a Negro, the same record shows that during all these years, and for all these murders only three white men have been tried, convicted, and executed. As no white man has been lynched for the murder of colored people, these three executions are the only instances of the death penalty being visited upon white men for murdering Negroes.

From Ida B. Wells, *A Red Record. Tabulated Statistics and Alleged Causes of Lynchings in the United States, 1892–1893–1894* (Chicago, n.d.), 9–15, 20, 43, 45–48.

Four sharecroppers hanging from a tree in Russellville, Kentucky, 1908. Their "crime" was to express sympathy for a black man who had killed his white employer in self-defense. Thousands of black lynching victims died the same way, prompting the antilynching crusade of Ida B. Wells and other reformers. (Gilman Paper Company Collection)

Naturally enough the commission of these crimes began to tell upon the public conscience, and the Southern white man, as a tribute to the nineteenth century civilization, was in a manner compelled to give excuses for his barbarism.

The first excuse given to the civilized world for the murder of unoffending Negroes was the necessity of the white man to repress and stamp out alleged "race riots." For years immediately succeeding the war there was an appalling slaughter of colored people, and the wires usually conveyed to northern people and the world the intelligence, first, that an insurrection was being planned by Negroes, which, a few hours later, would prove to have been vigorously resisted by white men, and controlled with a resulting loss of several killed and wounded. It was always a remarkable feature in these insurrections and riots that only Negroes were killed during the rioting, and that all the white men escaped unharmed. . . .

Then came the second excuse, which had its birth during the turbulent times of reconstruction. By an amendment to the Constitution the Negro was given the right of franchise, and, theoretically at least, his ballot became his invaluable emblem of citizenship. In a government "of the people, for the people, and by the people," the Negro's vote became an important factor in all matters of state and national politics. But this did not last long. The southern white man would not consider that the Negro had any right which a white man was bound to respect, and the idea of a republican form of government in the southern states grew into general contempt.

The white man's victory soon became complete by fraud, violence, intimidation and murder. The franchise vouchsafed to the Negro grew to be a "barren ideality," and regardless of numbers, the colored people found themselves voiceless in the councils of those whose duty it was to rule. With no longer the fear of "Negro Domination" before their eyes, the white man's second excuse became valueless. With the Southern governments all subverted and the Negro actually eliminated from all participation in state and national elections, there could be no longer an excuse for killing Negroes to prevent "Negro Domination."

Brutality still continued; Negroes were whipped, scourged, exiled, shot and hung whenever and wherever it pleased the white man so to treat them, and as the civilized world with increasing persistency held the white people of the South to account for its outlawry, the murderers invented the third excuse—that Negroes had to be killed to avenge their assaults upon women. There could be framed no possible excuse more harmful to the Negro and more unanswerable if true in its sufficiency for the white man.

Humanity abhors the assailant of womanhood, and this charge upon the Negro at once placed him beyond the pale of human sympathy. With such unanimity, earnestness, and apparent candor was this charge made and reiterated that the world has accepted the story that the Negro is a monster which the Southern white man has painted him. . . .

A word as to the charge itself. In considering the third reason assigned by the Southern white people for the butchery of blacks, the question must be asked, what the white man means when he charges the black man with rape. Does he mean the crime which the statutes of the civilized states describe as such? Not by any means. With the Southern white man, any mésalliance existing between a white woman and a black man is a sufficient foundation for the charge of rape. The Southern white man says that it is impossible for a voluntary alliance to exist between a white woman and a colored man, and therefore, the fact of an alliance is a proof of force. In numerous instances where colored men have been lynched on the charge of rape, it was positively known at the time of lynching, and indisputably proven after the victim's death, that the relationship sustained between the man and woman was voluntary and clandestine, and that in no court of law could even the charge of assault have been successfully maintained.

It was for the assertion of this fact, in the defense of her own race, that the writer hereof became an exile; her property destroyed and her return to her home forbidden under penalty of death. . . .

But threats cannot suppress the truth, and while the Negro suffers the soul deformity, resultant from two and a half centuries of slavery, he is no more guilty of this vilest of all vile charges than the white man who would blacken his name.

During all the years of slavery, no such charge was ever made, not even during the dark days of the rebellion, when the white man, following the fortunes of war went to do battle for the maintenance of slavery. While the master was away fighting to forge the fetters upon the slave, he left his wife and children with no protectors save the Negroes themselves. And yet during those years of trust and peril, no Negro proved recreant to his trust and no white man returned to a home that had been dispoiled.

Likewise during the period of alleged "insurrection," and alarming "race riots," it never occurred to the white man, that his wife and children were in danger of assault. Nor in the Reconstruction era, when the hue and cry was against "Negro Domination," was there ever a thought that the domination would ever contaminate a fireside or strike to death the virtue of womanhood. . . .

In his remarkable apology for lynching, Bishop Haygood, of Georgia, says: "No race, not the most savage, tolerates the rape of woman, but it may be said without reflection upon any other people that the Southern people are now and always have been most sensitive concerning the honor of their women—their mothers, wives, sisters and daughters." It is not the purpose of this defense to say one word against the white women of the South. Such need not be said, but it is their misfortune that the chivalrous white men of that section, in order to escape the deserved execration of the civilized world, should shield themselves by their cowardly and infamously false excuse, and call into question that very honor about which their distinguished priestly apologist claims they are most sensitive. To justify their own barbarism they assume a chivalry which they do not possess. . . .

When emancipation came to the Negroes, there arose in the northern part of the United States an almost divine sentiment among the noblest, purest and best white women of the North, who felt called to a mission to educate and Christianize the millions of southern ex-slaves. From every nook and corner of the North, brave young white women answered that call and left their cultured homes, their happy associations and their lives of ease, and with heroic determination went to the South to carry light and truth to the benighted blacks. It was a heroism no less than that which calls for volunteers for India, Africa, and the Isles of the sea. To educate their unfortunate charges; to teach them the Christian virtues and to inspire in them the moral sentiments manifest in their own lives, these young women braved dangers whose record reads more like fiction than fact. They became social outlaws in the South. The peculiar sensitiveness of the southern white men for women, never shed its protecting influence about them. No friendly word from their own race cheered them in their work; no hospitable doors gave them the companionship like that from which they had come. No chivalrous white man doffed his hat in honor or respect. They were "Nigger teachers" —unpardonable offenders in the social ethics of the South, and were insulted, persecuted and ostracized, not by Negroes, but by the white manhood which boasts of its chivalry toward women.

And yet these northern women worked on, year after year, unselfishly, with a heroism which amounted almost to martyrdom. Threading their way through dense forests, working in schoolhouse, in the cabin and in the church, thrown at all times and in all places among the unfortunate and lowly Negroes, whom they had come to find and to serve, these northern women, thousands and thousands of them, have spent more than a quarter of a century in giving to the colored people their splendid lessons for home and heart and soul. Without protection, save that which innocence gives to every good woman, they went about their work, fearing no assault and suffering none. . . . Before the world adjudges the Negro a moral monster, a vicious assailant of womanhood and a menace to the sacred precints of home, the colored people ask the consideration of the silent record of gratitude, respect, protection, and devotion of the millions of the race in the South, to the thousands of northern white women who have served as teachers and missionaries since the war. . . .

These pages are written in no spirit of vindictiveness, for all who give the subject consideration must concede that far too serious is the condition of that civilized government in which the spirit of unrestrained outlawry constantly increases in violence, and casts its blight over a continually growing area of territory. We plead not for the colored people alone, but for all victims of the terrible injustice which puts men and women to death without form of law. During the year 1894, there were 132 persons executed in the United States by due form of law, while in the same year, 197 persons were put to death by mobs who gave the victims no opportunity to make a lawful defense. No comment need be made upon a condition of public sentiment responsible for such alarming results.

The Segregated South

After the *Dred Scott* decision in 1857, the tide of federal decision making turned, becoming more favorable for blacks, at least through 1870 when the ratification of the Fifteenth Amendment to the Constitution guaranteed them the right to vote. But with President Rutherford B. Hayes's withdrawal of federal troops from the South in 1877, the current gradually shifted once more toward disfranchisement, exploitation, and increasingly, segregation. In the *Plessy* v. *Ferguson* case in 1896, the Supreme Court upheld a Louisiana law requiring separate railroad cars for blacks and whites.

Homer Plessy was one-eighth black; by sitting in the white section of a railway car en route from New Orleans to Covington, Louisiana, he violated a Louisiana "Jim Crow" (racial separation) law. He was arrested for refusing to move into a black section, and John H. Ferguson, the Louisiana judge who tried the case, found him guilty. Believing that the Jim Crow law violated the Fourteenth Amendment, Plessy appealed the decision. But the Supreme Court upheld the Louisiana law, stating that the Fourteenth Amendment, which forbids states to abridge the civil rights and liberties of citizens, requires only that separate facilities be equal.

This "separate but equal" doctrine allowed segregation not only of private commercial facilities like hotels, but also of public schools and even towns and cities. In practice it permitted the creation of facilities that were surely separate but hardly equal. The decision stood until 1954, when it was overturned by the Supreme Court in the landmark decision in *Brown* v. *The Board of Education of Topeka.*

Henry Billings Brown, the author of the *Plessy* decision, was born to wealthy parents in Massachusetts in 1836. He attended Yale College and set up a law practice in Detroit. Appointed to the Supreme Court by President Benjamin Harrison in 1890, Brown retired from the Court in 1906 and lived in New York until his death in 1913. His chief opinion besides *Plessy* was a concurrence in the decision in *Dawson* v. *Bidwell* (1901) that inhabitants of annexed territories, such as Puerto Rico, had no constitutional rights.

Questions to Consider. Several aspects of the *Plessy* opinion merit special attention. Note, for example, the dual themes of racism and growth. Did Henry Billings Brown believe his decision would segregate facilities in the South? Was it not, in fact, Southern industrial progress—new railroads, streetcars, hotels, and schools—and its effect on race relations that had brought the issue before the Court in the first place? Brown stated that although all citizens have a kind of "property" interest in their reputations because these can affect their future, segregation will not harm blacks' reputations unless they allow it to hurt their self-esteem. Whites in a minority position, said Brown, would not suffer diminished self-esteem; neither should blacks. What evidence is cited for this opinion? Note Brown's narrow view of the scope of the law. Law, he argued, can neither equalize nor unify society. In its *Plessy* decision, therefore, the Supreme Court declared actual racial experience—slavery, terrorism, and exploitation—to be irrelevant to the legal consideration of race relations. Do you agree with this reasoning?

Plessy v. *Ferguson* (1896)

HENRY BILLINGS BROWN

This case turns upon the constitutionality of an act of the general assembly of the state of Louisiana, passed in 1890, providing for separate railway carriages for the white and colored races. . . .

The constitutionality of this act is attacked upon the ground that it conflicts both with the 13th Amendment of the Constitution, abolishing slavery, and the 14th Amendment, which prohibits certain restrictive legislation on the part of the states.

That it does not conflict with the 13th Amendment, which abolished slavery and involuntary servitude, except as a punishment for crime, is too clear for argument. . . .

The object of the [14th] amendment was undoubtedly to enforce the absolute equality of the two races before the law, but in the nature of things it could not have been intended to abolish distinctions based upon color, or to enforce social, as distinguished from political, equality, or a commingling of the two races upon terms unsatisfactory to either. Laws permitting, and even requiring their separation in places where they are liable to be brought into contact do not necessarily imply the inferiority of either race to the other, and have been generally, if not universally, recognized as within the competency of the state legislatures in the exercise of their police power. The most common instance of this is connected with the establishment of separate schools for white and colored children, which have been held to be a valid exercise of

Plessy v. *Ferguson,* 163 U.S. 537 (1896).

the legislative power even by courts of states where the political rights of the colored race have been longest and most earnestly enforced. . . .

It is claimed by the plaintiff in error that, in any mixed community, the reputation of belonging to the dominant race, in this instance the white race, is property, in the same sense that a right of action, or of inheritance, is property. Conceding this to be so, for the purposes of this case, we are unable to see how this statute deprives him of, or in any way affects his right to, such property. If he be a white man and assigned to a colored coach, he may have his action for damages against the company for being deprived of his so-called property. Upon the other hand, if he be a colored man and be so assigned, he has been deprived of no property, since he is not lawfully entitled to the reputation of being a white man. . . .

So far, then, as a conflict with the 14th Amendment is concerned, the case reduces itself to the question whether the statute of Louisiana is a reasonable regulation, and with respect to this there must necessarily be a large discretion on the part of the legislature. In determining the question of reasonableness it is at liberty to act with reference to the established usages, customs, and traditions of the people, and with a view to the promotion of their comfort, and the preservation of the public peace and good order. Gauged by this standard, we cannot say that a law which authorizes or even requires the separation of the two races in public conveyances is unreasonable or more obnoxious to the 14th Amendment than the acts of Congress requiring separate schools for colored children in the District of Columbia, the constitutionality of which does not seem to have been questioned, or the corresponding acts of state legislatures.

We consider the underlying fallacy of the plaintiff's argument to consist in the assumption that the enforced separation of the two races stamps the colored race with a badge of inferiority. If this be so, it is not by reason of anything found in the act, but solely because the colored race chooses to put that construction upon it. The argument necessarily assumes that if, as has been more than once the case, and is not unlikely to be so again, the colored race should become the dominant power in the state legislature, and should enact a law in precisely similar terms, it would thereby relegate the white race to an inferior position. We imagine that the white race, at least, would not acquiesce in this assumption. The argument also assumes that social prejudice may be overcome by legislation, and that equal rights cannot be secured to the Negro except by an enforced commingling of the two races. We cannot accept this proposition. If the two races are to meet on terms of social equality, it must be the result of natural affinities, a mutual appreciation of each other's merits and a voluntary consent of individuals. . . .

Legislation is powerless to eradicate racial instincts or to abolish distinctions based upon physical differences, and the attempt to do so can only result in accentuating the difficulties of the present situation. If the civil and political right of both races be equal, one cannot be inferior to the other civilly or politically. If one race be inferior to the other socially, the Constitution of the United States cannot put them upon the same plane.

10

Bearing Gifts

Nativist bigotry was widespread in turn-of-the-century America, attaching itself with special force to immigrants from Eastern or Catholic Europe and perhaps most venomously to Jews. Anti-Semitism was a powerful current from czarist Russia to the democratic United States in the late nineteenth century, intensifying in the United States with the beginning of large-scale Jewish immigration in the 1880s. Thereafter, anti-Semitism emerged in all regions, classes, and parties. Resort hotels and exclusive men's clubs barred Jewish businessmen, and upper-class colleges established quota systems. Small-town Midwesterners and Southern farmers criticized not just Wall Street bankers but international Jewish bankers. Radical writers like Jack London cast a racist net that snared Jews as well as blacks. Even urban Catholic immigrants, who themselves experienced religious and nativist discrimination, harassed the "Christ-killers" and "Shylocks" who shared their ethnic slums.

Spokespersons for the various immigrant groups labored hard to counter nativist bigotry. They challenged stereotypes where they could, chiefly by publicizing their group's successes, including successful examples of Americanization. They also tried to portray the group's distinctive characteristics in positive terms, stressing how the country would benefit from Italian musical genius, for example, or Polish religious fervor. The Jewish community had no finer advocate than Mary Antin, a young writer and political activist whose speech before a New York convention of the General Federation of Women's Clubs is excerpted below.

Mary Antin was born in Russia in 1881 and emigrated with her parents to the United States in 1894. When she was still a teenager, Antin wrote her first book—in Yiddish—about the Jewish immigrant experience. After studying at Teachers College and Barnard College in New York City, she published *The Promised Land* (1912), perhaps our most beautiful version of the immigrant saga. An ardent socialist and union supporter, Antin continued to write and lecture on the subject of immigration; she was a notable opponent of congressional efforts to pass restrictive immigration laws. She died in Suffern, New York, on May 15, 1949.

Questions to Consider. Why didn't Mary Antin argue for the value of Jewish immigration by offering case studies, as immigrant defenders sometimes did, of successful individual Jews? What point was she trying to make by implicitly reinforcing a stereotype about Jews—that as a group they produced a disproportionate number of scholars, lawyers, and debaters? How did she attempt to connect the discussion about Jews and the law with her discussion later about the organization of the clothing industry? Was she right to argue that the passion for justice was fundamental to being a Jew, so that Jews were, in a sense, heirs to the "Spirit of '76" and therefore naturally American? What were the "false gods" Antin referred to in her final sentence?

Russian Jews (1916)

MARY ANTIN

On the whole the Russian immigrant in this country is the Jewish immigrant, since we are the most numerous group out of Russia. But to speak for the Jews—the most misunderstood people in the whole of history—ten minutes, in which to clear away 2,000 years of misunderstanding! Your President has probably in this instance, as in other instances, been guided by some inspiration, the source of which none of us may know. I was called by name long before your President notified me that she would call me to this assembly. I was called by name to say what does the Jew bring to America—by a lady from Philadelphia. Miss Repplier, not long ago, in an article in her inimitable fashion, called things by their name, and sometimes miscalled them, spoke of "the Jew in America who has received from us so much and has given us so little." This comment was called down by something that I had said about certain things in American life that did not come up to the American standard. "The Jew who has given so little." Tonight I am the Jew—you are the Americans. Let us look over these things.

What do we bring you besides our poverty and our rags? Men, women, and children—the stuff that nations are built of. What sort of men and women? I shall not seek to tire you with a list of shining names of Jewish notables. If you want to know who's who among the Jews, I refer you to your biographical dictionary. You are as familiar as I am with the name of Jews who shine in the professions, who have done notable service to the state, in politics, in diplomacy, and where you will. . . .

You know as well as I what numbers of Jewish youth are always taking high ranks, high honors in the schools, colleges and universities. You know

From General Federation of Women's Clubs, *Thirteenth Biennial Convention* (New York, 1916).

as well as I do in what numbers our people crowd your lecture halls and your civic centers, in all those places where the spiritual wine of life may be added to our daily bread. These are things that you know. I don't want you to be thinking of any list of Jewish notables.

A very characteristic thing of Jewish life is the democracy of virtue that you find in every Jewish community. We Jews have never depended for our salvation on the supreme constellations of any chosen ones. . . . Our shining ones were to us always examples by means of which the whole community was to be disciplined to what was Jewish virtue.

Take a group of Jews anywhere, and you will have the essence of their Jewishness, though there be not present one single shining luminary. The average Jew presents the average of whatsoever there is of Jewish virtue, talent or capacity.

What is this peculiar Jewish genius? If I must sum it up in a word, I will say that the Jewish genius is a love for living out the things that they believe. What do we believe? We Jews believe that the world is a world of law. Law is another name for our God, and the quest after the law, the formulation of it, has always permeated our schools, and the incorporation of the laws of life, as our scholars noted it down, has been the chief business of the Jewish masses. No wonder that when we come to America, a nation founded as was our ancient nation, a nation founded on law and principle, on an ideal—no wonder that we so quickly find ourselves at home, that presently we fall into the regulation habit of speaking of America as our own country, until Miss Repplier reproves us, and then we do it no more. I used formerly when speaking of American sins, tribulations, etc., I used to speak of them as "ours"; no more—your sins. I have been corrected.

Why then, now that we have come here, to this nation builded on the same principle as was our nation, no wonder that we so quickly seize on the fundamentals. We make no virtue of the fact—it is the Jewishness in us—that has been our peculiar characteristics, our habit. We need no one from outside of our ranks to remind us of the goodly things we have found and taken from your hands. We have been as eloquent as any that has spoken in appreciation of what we have found here, of liberty, justice, and a square deal. We give thanks. We have rendered thanks, we Jews, some of you are witnesses. We know the value of the gifts that we have found here.

Who shall know the flavor of bread if not they that have gone hungry, and we, who have been for centuries without the bread of justice, we know the full flavor of American justice, liberty, and equality.

To formulate and again formulate, and criticise the law,—what do our Rabbis in the Ghetto besides the study of law? To them used to come our lawyers, to our Rabbis, not to find the way how to get around the law, but to be sure that we were walking straight in the path indicated by the law. So today in America we are busy in the same fashion.

The Jewish virtues, such as they are, are widespread throughout the Jewish masses. Here in New York City is congregated the largest Jewish community in the whole world, and what is true of the Jews of New York, is true of the Jews of America, and the Jews of the world. If I speak of the characteristics of Jewish life on the East side, one of the great characteristics is its restlessness in physical form, due to the oppression of city life, and the greater restlessness, due to the unquenchable, turbulent quest for the truth, and more truth. You know that the East side of New York is a very spawning ground for debate, and debating clubs. There are more boys and girls in debating clubs than in boys' basket ball teams, or baseball teams. I believe in boys playing baseball, but I also believe in that peculiar enthusiasm of our Jewish people for studying the American law, just as they used to study their own law, to see whether any of the American principles find incorporation in American institutions and habits. We are the critics. We are never satisfied with things as they are. Go out and hear the boys and girls. They like to go to school and learn the names of liberty, and equality and justice, and after school they gather in their debating circles and discuss what might be the meaning of these names, and what is their application to life. That is the reason there is so much stirring, rebellion, and protest that comes out of the East side.

In the great labor movement, it is the effort of the people to arrive at a program of economic justice that shall parallel the political justice. Consider for a moment the present condition of the garment-making trade. That is a Jewish trade. Ages ago when the lords of the nations, among whom we lived, were preventing us from engaging in other occupations, they thrust into the hands of our people the needle, and the needle was our tool, why through the needle we have still thought to give expression to the Jewish genius in our life.

This immense clothing industry—a Jewish industry primarily—is today in a better condition as regards unionization, is further on the road to economic justice than any other great industry that you could name. Mind you, the sweatshop we found here when we came here. We took it just as it was, but the barring of the sweatshop and the organization of the clothing industry in such fashion that it is further in advance, more nearly on a basis that affords just treatment to all concerned—that has been the contribution of our tailor men and tailor women. We have done this thing. . . . The Protocol[1] is a piece of machinery for bringing about justice in this great industry. We have invented that thing, we Jews. We are putting it in operation, we are fighting for its perpetuation. Whatsoever good comes from it, we have done it. . . .

Consider us, if you will, in the most barbarous sense, but I point to this as our great contribution, we are always protesting, and if you want to know the value of that contribution, I remind you that the formulae of the rights of men, which was a criticism of things as they used to be, and a formularizing of things as they ought to be, was at least as efficient as all the armies of the continent put together in the revolutionary war. The Spirit of '76 is the spirit of criticism. We Jews in America are busy at our ancient business of pulling down false gods.

1. **The Protocol:** A labor-management agreement recognizing union rights and providing for improved working conditions in the garment industry.—*Eds.*

11

A MULTICULTURAL VISION

> Fully half of white Americans with native grandparents have one or more pioneers among their ancestors. Whatever valuable race traits distinguish the American people from the parent European stocks are due to the efflorescence of this breed. . . . Now we confront the melancholy spectacle of this pioneer breed being swamped and submerged by an overwhelming tide of latecomers from the old-world hive. . . . The new blood now being injected into the veins of our people is "sub-common." Observe immigrants . . . in their Sunday best. You are struck by the fact that from ten to twenty per cent are . . . big-faced persons of low mentality. . . . Clearly they belong in skins, in wattled huts at the close of the Great Ice Age.

So Edward A. Ross argued in 1914 in *The Old World in the New,* an influential treatise based on the notion of Anglo-Saxon racial superiority. Like so many Americans during the era of World War I, Ross was convinced that the mingling of immigrant blood, that of southeastern Europeans in particular, with that of Anglo-Saxons would not only arrest the development of the United States, but would extinguish the Anglo-Saxon race. Thus he argued for restricted immigration in order to preserve America's quality of life. To fail to do so was to invite disaster.

More thoughtful persons were not threatened by the so-called new immigrants who came to American shores from Poland, Russia, Greece, Italy, and other nations. Many understood the immigration of diverse peoples as an opportunity to create not a "melting-pot" society, but one that was pluralistic and "cosmopolitan," according to Randolph A. Bourne. In contrast to Ross, he argued that Anglo-Saxon or "English-American conservatism" was America's "chief obstacle to social advance."

Writing two years after Ross wrote on restriction, Bourne made a case for what today we call "multiculturalism." Emphatically rejecting any notion that democratic tendencies reside in any particular race, he argued in *Trans-National America,* a part of which is reproduced below, that the capacity for excellence resides in all people. The United States, so attractive to immigrants, therefore had a unique opportunity to build a society that would reflect "a new ideal": a dynamic, tolerant community in which distinctive ethnic groups would make unique contributions to the whole. Although Ross and his supporters were to have their way—the Immigration Act of 1924 restricted European immigration and favored persons from northern and western European countries—it is Bourne's observations that ring true for most modern readers. It was he who reminded Americans that "we are all foreign-born or the descendants of foreign-born."

As a result of a fall in infancy, Bourne was hunchbacked and stunted and his head was deformed; persons he encountered were often unable to overlook his physical features. In writing of the "inferior" southeastern European, Ross had observed that "in every face there was something wrong. . . . There were so many sugarloaf heads, moon-faces, slit mouths, lantern-jaws, and goose-bill noses that one might imagine a malicious jinn had amused himself by casting human beings in a set of skew-molds discarded by the Creator." Cruel and unthinking statements like these doubtless went straight to Bourne's heart, and one might speculate that his sympathy for minorities may very well have derived from the reactions of others to his appearance.

Bourne was a native of New Jersey and attended Columbia University. As a writer for *The Masses* and *Seven Arts,* he attacked America's entry into World War I, but when the latter periodical was suspended in 1917, Bourne had trouble finding outlets for his writing and sank into dire poverty. Having made a name for himself as a brilliant social and literary critic with the publication of several books, Bourne died in 1918 at age thirty-two in the influenza pandemic that claimed the lives of millions.

Questions to Consider. To what extent was Bourne skeptical of American institutions? How do Bourne's ideas compare with the popular notion of America as a "melting pot"? According to Bourne, of what value was cultural pluralism? Is his thinking persuasive?

Trans-National America (1916)

RANDOLPH BOURNE

No reverberatory effect of the great war has caused American public opinion more solicitude than the failure of the "melting-pot." The discovery of diverse nationalistic feelings among our great alien population has come to

From *Atlantic Monthly,* July 1916.

European immigrants at Ellis Island, 1905. Women often wore head scarves aboard ship because of the damp cold and because they had worn them in public in Europe to avoid appearing immodest. Women seldom traveled to the United States alone with small children. The man of the family may have died on the voyage or may have been looking for lost luggage when the photographer snapped this picture. (George Eastman House)

most people as an intense shock. It has brought out the unpleasant inconsistencies of our traditional beliefs. We have had to watch hard-hearted old Brahmins virtuously indignant at the spectacle of the immigrant refusing to be melted, while they jeer at patriots like Mary Antin who write about "our forefathers." We have had to listen to publicists who express themselves as stunned by the evidence of vigorous nationalistic and cultural movements in this country among Germans, Scandinavians, Bohemians, and Poles, while in the same breath they insist that the alien shall be forcibly assimilated to that Anglo-Saxon tradition which they unquestioningly label "American."

As the unpleasant truth has come upon us that assimilation in this country was proceeding on lines very different from those we had marked out for it, we found ourselves inclined to blame those who were thwarting our prophecies. The truth became culpable. We blamed the war, we blamed the Germans. And then we discovered with a moral shock that these movements had been making great headway before the war even began. We found that the tendency, reprehensible and paradoxical as it might be, has been for the national clusters of immigrants, as they became more and more firmly established and more and more prosperous, to cultivate more and more assiduously the literatures and cultural traditions of their homelands. Assimilation, in other words, instead of washing out the memories of Europe, made them more and more intensely real. Just as these clusters became more and more objectively American, did they become more and more German or Scandinavian or Bohemian or Polish.

To face the fact that our aliens are already strong enough to take a share in the direction of their own destiny, and that the strong cultural movements represented by the foreign press, schools, and colonies are a challenge to our facile attempts, is not, however, to admit the failure of Americanization. It is not to fear the failure of democracy. It is rather to urge us to an investigation of what Americanism may rightly mean. It is to ask ourselves whether our ideal has been broad or narrow—whether perhaps the time has not come to assert a higher ideal than the "melting-pot." Surely we cannot be certain of our spiritual democracy when, claiming to melt the nations within us to a comprehension of our free and democratic institutions, we fly into panic at the first sign of their own will and tendency. We act as if we wanted Americanization to take place only on our own terms, and not by the consent of the governed. All our elaborate machinery of settlement and school and union, of social and political naturalization, however, will move with friction just in so far as it neglects to take into account this strong and virile insistence that America shall be what the immigrant will have a hand in making it, and not what a ruling class, descendant of those British stocks which were the first permanent immigrants, decide that America shall be made. This is the condition which confronts us, and which demands a clear and general readjustment of our attitude and our ideal. . . .

Mary Antin is right when she looks upon our foreign-born as the people who missed the Mayflower and came over on the first boat they could find. But she forgets that when they did come it was not upon other Mayflowers, but upon a "Maiblume," a "Fleur de Mai," a "Fior di Maggio," a "Majblomst." These people were not mere arrivals from the same family, to be welcomed as understood and long-loved, but strangers to the neighborhood, with whom a long process of settling down had to take place. For they brought with them their national and racial characters, and each new national quota had to wear slowly away the contempt with which its mere alienness got itself greeted. Each had to make its way slowly from the lowest strata of unskilled labor up to a level where it satisfied the accredited norms of social success.

We are all foreign-born or the descendants of foreign-born, and if distinctions are to be made between us they should rightly be on some other ground than indigenousness. The early colonists came over with motives no less colonial than the later. They did not come to be assimilated in an American melting-pot. They did not come to adopt the culture of the American Indian. They had not the smallest intention of "giving themselves without reservation" to the new country. They came to get freedom to live as they wanted to. They came to escape from the stifling air and chaos of the old world; they came to make their fortune in a new land. They invented no new social framework. Rather they brought over bodily the old ways to which they had been accustomed. Tightly concentrated on a hostile frontier, they were conservative beyond belief. Their pioneer daring was reserved for the objective conquest of material resources. In their folkways, in their social and political institutions, they were, like every colonial people, slavishly imitative of the mother-country. So that, in spite of the "Revolution," our whole legal and political system remained more English than the English, petrified and unchanging, while in England law developed to meet the needs of the changing times.

It is just this English-American conservatism that has been our chief obstacle to social advance. We have needed the new peoples—the order of the German and Scandinavian, the turbulence of the Slav and Hun—to save us from our own stagnation. I do not mean that the illiterate Slav is now the equal of the New Englander of pure descent. He is raw material to be educated, not into a New Englander, but into a socialized American along such lines as those thirty nationalities are being educated in the amazing schools of Gary. I do not believe that this process is to be one of decades of evolution. The spectacle of Japan's sudden jump from mediaevalism to post-modernism should have destroyed that superstition. We are not dealing with individuals who are to "evolve." We are dealing with their children, who, with that education we are about to have, will start level with all of us. Let us cease to think of ideals like democracy as magical qualities inherent in certain peoples. Let us speak, not of inferior races, but of inferior civilizations. We are all to educate and to be educated. These peoples in America are in a common enterprise. It is not what we are now that concerns us, but what this plastic next generation may become in the light of a new cosmopolitan ideal. . . .

The failure of the melting-pot, far from closing the great American democratic experiment, means that it has only just begun. Whatever American nationalism turns out to be, we see already that it will have a color richer and more exciting than our ideal has hitherto encompassed. In a world which has dreamed of internationalism, we find that we have all unawares been building up the first international nation. The voices which have cried for a tight and jealous nationalism of the European pattern are failing. From the ideal, however valiantly and disinterestedly it has been set for us, time and tendency have moved us further and further away. What we have achieved has been rather a cosmopolitan federation of national colonies, of foreign cultures, from whom the sting of devastating competition has been removed. America is already the world-federation in miniature, the continent where for the first time in history has been achieved that miracle of hope, the peaceful living side by side, with character substantially preserved, of the most heterogenous peoples under the sun. Nowhere else has such contiguity been anything but the breeder of misery. Here, notwithstanding our tragic failures of adjustment, the outlines are already too clear not to give us a new vision and a new orientation of the American mind in the world.

It is for the American of the younger generation to accept this cosmopolitanism, and carry it along with self-conscious and fruitful purpose. In his colleges, he is already getting, with the study of modern history and politics, the modern literatures, economic geography, the privilege of a cosmopolitan outlook such as the people of no other nation of today in Europe can possibly secure. If he is still a colonial, he is no longer the colonial of one partial culture, but of many. He is a colonial of the world. Colonialism has grown into cosmopolitanism, and his motherland is no one nation, but all who have anything life-enhancing to offer to the spirit. That vague sympathy which the France of ten years ago was feeling for the world—a sympathy which was drowned in the terrible reality of war—may be the modern American's, and that in a positive and aggressive sense. If the American is parochial, it is in sheer wantonness or cowardice. His provincialism is the measure of his fear of bogies or the defect of his imagination. . . .

All our idealisms must be those of future social goals in which all can participate, the good life of personality lived in the environment of the Beloved Community. No mere doubtful triumphs of the past, which redound to the glory of only one of our transnationalities, can satisfy us. It must be a future America, on which all can unite, which pulls us irresistibly toward it, as we understand each other more warmly.

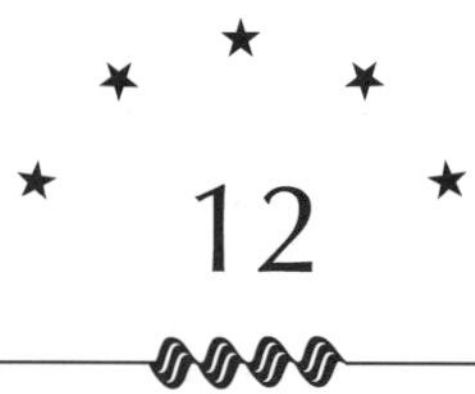

12

Closing the Doors

For a half-century after the Civil War the United States maintained a relatively unrestrictive policy toward immigration from Europe. Yet the coming of so many millions of immigrants, particularly so many who were neither Protestant nor northern Europeans, caused growing alarm among "old-stock" Americans, who associated the newcomers with saloons, political corruption, and other "ills" of urban society. Labor leaders feared such floods of uncontrollable cheap labor; upper-class spokesmen were concerned about the possible "mongrelization" of the country.

The first broad effort to restrict immigration was the Literacy Test of 1917, which actually had little effect because most immigrants could in fact read and write. In 1921, Congress limited immigration from any country to 3 percent of that country's proportion of the American population as of 1910. By 1924 the public favored even more restrictive measures. The sweeping National Origins Act, excerpted below, brought the tradition of unrestricted entry by Europeans to a definitive close. Only people from the Western Hemisphere could come freely now. (A separate Oriental Exclusion Act later banned Asians altogether.) The national-origins standard, though modified, persisted until 1965, when the emphasis shifted from national origin to refugees, relatives, and occupational skills.

Questions to Consider. The Immigration Act of 1924 shows how American society rated the different nationalities at that time. According to the quotas listed in the act, for example, a Czech was worth thirty Chinese, a Swiss equaled twenty Syrians, and an Irishman ten Italians. Is this a fair interpretation of the act? Not even at this peak of feverish nationalism did the U.S. government discriminate arbitrarily between nationalities or allot immigration space on a random basis. With the notable exception of Asians, national quotas were figured on a percentage basis: limiting Armenians also meant limiting Austrians. Most of the Western Hemisphere, moreover, was exempt from the act. Nevertheless, by basing quotas on the 1890 rather than the 1910 census, the act did embody clear racial preferences. Why, then, was such care taken to employ percentages rather than absolute numbers?

Immigration Act of 1924

It will be remembered that the quota limit act of May 1921, provided that the number of aliens of any nationality admissible to the United States in any fiscal year should be limited to 3 per cent of the number of persons of such nationality who were resident in the United States according to the census of 1910, it being also provided that not more than 20 per cent of any annual quota could be admitted in any one month. Under the act of 1924 the number of each nationality who may be admitted annually is limited to 2 per cent of the population of such nationality resident in the United States according to the census of 1890, and not more than 10 per cent of any annual quota may be admitted in any month except in cases where such quota is less than 300 for the entire year.

Under the act of May, 1921, the quota area was limited to Europe, the Near East, Africa, and Australasia. The countries of North and South America, with adjacent islands, and countries immigration from which was otherwise regulated, such as China, Japan, and countries within the Asiatic barred zone, were not within the scope of the quota law. Under the new act, however, immigration from the entire world, with the exception of the Dominion of Canada, Newfoundland, the Republic of Mexico, the Republic of Cuba, the Republic of Haiti, the Dominican Republic, the Canal Zone, and independent countries of Central and South America, is subject to quota limitations. The various quotas established under the new law are shown in the . . . proclamation of the President, issued on the last day of the present fiscal year: . . .

Country or Area of Birth	*Quota 1924–1925*
Afghanistan	100
Albania	100
Andorra	100
Arabian peninsula	100
Armenia	124
Australia, including Papua, Tasmania, and all islands appertaining to Australia	121
Austria	785
Belgium	512
Bhutan	100
Bulgaria	100
Cameroon (proposed British mandate)	100
Cameroon (French mandate)	100
China	100
Czechoslovakia	3,073

From the *Annual Report of the Commissioner-General of Immigration* (Government Printing Office, Washington, D.C., 1924).

Danzig, Free City of	228
Denmark	2,789
Egypt	100
Estonia	124
Ethiopia (Abyssinia)	100
Finland	170
France	3,954
Germany	51,227
Great Britain and Northern Ireland	34,007
Greece	100
Hungary	473
Iceland	100
India	100
Iraq (Mesopotamia)	100
Irish Free State	28,567
Italy, including Rhodes, Dodekanesia, and Castellorizzo	3,845
Japan	100
Latvia	142
Liberia	100
Liechtenstein	100
Lithuania	344
Luxemburg	100
Monaco	100
Morocco (French and Spanish Zones and Tangier)	100
Muscat (Oman)	100
Nauru (Proposed British mandate)	100
Nepal	100
Netherlands	1,648
New Zealand (including appertaining islands)	100
Norway	6,453
New Guinea, and other Pacific Islands under proposed Australian mandate	100
Palestine (with Trans-Jordan, proposed British mandate)	100
Persia	100
Poland	5,982
Portugal	503
Ruanda and Urundi (Belgium mandate)	100
Rumania	603
Russia, European and Asiatic	2,248
Samoa, Western (proposed mandate of New Zealand)	100
San Marino	100
Siam	100
South Africa, Union of	100
South West Africa (proposed mandate of Union of South Africa)	100
Spain	131
Sweden	9,561
Switzerland	2,081
Syria and The Lebanon (French mandate)	100
Tanganyika (proposed British mandate)	100
Togoland (proposed British mandate)	100
Togoland (French mandate)	100
Turkey	100
Yap and other Pacific islands (under Japanese mandate)	100
Yugoslavia	671

"The Only Way to Handle It." This 1921 cartoon from the *Providence Evening Bulletin* urged support for measures to restrict immigration according to the size of resident nationality groups. New England Yankees, such as the readers of the *Bulletin,* helped lead the restrictionist movement, with considerable assistance from Midwesterners and Californians. Restrictionists felt especially threatened by the renewal of mass European migration to America following the end of World War I. (Library of Congress)

A Bessemer steel converter, heart of Andrew Carnegie's steel empire, with the machinery dwarfing the human steelworkers, about 1890. (Hagley Museum & Library)

CHAPTER THREE

Industry, Expansion, and Reform

13

LABOR'S VISION

The decades following the Civil War brought an enormous expansion of activity in railroads, coal, steel, and other basic industries. This rapid rise in the development of America's natural resources was accompanied by a sharp rise in the country's per capita wealth and income and, in the long run, a higher standard of living for most people. But it resulted in other things as well: greater wealth and power for "capitalists," as the new leaders of industry were called; a deterioration in conditions for many workers; and a society repeatedly torn by class conflict.

The Noble Order of the Knights of Labor, formed as a secret workingmen's lodge in 1869, represented an early response to these trends. Secrecy seemed essential at first because of the hostility of employers toward labor unions. Not until 1881 did the Knights of Labor abandon secrecy and announce its objectives to the world. Its slogan was "An injury to one is the concern of all." The Knights took pride in their admission of all workers—regardless of race, sex, or level of skill—and in their moderate, public-spirited vision of a cooperative economic order. These factors, together with their support of successful railroad strikes, swelled the Knights of Labor membership rolls to nearly 800,000 by 1886. After that, however, a wave of antiradicalism, combined with internal problems and the loss of several bitter industrial struggles, sent membership plummeting. By 1900 the organization was gone. It was replaced by two other labor organizations: the American Federation of Labor (AFL), founded in 1886, which organized skilled labor and struck over wages and working conditions, and the Industrial Workers of the World (IWW), founded in 1905, which appealed to the unskilled and stood for industrial reorganization. The AFL, which opposed most of the Knights principles, endured; the IWW, which shared many of them, did not.

The American Federation of Labor was a combination of national craft unions with an initial membership of about 140,000. It was the result of craft disagreement with the Knights of Labor partly over tactics and partly over leadership. The unions that constituted the AFL were central players in a nationwide campaign in support of an eight-hour workday. Centered in Chicago but spreading rapidly to other cities, the campaign (whose major statement appears below) culminated in a series of mass strikes and demonstrations on May 1, 1886. The campaign failed in its efforts to impose a uniform eight-hour day throughout American industry. It succeeded, however, in making a shortened workday one of the cardinal ongoing demands of union organizers and negotiators. When major breakthroughs in union representation and influence came during the 1930s and 1940s, eight hours—"nine to five" with an hour for lunch—became in fact the standard workday everywhere.

Because the Knights of Labor was at first a secret organization, the preamble to its constitution, reprinted below, contained asterisks instead of the organization's name. The author of the preamble was Terence V. Powderly, Grand Master Workman of the Knights from 1879 to 1893. Powderly was born in Carbondale, Pennsylvania, in 1849 to Irish immigrant parents. After ten years as a railroad laborer and machinist, he became active in union affairs, joining the Knights in 1874 and rising rapidly in the organization. He was also a political activist during these years. He served as mayor of Scranton, Pennsylvania, supporting many prolabor candidates in the 1880s, though, like most American labor leaders, he refused to support a separate labor party. After the Knights' decline, Powderly studied law and then served in the Federal Bureau of Immigration. He died in Washington, D.C., in 1924.

Samuel Gompers was the president of the AFL in 1886 and a key figure in the Eight-Hour Association. Gompers was a German-born cigarmaker who emigrated to New York City with his parents at age thirteen. At first a strong socialist, he became a leader of the Cigarmakers' Union in the 1870s, moving it away from social and political reform and toward "pure and simple unionism" based on demands for higher wages, benefits, and security. Gompers was president of the AFL every year but one from 1886 to 1924. During this time, he built an organization that was both powerful and conservative—one that was hostile to radicalism, party alignments, and the admission of the unskilled. He died in San Antonio, Texas, in 1924.

Questions to Consider. What general objectives did the Knights preamble set forth? What do the Knights' practical demands reveal about working conditions in America during the Gilded Age (the period from 1870 to 1890)? To what extent was the preamble idealistic? How radical was it? Does the preamble explain why the Knights barred doctors, lawyers, bankers, gamblers, and liquor dealers from membership, although it allowed farmers, merchants, and small capitalists to join? If you wanted to quote something from the preamble giving the gist of the Knights' philosophy, which passage would you select?

The statement of the Eight-Hour Association opened with a demand to reduce the workday from ten hours to eight. How long had the standard workday been ten hours? Was the ten-hour workday a national standard in 1886? How, according to the statement, would the U.S. economy be able to tolerate so drastic a shrinkage in the workweek? For whose eyes does this portion of the statement appear to have been written? How could a shorter workday benefit laborers? Who besides the individual workers would benefit from the new day?

★★★★

Preamble to the Constitution of the Knights of Labor (1878)

The recent alarming development and aggression of aggregated wealth, which, unless checked, will invariably lead to the pauperization and hopeless degradation of the toiling masses, render it imperative, if we desire to enjoy the blessings of life, that a check should be placed upon its power and upon unjust accumulation, and a system adopted which will secure to the laborer the fruits of his toil; and as this much-desired object can only be accomplished by the thorough unification of labor, and the united efforts of those who obey the divine injunction that "In the sweat of thy brow shalt thou eat bread," we have formed the ***** with a view of securing the organization and direction, by co-operative effort, of the power of the industrial classes; and we submit to the world the object sought to be accomplished by our organization, calling upon all who believe in securing "the greatest good to the greatest number" to aid and assist us:—

I. To bring within the folds of organization every department of productive industry, making knowledge a standpoint for action, and industrial and moral worth, not wealth, the true standard of individual and national greatness.

II. To secure to the toilers a proper share of the wealth that they create; more of the leisure that rightfully belongs to them; more societary advantages; more of the benefits, privileges, and emoluments of the world; in a word, all those rights and privileges necessary to make them capable of enjoying, appreciating, defending, and perpetuating the blessing of good government.

III. To arrive at the true condition of the producing masses in their educational, moral, and financial condition, by demanding from the various governments the establishment of bureaus of Labor Statistics.

IV. The establishment of co-operative institutions, productive and distributive.

From Terence V. Powderly, *Thirty Years of Labor* (Excelsior Publishing House, Columbus, Ohio, 1890), 243–246.

Strikebreakers dragged from a train in Pittsburgh, 1877. The 1877 railroad strike was the first nationwide strike. Two weeks of fierce fighting left hundreds dead and damage in the millions of dollars. Industrial conflicts continued to convulse the industry in the 1880s, with workers sometimes winning concessions and sometimes losing them. (Library of Congress)

V. The reserving of the public lands—the heritage of the people—for the actual settler;—not another acre for railroads or speculators.

VI. The abrogation of all laws that do not bear equally upon capital and labor, the removal of unjust technicalities, delays, and discriminations in the administration of justice, and the adopting of measures providing for the health and safety of those engaged in mining, manufacturing, or building pursuits.

VII. The enactment of laws to compel chartered corporations to pay their employees weekly, in full, for labor performed during the preceding week, in the lawful money of the country.

VIII. The enactment of laws giving mechanics and laborers a first lien on their work for their full wages.

IX. The abolishment of the contract system on national, state, and municipal work.

X. The substitution of arbitration for strikes, whenever and wherever employers and employees are willing to meet on equitable grounds.

XI. The prohibition of the employment of children in workshops, mines, and factories before attaining their fourteenth year.

XII. To abolish the system of letting out by contract the labor of convicts in our prisons and reformatory institutions.

XIII. To secure for both sexes equal pay for equal work.

XIV. The reduction of the hours of labor to eight per day, so that the laborers may have more time for social enjoyment and intellectual improvement, and be enabled to reap the advantages conferred by the labor-saving machinery which their brains have created.

XV. To prevail upon governments to establish a purely national circulating medium, based upon the faith and resources of the nation, and issued directly to the people, without the intervention of any system of banking corporations, which money shall be a legal tender in payment of all debts, public or private.

Statement of the Eight-Hour Association (1886)

The Eight-Hour Association asks for a reduction of all daily toil from ten hours to eight, for the reason that such reduction of time will give opportunity for two more men to work for every eight now employed. In other words, the work now performed by eight men will require ten men to achieve the same result. This will be twenty more men employed for every eighty, thus giving immediate, and for some years, constant labor to all who are willing and able to work.

That every one shall have steady employment at good wages, working eight hours daily, it is necessary that all agree and unite in this movement. In order for each workman to prosper it is essential that all other workmen prosper; because all people support each other by exchanging each others' production and services. Therefore everybody who has commodities or services for sale is interested in having everybody else have a sufficient income from his own earnings to make a mutual exchange. United action in this effort means not only strength but prosperity for all.

The advocates of eight hours for a day's labor advise all workers to take for this number of hours an eight-hour price, allowing the law of supply and demand to regulate wages in the future. We fully believe that while

From *John Swinton's Paper* (May 2, 1886).

merchants, manufacturers and all employers will be benefited, the wages for laborers will soon be higher than ever heretofore, for the following reasons: A reduction of one-fifth of laboring-time for all that work will make a reduction of one-fifth of all kinds of products in the near future, which will make proportionate scarcity. With scarcity will come advance in prices for every commodity, giving merchants and manufacturers a fair profit, and wage-workers an advance in wages. Ere long, all being employed, the production will be as great as now, but, all earning wages, the consumption and demand will be greater than now, so that prices and wages will still continue better than at present.

Eight hours, instead of ten, means a gain of two hours each day—more than one day each week—*seventy-eight days a year!*—a time sufficient to enable every unlettered person to learn to read and write; time in which every foreigner can learn to speak the English language and familiarize himself with his political duty as an American citizen. The extra time thus gained in the year will afford every workingman not only a sufficient recreation, but opportunity to attend the State and county fairs, the National Exposition, and make a visit to the childhood home, with time to spare for a journey to Europe.

This appeal is in the interest of capital as well as labor. The plain facts are that the strikes, lock-outs, business failures, general business depression throughout the world, overflowing prisons and poor-houses, are the result of the producing power of the country being far in excess of the practical ability to consume. We make, raise and produce more than we can readily eat, wear, or dispose of. This results, first, in a falling of prices; then a lowering of wages, succeeded by strikes and resistance of wage-workers, and a final discharge of workmen into idleness. Then, as men are unable to buy, there is a great under-consumption, goods piling up on one side, while great want and destitution exist on the other. To remedy this, productive power, temporarily, must be lessened. To do this by destroying machinery is barbarous. It is wiser far to accomplish this result, and benefit all mankind, by lessening the hours in which machines and men labor in the work of production. . . .

The advantage of eight hours to the laboring classes will be (1st) employment; (2d) steady employment; (3d) better wages; (4th) relief from anxiety that comes from idleness and poverty; (5th) an opportunity to lay aside the means for the purchase of a home; (6th) opportunity to see and get acquainted with the family by day-light; (7th) more time for intellectual improvement; (8th) a chance for outdoor recreation on the secular day, without being compelled to take Sunday for that purpose; (9th) the ability to obtain respectable dress and make a good appearance, whereby encouragement is given to attend church and social gatherings, resulting in intellectual, moral and spiritual improvement. . . .

To fully lay this matter before the people, through literature, discussion, lecture, sermon and study, *we recommend Saturday, April 24, 1886, as a general holiday for the laboring classes, preparatory to inaugurating the Eight-Hour Movement seven days afterwards, on the first day of May.*

In this effort we fervently invoke the aid of the press, the clergy, legislators, teachers, employers, and all persons in authority. Give us employment for the idle masses who are struggling for bread; give us a chance to send pauper and criminal back to shop, and field, and factory, where they may get an honest living; give us back again health and bloom for the sunken-eyed, starving sewing-woman; give us homes for working-people, and a chance to earn them; give us an honest opportunity for every human being to possess the reasonable comforts of life—GIVE US EIGHT HOURS!

Production and Wealth

During the late nineteenth century the United States experienced remarkable industrial development. In 1860 it was largely a nation of farms, villages, small businesses, and small-scale manufacturing establishments; by 1900 it had become a nation of cities, machines, factories, offices, shops, and powerful business combinations. Between 1860 and 1900, railroad trackage increased, annual production of coal rose steadily, iron and steel production soared, oil refining flourished, and development of electric power proceeded apace. "There has never been in the history of civilization," observed economist Edward Atkinson in 1891, "a period, or a place, or a section of the earth in which science and invention have worked such progress or have created such opportunity for material welfare as in these United States in the period which has elapsed since the end of the Civil War." By the end of the century, America's industrial production exceeded that of Great Britain and Germany combined, and the United States was exporting huge quantities of farm and factory goods to all parts of the world. The country had become one of the richest and most powerful nations in history.

More than any other single element, steel permitted and laid the foundation for industrialization. The process of steel production powered industrial development, because it was from steel that railroad tracks and cars, bridges and girders, machines and farm equipment, elevators, ships, and automobiles were all manufactured. One key to rising steel production was the adaptation of the so-called Bessemer process to American conditions. The emergence of mass steel manufacture by this method involved a dynamic interplay between foreign and domestic production ideas, patent law, firm capitalization and competition, creative marketing, and, perhaps most important, constant technical adaptation on the factory floor.

At the other end of the production scale was Andrew Carnegie, the "King of Steel." Carnegie liked to boast of the accomplishments of efficient business organization in the American steel industry, as he did in the excerpt below from *Triumphant Democracy* (1886), a best seller. "Two pounds of ironstone mined upon Lake Superior and transported nine hundred miles to Pittsburgh; one pound and a half of coal mined and manufactured into coke, and transported to Pittsburgh; one-half pound of lime, mined and transported to Pittsburgh; a small amount of manganese ore mined in Virginia and brought to Pittsburgh—and these four pounds of materials manufactured into one pound of steel, for which the consumer pays one cent."

Carnegie preached what he called a "gospel of wealth." His gospel emphasized individual initiative, private property, competition, and the accumulation of wealth in the hands of those with superior ability and energy. But in the last quarter of the nineteenth century, less than 1 percent of the population controlled more than 50 percent of the nation's wealth, the highest concentration in U.S. history up to that time, and the benefits of spectacular industrial growth were hardly shared equitably. The nation had been built on the assumption that all men were created equal, and most Americans took for granted that in a republican society property and power would be widely distributed. Yet the disparity between the very rich and the very poor had grown extreme.

Thoughtful observers, troubled by the concentration of wealth and power in the hands of so few, raised their voices in protest. Andrew Carnegie was unusual in that, on the one hand, he defended the absolute right of the entrepreneur to accumulate wealth and also the Social Darwinist notion of "survival of the fittest." But at the same time, like some of the radicals of his era, Carnegie argued that the rich should dispense their wealth in ways that would benefit society. The "man who dies rich," he asserted, "dies disgraced."

Andrew Carnegie, the son of a handloom weaver, was born in Scotland in 1835. With his family, he moved to Allegheny, Pennsylvania, at the age of twelve and got a job in a textile mill at $1.20 a week. During this period he studied telegraphy, a skill that landed him a position as the personal secretary and telegrapher of a leading raiload executive. Carnegie was himself a railroad executive for a time, and then amassed a fortune selling bonds, dealing in oil, and building bridges. In 1873 he concentrated his efforts on steel and gradually built his Carnegie Steel Company into a massive industrial giant. In 1901 he sold the firm to J. P. Morgan, who made it the core of the world's first billion-dollar company, the United States Steel Corporation. Over the next two decades Carnegie gave away some $350 million for libraries and other public works. He died in Lenox, Massachusetts, in 1919.

Questions to Consider. The excerpt from *Triumphant Democracy* is typical of the many articles and books Andrew Carnegie wrote celebrating the American system. Why did Carnegie think life "has become vastly better worth living" than it had been a century before? What particular aspects of American life did he single out for special mention? In what ways did he think life in the United States was better than life in Europe? Was he writing mainly about the life of the average or of the well-to-do American? How did he relate America's economic achievements to democracy?

Triumphant Democracy (1886)

ANDREW CARNEGIE

A community of toilers with an undeveloped continent before them, and destitute of the refinements and elegancies of life—such was the picture presented by the Republic sixty years ago. Contrasted with that of today, we might almost conclude that we were upon another planet and subject to different primary conditions. The development of an unequaled transportation system brings the products of one section to the doors of another, the tropical fruits of Florida and California to Maine, and the ice of New England to the Gulf States. Altogether life has become vastly better worth living than it was a century ago.

Among the rural communities, the change in the conditions is mainly seen in the presence of labor-saving devices, lessening the work in house and field. Mowing and reaping machines, horse rakes, steam plows and threshers, render man's part easy and increase his productive power. Railroads and highways connect him with the rest of the world, and he is no longer isolated or dependent upon his petty village. Markets for his produce are easy of access, and transportation swift and cheap. If the roads throughout the country are yet poor compared with those of Europe, the need of good roads has been rendered less imperative by the omnipresent railroad. It is the superiority of the iron highway in America which has diverted attention from the country roads. It is a matter of congratulation, however, that this subject is at last attracting attention. Nothing would contribute so much to the happiness of life in the country as such perfect roads as those of Scotland. It is a difficult problem, but its solution will well repay any amount of expenditure necessary. [British historian Thomas] Macaulay's test of the civilization of a people—the condition of their roads—must be interpreted, in this age of steam, to include railroads. Communication between great cities is now cheaper and more comfortable than in any other country. Upon the principal railway lines, the cars—luxurious drawing-rooms by day, and sleeping chambers by night—are ventilated by air, warmed and filtered in winter, and cooled in summer. Passenger steamers upon the lakes and rivers are of gigantic size, and models of elegance.

It is in the cities that the change from colonial conditions is greatest. Most of these—indeed all, excepting those upon the Atlantic coast—have been in

From Andrew Carnegie, *Triumphant Democracy* (Scribners, New York, 1886), 164–183.

Andrew Carnegie. Carnegie was the country's biggest industrialist in the late 1800s, with a fortune estimated to be a half-billion dollars. He was also industry's most articulate spokesman, writing books and articles that were widely read. Carnegie exemplified two cherished American ideals: self-help in the accumulation of wealth and stewardship in the disposal of it. He endowed hundreds of public libraries and donated to a wide range of charities. (The Bettmann Archive)

great measure the result of design instead of being allowed, like Topsy, to "just grow." In these modern days cities are laid out under definite, far-seeing plans; consequently the modern city presents symmetry of form unknown in mediaeval ages. The difference is seen by contrasting the crooked cowpaths of old Boston with the symmetrical, broad streets of Washington or Denver. These are provided with parks at intervals for breathing spaces; amply supplied with pure water, in some cases at enormous expense; the most modern ideas are embodied in their sanitary arrangements; they are well lighted, well policed, and the fire departments are very efficient. In these modern cities an extensive fire is rare. The lessening danger of this risk is indicated by the steady fall in the rate of fire insurance.

The variety and quality of the food of the people of America excels that found elsewhere, and is a constant surprise to Europeans visiting the States. The Americans are the best-fed people on the globe. Their dress is now of the richest character—far beyond that of any other people, compared class for class. The comforts of the average American home compare favorably with those of other lands, while the residences of the wealthy classes are unequaled. The first-class American residence of today in all its appointments excites the envy of the foreigner. One touch of the electric button calls a messenger; two bring a telegraph boy; three summon a policeman; four give the alarm of fire. Telephones are used to an extent undreamt of in Europe, the stables and other out-buildings being connected with the mansion; and the houses of friends are joined by the talking wire almost as often as houses of business. Speaking tubes connect the drawing-room with the kitchen; and the dinner is brought up "piping hot" by a lift. Hot air and steam pipes are carried all over the house; and by the turning of a tap the temperature of any room is regulated to suit the convenience of the occupant. A passenger lift is common. The electric light is an additional home comfort. Indeed, there is no palace or great mansion in Europe with half the conveniences and scientific appliances which characterize the best American mansions. New York Central Park is no unworthy rival of Hyde Park and the Bois de Boulogne in its display of fine equipages; and in winter the hundreds of graceful sleighs dashing along the drives form a picture. The opera-houses, theatres, and public halls of the country excel in magnificence those of other lands, if we except the latter constructions in Paris and Vienna, with which the New York, Philadelphia, and Chicago opera-houses rank. The commercial exchanges, and the imposing structures of the life insurance companies, newspaper buildings, hotels, and many edifices built by wealthy firms, not only in New York but in the cities of the West, never fail to excite the Europeans' surprise. The postal system is equal in every respect to that of Europe. Mails are taken up by express trains, sorted on board, and dropped at all important points without stopping. Letters are delivered several times a day in every considerable town, and a ten-cent special delivery stamp insures delivery at once by special messenger in the large cities. The uniform rate of postage for all distances, often exceeding three thousand miles, is only two cents . . . per ounce.

In short, the conditions of life in American cities may be said to have approximated those of Europe during the sixty years of which we are speaking. Year by year, as the population advances, the general standard of comfort in the smaller Western cities rises to that of the East. Herbert Spencer [an English philosopher] was astonished beyond measure at what he saw in American cities. "Such books as I had looked into," said he, "had given me no adequate idea of the immense developments of material civilization which I have found everywhere. The extent, wealth, and magnificence of your cities, and especially the splendors of New York, have altogether astonished me. Though I have not visited the wonder of the West, Chicago, yet some of your minor modern places, such as Cleveland, have sufficiently amazed me by the marvelous results of one generation's activity. Occasionally, when I have been in places of some ten thousand inhabitants, where the telephone is in general use, I have felt somewhat ashamed of our own unenterprising towns, many of which, of fifty thousand inhabitants and more, make no use of it."

Such is the Democracy; such its conditions of life. In the presence of such a picture can it be maintained that the rule of the people is subversive of government and religion? Where have monarchical institutions developed a community so delightful in itself, so intelligent, so free from crime or pauperism—a community in which the greatest good of the greatest number is so fully attained, and one so well calculated to foster the growth of self-respecting men—which is the end civilization seeks?

> "For ere man made us citizens
> God made us men."

The republican is necessarily self-respecting, for the laws of his country begin by making him a man indeed, the equal of other men. The man who most respects himself will always be found the man who most respects the rights and feelings of others.

The rural democracy of America could be as soon induced to sanction the confiscation of the property of its richer neighbors, or to vote for any violent or discreditable measure, as it could be led to surrender the President for a king. Equal laws and privileges develop all the best and noblest characteristics, and these always lead in the direction of the Golden Rule. These honest, pure, contented, industrious, patriotic people really do consider what they would have others do to them. They ask themselves what is fair and right. Nor is there elsewhere in the world so conservative a body of men; but then it is the equality of the citizen—just and equal laws—republicanism, they are resolved to conserve. To conserve these they are at all times ready to fight and, if need be, to die; for, to men who have once tasted the elixir of political equality, life under unequal conditions could possess no charm.

To every man is committed in some degree, as a sacred trust, the manhood of man. This he may not himself infringe or permit to be infringed by others. Hereditary dignities, political inequalities, do infringe the right of man, and hence are not to be tolerated. The true democrat must live the peer of his fellows, or die struggling to become so.

The American citizen has no further need to struggle, being in possession of equality under the laws in every particular. He has not travelled far in the path of genuine Democracy who would not scorn to enjoy a privilege which was not the common birthright of all his fellows.

15

Prairie Revolt

Rapid agricultural expansion was a crucial part of the nation's amazing economic growth in the late nineteenth century. Yet average farm income went down during this era, and farmers gradually lost their high status in American society. Farmers in the Midwest suffered from bad weather; farmers in the South suffered from weevils and other pests. Everywhere growers received lower prices because of overproduction but paid higher borrowing and shipping costs because of what they saw as greedy, unresponsive banks and railroads. Targeting this network of transportation and finance in frustration, farmers joined organizations such as the Grange and the Farmers' Alliance to promote their own interests. In 1890 midwestern Alliances ran candidates for office against Republicans and Democrats. In the South, Alliance members, facing the problem of racial conflict, sought to take over the Democratic party. In 1892 they formed a national People's, or Populist, party.

Thundering against millionaires and "plutocrats," the Populists demanded major changes, including government ownership of all railroads, telegraph systems, and telephones; a graduated income tax; and a dramatic increase in the national currency by means of "free and unlimited" coinage of silver at a 16-to-1 ratio to gold. The Populists did well for a new party, carrying four states for president in 1892 and receiving a million popular votes as well as electing several congressmen and state officials.

Two developments conspired against further success. First, the party shattered violently along racial lines in the South, with black voters steadily losing the franchise and whites drifting, of necessity, towards the white supremacist Democrats. Second, in the Midwest the two main parties appropriated key Populist positions for their own use. The Democrats proved especially deft at this game, using not only the Populists' class and sectional rhetoric but their call for inflation through the coinage of silver bullion. Western silver miners, not surprisingly, were major backers of the prairie Democrats. The turning point came in 1896 when William Jennings Bryan of Nebraska seized the Democratic nomination for president with a rousing, Populist-inspired speech to the party convention in Chicago. Bryan lost the ensuing election. But he helped the Democrats steal the Populists' thunder and drive them out of existence.

William Jennings Bryan was born in 1860 in Salem, Illinois. He attended college and law school in Illinois before moving to Nebraska. In 1890 he ran successfully for Congress from a Republican district. A free-silver advocate with clear agrarian sympathies, a good writer and orator, Bryan went to Chicago in 1896 as a Nebraska delegate and proceeded to stampede the hall with his "Cross of Gold" speech. The Eastern party barons hated the speech and Bryan; farm-state Democrats loved both. He traveled over 18,000 miles seeking the presidency that year before losing narrowly to William McKinley. He lost again for president in 1900 (against McKinley) and 1908 (against William Howard Taft). Bryan's reputation as an ardent Christian and temperance advocate earned him the nickname the "Great Commoner." He was also a pacifist, a position he generally adhered to even as secretary of state in Woodrow Wilson's first administration. A long-time editor and speaker, he recited his Cross of Gold speech thousands of times. Bryan died in Tennessee in 1925, shortly after prosecuting John T. Scopes for teaching Darwinian evolution instead of biblical creationism in high school.

Questions to Consider. What use did Bryan make of biblical rhetoric and references in his speech? What use did he make of episodes in American history? Were his biblical and historical usages legitimate and accurate? Why did he think government had to regulate the banks? To what extent was Bryan's appeal occupational as opposed to sectional or class-based? Why did bankers oppose Bryan's attack on the gold standard? Why did farmers want more currency in circulation? Could a politician seize a party's nomination by giving an electrifying convention speech today?

The Cross of Gold (1896)

WILLIAM JENNINGS BRYAN

This is not a contest between persons. The humblest citizen in all the land, when clad in the armor of a righteous cause, is stronger than all the hosts of error. I come to speak to you in defense of a cause as holy as the cause of liberty—the cause of humanity.

From William Jennings Bryan, *The First Battle* (Chicago, 1896), 199–205.

When this debate is concluded, a motion will be made to lay upon the table the resolution offered in commendation of the administration, and also the resolution offered in condemnation of the administration. We object to bringing this question down to the level of persons. The individual is but an atom; he is born, he acts, he dies; but principles are eternal; and this has been a contest over a principle.

Never before in the history of this country has there been witnessed such a contest as that through which we have just passed. Never before in the history of American politics has a great issue been fought out as this issue has been, by the voters of a great party. On the fourth of March, 1895, a few Democrats, most of them members of Congress, issued an address to the Democrats of the nation, asserting that the money question was the paramount issue of the hour; declaring that a majority of the Democratic party had the right to control the action of the party on this paramount issue; and concluding with the request that the believers in the free coinage of silver in the Democratic party should organize, take charge of, and control the policy of the Democratic party. Three months later, at Memphis, an organization was perfected, and the silver Democrats went forth openly and courageously proclaiming their belief, and declaring that, if successful, they would crystallize into a platform the declaration which they had made. Then began the conflict. With a zeal approaching the zeal which inspired the Crusaders who followed Peter the Hermit, our silver Democrats went forth from victory unto victory until they are now assembled, not to discuss, not to debate, but to enter up the judgement already rendered by the plain people of this country. . . .

The gentleman who preceded me [ex-Governor Russell] spoke of the State of Massachusetts; let me assure him that not one present in all this convention entertains the least hostility to the people of the State of Massachusetts, but we stand here representing the people who are the equals, before the law, of the greatest citizens in the State of Massachusetts. When you [the gold delegates] come before us and tell us that we are about to disturb your business interests, we reply that you have disturbed our business interests by your course.

We say to you that you have made the definition of a business man too limited in its application. The man who is employed for wages is as much a business man as his employer, the attorney in a country town is as much a business man as the corporation counsel in a great metropolis; the merchant at the cross-roads store is as much a business man as the merchant of New York; the farmer who goes forth in the morning and toils all day—who begins in the spring and toils all summer—and who by the application of brain and muscle to the natural resources of the country creates wealth, is as much a business man as the man who goes upon the board of trade and bets upon the price of grain; the miners who go down a thousand feet into the earth, or climb two thousand feet upon the cliffs, and bring forth from their hiding places the precious metals to be poured into the channels of trade are as much business men as the few financial magnates who, in a back room, corner the money of the world. We come to speak for this broader class of business men.

Ah, my friends, we say not one word against those who live upon the Atlantic coast, but the hardy pioneers who have braved all the dangers of the wilderness, who have made the desert to blossom as the rose—the pioneers away out there [pointing to the West], who rear their children near to Nature's heart, where they can mingle their voices with the voices of the birds—out there where they have erected school houses for the education of their young, churches where they praise their Creator, and cemeteries where rest the ashes of their dead—these people, we say, are as deserving of the consideration of our party as any people in this country. It is for these that we speak. We do not come as aggressors. Our war is not a war of conquest; we are fighting in the defense of our homes, our families, and posterity. We have petitioned, and our petitions have been scorned; we have entreated, and our entreaties have been disregarded; we have begged, and they have mocked when our calamity came. We beg no longer; we petition no more. We defy them.

They tell us that this platform was made to catch votes. We reply to them that changing conditions make new issues; that the principles on which Democracy rests are as everlasting as the hills, but that they must be applied to new conditions as they arise. Conditions have arisen, and we are here to meet those conditions. They tell us that the income tax ought not be brought in here; that it is a new idea. They criticize us for our criticism of the Supreme Court of the United States. My friends, we have not criticized; we have simply called attention to what you already know. If you want criticisms, read the dissenting opinions of the court. There you will find criticisms. They say that we passed an unconstitutional law; we deny it. The income tax law was not unconstitutional when it was passed; it was not unconstitutional when it went before the Supreme Court for the first time; it did not become unconstitutional until one of the judges changed his mind, and we cannot be expected to know when a judge will change his mind. The income tax is just. It simply intends to put the burdens of government upon the backs of the people. I am in favor of an income tax. When I find a man who is not willing to bear his share of the burdens of the government which protects him, I find a man who is unworthy to enjoy the blessings of a government like ours.

They say that we are opposing national bank currency; it is true. If you will read what Thomas Benton said, you will find he said that, in searching history, he could find but one parallel to Andrew Jackson; that was Cicero, who destroyed the conspiracy of Cataline and saved Rome. Benton said that Cicero only did for Rome what Jackson did for us when he destroyed the bank conspiracy and saved America. We say in our platform that we believe that the right to coin and issue money is a function of government. We believe it. We believe that it is a part of sovereignty, and can no more with safety be delegated to private individuals than we could afford to delegate to private individuals the power to make penal statutes or levy taxes. Mr. Jefferson, who was once regarded as good Democratic authority, seems to have differed in opinion from the gentleman who has addrest us on the part of the minority. Those who are opposed to this proposition tell us that the issue of paper money is a function of the bank, and that the Government ought to go out of the banking business. I stand with Jefferson rather than with them, and tell them, as he did, that the issue of money is a function of government, and that banks ought to go out of the governing business. . . .

And now, my friends, let me come to the paramount issue. If they ask us why it is that we say more on the money question than we say upon the tariff question, I reply that, if protection has slain its thousands, the gold standard has slain its tens of thousands. If they ask us why we do not embody in our platform all the things that we believe in, we reply that when we have restored the money of the Constitution all other necessary reforms will be possible; but that until this is done there is no other reform that can be accomplished. . . .

Why this change? Ah, my friends, is not the reason for the change evident to any one who will look at the matter? No private character, however pure, no personal popularity, however great, can protect from the avenging wrath of an indignant people a man who will declare that he is in favor of fastening the gold standard upon this country, or who is willing to surrender the right of self-government and place the legislative control of our affairs in the hands of foreign potentates and powers. . . .

Here is the line of battle, and we care not upon which issue they force the fight; we are prepared to meet them on either issue or on both. If they tell us that the gold standard is the standard of civilization, we reply to them that this, the most enlightened of all the nations of the earth, has never declared for a gold standard and that both the great parties this year are declaring against it. If the gold standard is the standard of civilization, why, my friends, should we not have it? If they come to meet us on that issue we can present the history of our nation. More than that; we can tell them that they will search the pages of history in vain to find a single instance where the common people have ever declared themselves in favor of the gold standard. They can find where the holders of fixt investments have declared for a gold standard, but not where the masses have.

Mr. Carlisle said in 1878 that this was a struggle between "the idle holders of idle capital" and "the struggling masses, who produce the wealth and pay the taxes of the country"; and, my friends, the question we are to decide is: Upon which side will the Democratic party fight; upon the side of "the idle holders of idle capital" or upon the side of "the struggling masses"? That is the question which the party must answer first, and then it must be answered by each individual hereafter. The sympathies of the Democratic party, as shown by the platform, are on the side of the struggling masses who have ever been the foundation of the Democratic party. There are two ideas of government. There are those who believe that, if you will only legislate to make the well-to-do prosperous, their prosperity will leak through on those below. The Democratic idea, however, is that if you legislate to make the masses prosperous, their prosperity will find its way up through every class which rests upon them.

You come to us and tell us that the great cities are in favor of the gold standard; we reply that the great cities rest upon our broad and fertile prairies. Burn down your cities and leave our farms, and your cities will spring up again as if by magic; but destroy our farms and the grass will grow in the streets of every city in the country.

My friends, we declare that this nation is able to legislate for its own people on every question, without waiting for the aid or consent of any other nation on earth; and upon that issue we expect to carry every State in the Union. I shall not slander the inhabitants of the fair State of Massachusetts nor the inhabitants of the State of New York by saying that, when they are confronted with the proposition, they will declare that this nation is not able to attend to its own business. It is the issue of 1776 over again. Our ancestors, when but three millions in number, had the courage to declare their political independence of every other nation; shall we, their descendants, when we have grown to seventy millions, declare that we are less independent than our forefathers? No, my friends, that will never be the verdict of our people. Therefore we care not upon what lines the battle is fought. If they say bimetalism is good, but that we cannot have it until the other nations help us, we reply that, instead of having a gold standard because England has, we will restore bimetalism, and then let England have bimetalism because the United States has it. If they dare to come out in the open field and defend the gold standard as a good thing, we will fight them to the uttermost. Having behind us the producing masses of this nation and the world, supported by the commercial interests, the laboring interests, and the toilers everywhere, we will answer their demand for a gold standard by saying to them: You shall not press down upon the brow of labor this crown of thorns, you shall not crucify mankind upon a cross of gold.

The Lure of the East

The United States went to war with Spain over Cuba in 1898. But the U.S. victory in the brief war brought acquisitions in the Pacific (the Philippines and Guam) as well as in the Caribbean (Puerto Rico); at this time the United States also got control of the Hawaiian Islands and Wake Island. In part these acquisitions represented the resumption of a long tradition of westward territorial expansion that had been abandoned since the purchase of Alaska in 1867. In part they represented America's desire for "great power" status at a time when the European nations were winning colonies in Asia and Africa. But powerful economic forces were at work, too, as they had been in the formulation of the recent Open Door policy or, for that matter, in President James Monroe's assertion of his famous Doctrine in 1823.

At the beginning of the war, President William McKinley was unsure himself whether or not the United States should take over the Philippines, and if it did, whether its forces would take only Manila, or the whole island of Luzon, or the entire archipelago. Not until December 1898 did the president finally announce that the United States would pursue a policy of "benevolent assimilation" toward the whole territory. This decision gave rise to a small but vocal anti-imperialist movement at home and, more important, a strong Filipino resistance struggle against the American occupation.

At this point, however, forceful advocates of imperialism rose to defend the president in the most vigorous terms. Of these none was more forceful or more important than Senator Albert J. Beveridge. His Senate speech of January 1900 in support of a (successful) resolution urging colonial status for the Philippines, excerpted below, provided the broadest possible grounds for the president's policy. With the fight thus in hand at home, McKinley turned to winning the fight abroad. Having made his decision, moreover, he stuck doggedly with it. In fact, the Americans overcame the insurgents only after another year's hard fighting and the death of more than a hundred thousand Filipinos.

President McKinley's ally and fellow Ohioan, Albert Beveridge, was only thirty-seven at the time of his imperialist speech of 1900, but he was already known as a proponent of military strength and Anglo-Saxon supremacy. This speech further enhanced his standing in Republican circles. Beveridge left the Senate in 1912 to devote himself to writing. In 1919, eight years before his death in Indiana, his *Life of John Marshall* was awarded the Pulitzer Prize for historical biography.

Questions to Consider. Beveridge's speech makes enormous claims for the strategic importance of the Philippines. On what grounds did Beveridge make these claims? Has history borne out Beveridge's predictions about the Pacific Ocean and world commerce? Did Beveridge think acquiring the Philippines would increase or reduce the chances of war? How did he seem to view the Declaration of Independence and the Constitution? Was Beveridge's main concern economics or race?

America's Destiny (1900)

ALBERT BEVERIDGE

Mr. President, the times call for candor. The Philippines are ours forever, "territory belonging to the United States," as the Constitution calls them. And just beyond the Philippines are China's illimitable markets. We will not retreat from either. We will not repudiate our duty in the archipelago. We will not abandon our opportunity in the Orient. We will not renounce our part in the mission of our race, trustee, under God, of the civilization of the world. And we will move forward to our work, not howling out regrets like slaves whipped to their burdens, but with gratitude for a task worthy of our strength, and thanksgiving to Almighty God that He has marked us as His chosen people, henceforth to lead in the regeneration of the world.

This island empire is the last land left in all the oceans. If it should prove a mistake to abandon it, the blunder once made would be irretrievable. If it proves a mistake to hold it, the error can be corrected when we will. Every other progressive nation stands ready to relieve us.

But to hold it will be no mistake. Our largest trade henceforth must be with Asia. The Pacific is our ocean. More and more Europe will manufacture the most it needs, secure from its colonies the most it consumes. Where shall we turn for consumers of our surplus? Geography answers the question. China is our natural customer. She is nearer to us than to England, Germany, or Russia, the commercial powers of the present and the future. They have

From the *Congressional Record,* 56th Congress, 1st session, 704–712.

moved nearer to China by securing permanent bases on her borders. The Philippines give us a base at the door of all the East.

Lines of navigation from our ports to the Orient and Australia; from the Isthmian Canal to Asia; from all Oriental ports to Australia, converge at and separate from the Philippines. They are a self-supporting, dividend-paying fleet, permanently anchored at a spot selected by the strategy of Providence, commanding the Pacific. And the Pacific is the ocean of the commerce of the future. Most future wars will be conflicts for commerce. The power that rules the Pacific, therefore, is the power that rules the world. And, with the Philippines, that power is and will forever be the American Republic. . . .

Nothing is so natural as trade with one's neighbors. The Philippines make us the nearest neighbors of all the East. Nothing is more natural than to trade with those you know. This is the philosophy of all advertising. The Philippines bring us permanently face to face with the most sought-for customers of the world. National prestige, national propinquity, these and commercial activity are the elements of commercial success. The Philippines give the first; the character of the American people supply the last. It is a providential conjunction of all the elements of trade, of duty, and of power. If we are willing to go to war rather than let England have a few feet of frozen Alaska, which affords no market and commands none, what should we not do rather than let England, Germany, Russia, or Japan have all the Philippines? And no man on the spot can fail to see that this would be their fate if we retired. . . .

Here, then, Senators, is the situation. Two years ago there was no land in all the world which we could occupy for any purpose. Our commerce was daily turning toward the Orient, and geography and trade developments made necessary our commercial empire over the Pacific. And in that ocean we had no commercial, naval, or military base. Today we have one of the three great ocean possessions of the globe, located at the most commanding commercial, naval, and military points in the eastern seas, within hail of India, shoulder to shoulder with China, richer in its own resources than any equal body of land on the entire globe, and peopled by a race which civilization demands shall be improved. Shall we abandon it? That man little knows the common people of the Republic, little understands the instincts of our race, who thinks we will not hold it fast and hold it forever, administering just government by simplest methods. We may trick up devices to shift our burden and lessen our opportunity; they will avail us nothing but delay. We may tangle conditions by applying academic arrangements of self-government to a crude situation; their failure will drive us to our duty in the end. . . .

But, Senators, it would be better to abandon this combined garden and Gibraltar of the Pacific, and count our blood and treasure already spent a profitable loss, than to apply any academic arrangement of self-government to these children. They are not capable of self-government. How could they be? They are not of a self-governing race. They are Orientals, Malays, instructed by Spaniards in the latter's worst estate.

They know nothing of practical government except as they have witnessed the weak, corrupt, cruel, and capricious rule of Spain. What magic will anyone employ to dissolve in their minds and characters those impressions of governors and governed which three centuries of misrule have created? What alchemy will change the oriental quality of their blood and set the self-governing currents of the American pouring through their Malay veins? How shall they, in the twinkling of an eye, be exalted to the heights of self-governing peoples which required a thousand years for us to reach, Anglo-Saxon though we are . . . ?

The Declaration of Independence does not forbid us to do our part in the regeneration of the world. If it did, the Declaration would be wrong, just as the Articles of Confederation, drafted by the very same men who signed the Declaration, was found to be wrong. The Declaration has no application to the present situation. It was written by self-governing men for self-governing men. . . .

Senators in opposition are stopped from denying our constitutional power to govern the Philippines as circumstances may demand, for such power is admitted in the case of Florida, Louisiana, Alaska. How, then, is it denied in the Philippines? Is there a geographical interpretation to the Constitution? Do degrees of longitude fix constitutional limitations? Does a thousand miles of ocean diminish constitutional power more than a thousand miles of land . . . ?

No; the oceans are not limitations of the power which the Constitution expressly gives Congress to govern all territory the nation may acquire. The Constitution declares that "Congress shall have power to dispose of and make all needful rules and regulations respecting the territory belonging to the United States." . . .

Mr. President, this question is deeper than any question of party politics; deeper than any question of the isolated policy of our country even; deeper even than any question of constitutional power. It is elemental. It is racial. God has not been preparing the English-speaking and Teutonic peoples for a thousand years for nothing but vain and idle self-contemplation and self-admiration. No! He has made us the master organizers of the world to establish system where chaos reigns. He has given us the spirit of progress to overwhelm the forces of reaction throughout the earth. He has made us adepts in government that we may administer government among savage and senile peoples. Were it not for such a force as this the world would relapse into barbarism and night. And of all our race He has marked the American people as His chosen nation to finally lead in the regeneration of the world. This is the divine mission of America, and it holds for us all the profit, all the glory, all the happiness possible to man. We are trustees of the world's progress, guardians of its righteous peace. The judgment of the Master is upon us: "Ye have been faithful over a few things; I will make you ruler over many things."

What shall history say of us? Shall it say that we renounced that holy trust, left the savage to his base condition, the wilderness to the reign of waste, deserted duty, abandoned glory, forgot our sordid profit even, because we feared our strength and read the charter of our powers with the doubter's eye and the quibbler's mind? Shall it say that, called by events to captain and command the proudest, ablest, purest race of history in history's noblest work, we declined that great commission? Our fathers would not have had it so. No! They founded no paralytic government, incapable of the simplest acts of administration. They planted no sluggard people, passive while the world's work calls them. They established no reactionary nation. They unfurled no retreating flag. . . .

Mr. President and Senators, adopt the resolution offered, that peace may quickly come and that we may begin our saving, regenerating, and uplifting work. . . . Reject it, and the world, history, and the American people will know where to forever fix the awful responsibility for the consequences that will surely follow such failure to do our manifest duty. . . .

17

The Right to Vote

Abigail Adams and other isolated voices urged voting rights for women at the time of the American Revolution, to no avail. In 1848 women convened at Seneca Falls, New York, to demand legal and political rights, including the vote, and they kept up their demand during the postwar debate on the enfranchisement of the freedmen. In 1869 two organizations emerged, the National Woman Suffrage Association, which fought for federal voting rights via a Constitutional amendment, and the American Woman Suffrage Association, which sought victories in the states. A woman suffrage amendment was introduced in the Senate in 1878 but gained little backing and was seldom debated. By the 1890s nineteen states allowed women to vote on school issues; three allowed them to vote on tax and bond issues; Wyoming, Colorado, Utah, and Idaho allowed full political rights.

In 1890, fearing (correctly) that the movement was about to stall in the face of the typical male view that "equal suffrage is a repudiation of manhood," the two main suffrage organizations combined in the National American Woman Suffrage Association, which focused on both promising states and Congress. Raising the level of argument and agitation as best they could, suffrage leaders met annually to resolve, write, speak, and strategize. One of the most important statements came in the 1904 "Declaration of Principles," reproduced below. Several other states now gave women the vote, including the key battleground of Illinois and New York. Pressure thus built in Congress to pass a suffrage amendment.

World War I proved the turning point. President Woodrow Wilson, an opponent of woman suffrage, wanted women's organizations to support the war. Most of them did so and even served in the government—but only if he promised to support a suffrage amendment. Wilson told the Senate in 1918 that the vote for women was "vital to the winning of the war." In 1919 Congress passed the 19th Amendment. Ratification came the next year. After a century of struggle, women had the vote.

The 1904 Declaration of Principles was the handiwork of four great leaders of the women's rights movement: Carrie Chapman Catt, Alice Stone Blackwell, Ida Husted Harper, and Anna Howard Shaw. Carrie

Chapman Catt (1859–1947) was born in Wisconsin, became one of the country's first female school superintendents, and worked as a suffragist organizer in Iowa. The wife of an engineer, Catt was elected president of the National American Woman Suffrage Association in 1900, served Woodrow Wilson on the Council of National Defense, and was instrumental in establishing the League of Women Voters after 1920. Alice Stone Blackwell (1857–1950), daughter of a Cincinnati merchant and the legendary suffragist pioneer Lucy Stone, attended Boston University, where she excelled, and became a major feminist editor. She served as secretary of the new National American Woman Suffrage Association. She was also active in the causes of prohibition, peace, and organized labor, moving, after the adoption of the 19th Amendment, toward more progressive, even socialist politics.

Ida Husted Harper (1851–1931) was born on an Indiana farm, attended Indiana University, and became a high school principal. A gifted writer whose husband was a noted labor lawyer, Harper worked chiefly as a journalist and suffragist. She wrote the definitive early biography of Susan B. Anthony and a monumental *History of Woman Suffrage* and was influential in the drive for the 19th Amendment. English-born Anna Howard Shaw (1847–1919) arrived in the United States as a 12-year-old with her father, a Unitarian minister and reformer. Self-schooled but an avid reader, Shaw became a Unitarian minister herself in 1871, later switching to Methodism before entering medical school at Boston University. In the end she chose suffrage work over preaching or medicine, became friends with Susan B. Anthony and Lucy Stone, and traveled to every state in the union on behalf of national suffrage. She died of exhaustion only days after Congress passed the 19th Amendment.

Questions to Consider. The "Declaration of Principles" argued that women should have the vote in part because of new social, economic, and diplomatic circumstances. What were these new circumstances? Which of them did the authors seem to think would have the greatest appeal? Would woman suffragists fifty years earlier have used the same arguments? Do you find them still persuasive? What might the authors have said that they did not say?

Declaration of Principles (1904)

CARRIE CHAPMAN CATT, ALICE STONE BLACKWELL, IDA HUSTED HARPER, ANNA HOWARD SHAW

When our forefathers gained the victory in a seven years' war to establish the principle that representation should go hand in hand with taxation, they marked a new epoch in the history of man; but though our foremothers bore an equal part in that long conflict its triumph brought to them no added rights and through all the following century and a quarter, taxation without representation has been continuously imposed on women by as great tyranny as King George exercised over the American colonists.

So long as no married woman was permitted to own property and all women were barred from the money-making occupations this discrimination did not seem so invidious; but to-day the situation is without a parallel. The women of the United States now pay taxes on real and personal estate valued at billions of dollars. In a number of individual States their holdings amount to many millions. Everywhere they are accumulating property. In hundreds of places they form one-third of the taxpayers, with the number constantly increasing, and yet they are absolutely without representation in the affairs of the nation, of the State, even of the community in which they live and pay taxes. We enter our protest against this injustice and we demand that the immortal principles established by the War of the Revolution shall be applied equally to women and men citizens.

As our new republic passed into a higher stage of development the gross inequality became apparent of giving representation to capital and denying it to labor; therefore the right of suffrage was extended to the workingman. Now we demand for the 4,000,000 wage-earning women of our country the same protection of the ballot as is possessed by the wage-earning men.

The founders took an even broader view of human rights when they declared that government could justly derive its powers only from the consent of the governed, and for 125 years this grand assertion was regarded as a corner-stone of the republic, with scarcely a recognition of the fact that one-half of the citizens were as completely governed without their consent as were the people of any absolute monarchy in existence. It was only when our government was extended over alien races in foreign countries that our people awoke to the meaning of the principles of the Declaration of Independence. In response to its provisions, the Congress of the United States hastened to invest with the power of consent the men of this new territory, but committed the flagrant injustice of withholding it from the women. We demand that the ballot shall be extended to the women of our foreign possessions on the same terms as to the men. Furthermore, we demand that the women of the United States shall no longer suffer the degradation of being held not so competent to exercise the suffrage as a Filipino, a Hawaiian or a Porto Rican man.

The remaining Territories within the United States are insisting upon admission into the Union on the ground that their citizens desire "the right to select their own governing officials, choose their own judges, name those who are to make their laws and levy, collect, and disburse their taxes." These are

From *History of Woman Suffrage* (1881–1922), 5: 130.

just and commendable desires but we demand that their women shall have full recognition as citizens when these Territories are admitted and that their constitutions shall secure to women precisely the same rights as to men.

When our government was founded the rudiments of education were thought sufficient for women, since their entire time was absorbed in the multitude of household duties. Now the number of girls graduated by the high schools greatly exceeds the number of boys in every State and the percentage of women students in the colleges is vastly larger than that of men. Meantime most of the domestic industries have been taken from the home to the factory and hundreds of thousands of women have followed them there, while the more highly trained have entered the professions and other avenues of skilled labor. We demand that under this new régime, and in view of these changed conditions in which she is so important a factor woman shall have a voice and a vote in the solution of their innumerable problems.

The laws of practically every State provide that the husband shall select the place of residence for the family, and if the wife refuse to abide by his choice she forfeits her right to support and her refusal shall be regarded as desertion. We protest against the recent decision of the courts which has added to this injustice by requiring the wife also to accept for herself the citizenship preferred by her husband, thus compelling a woman born in the United States to lose her nationality if her husband choose to declare his allegiance to a foreign country.

As women form two-thirds of the church membership of the entire nation; as they constitute but one-eleventh of the convicted criminals; as they are rapidly becoming the educated class and as the salvation of our government depends upon a moral, law-abiding, educated electorate, we demand for the sake of its integrity and permanence that women be made a part of its voting body.

In brief, we demand that all constitutional and legal barriers shall be removed which deny to women any individual right or personal freedom which is granted to man. This we ask in the name of a democratic and a republican government, which, its constitution declares, was formed "to establish justice and secure the blessings of liberty."

18

Side Effects

Industrialization brought, among other things, the factory system: big machines in large buildings where thousands of workers did specialized tasks under strict supervision. The factory system vastly increased America's output of such products as glass, machinery, newspapers, soap, cigarettes, beef, and beer. Factories thus provided innumerable new goods and millions of new jobs for Americans. But factories also reduced workers' control over their place of work, made the conditions of labor more dangerous, and played no small part in destroying the dignity of that labor. The first part of the following excerpt from Upton Sinclair's novel *The Jungle* offers a glimpse into the factory system as it operated in a Chicago meat-packing plant around 1905.

Industrialization produced not only big factories but also big cities, particularly in the Northeast and Midwest. Sinclair therefore took pains to show the role of industry and new production techniques in creating urban transportation and other services. The second part of the excerpt suggests a few of the links between industrial growth and Chicago's leaders—the so-called gray wolves who controlled the city's government and businesses. Here again, Sinclair indicates the high toll in human life exacted by unrestrained development.

The Jungle caused a sensation when it was first published. The pages describing conditions in Chicago's meatpacking plants aroused horror, disgust, and fury, and sales of meat dropped precipitously. "I aimed at the public's heart," said Sinclair ruefully, "and hit it in the stomach." President Theodore Roosevelt ordered a congressional investigation of meat-packing plants in the nation, and Congress subsequently passed the Meat Inspection Act. But Sinclair, a socialist, did not seek to inspire reform legislation. He was concerned mainly with dramatizing the misery of workers under the capitalist mode of production and with winning recruits to socialism.

Upton Sinclair was born in Baltimore, Maryland, in 1878. After attending college in New York City, he began to write essays and fiction, experiencing his first real success with the publication of *The Jungle* in 1906. Dozens of novels on similar subjects—the coal and oil industries, newspapers, the liquor business, the persecution of radicals, the threat of dictatorship—poured from his pen in the following years, though none had the immediate impact of *The Jungle.* Sinclair's style, with its emphasis on the details of everyday life, resembles the realism of other writers of the time. But he also wrote as a "muckraker" (as Theodore Roosevelt called journalists who wrote exposés), trying to alert readers to the deceit and corruption then prevalent in American life. Unlike most muckrakers, however, Sinclair was politically active, running in California in the 1920s as a socialist candidate for the U.S. Congress. In 1934 he won the Democratic nomination for governor with the slogan "End Poverty in California"(EPIC), but he lost the election. During World War II he was a warm supporter of President Franklin D. Roosevelt and wrote novels about the war, one of which won a Pulitzer Prize. Not long before Sinclair's death in 1968 in Bound Brook, New Jersey, President Lyndon Johnson invited him to the White House to be present at the signing of the Wholesome Meat Act.

Questions to Consider. *The Jungle* has been regarded as propaganda, not literature, and has been placed second only to Harriet Beecher Stowe's *Uncle Tom's Cabin* in its effectiveness as a propagandistic novel. Why do you think the novel caused demands for reform rather than converts to socialism? What seems more shocking in the passages from the novel reprinted below, the life of immigrant workers in Chicago in the early twentieth century or the filthy conditions under which meat was prepared for America's dining tables? What did Sinclair reveal about the organization of the work force in Chicago's meatpacking plants? Sinclair centered his story on a Lithuanian worker named Jurgis Rudkus and his wife, Ona. In what ways did he make Jurgis's plight seem typical of urban workers of his time? Why did Jurgis deny that he had ever worked in Chicago before? What did Sinclair reveal about the attitude of employers toward labor unions at that time?

The Jungle (1906)

UPTON SINCLAIR

There was another interesting set of statistics that a person might have gathered in Packingtown—those of the various afflictions of the workers. When

From Upton Sinclair, *The Jungle* (Doubleday, Page and Co., New York, 1906), 116–117, 265–269. Published in the British Commonwealth by Penguin Books, Ltd. Reprinted by permission of the Estate of Upton Sinclair.

A meatpacking house. Trimmers wielding razor-sharp knives in a Chicago packing house in 1892, more than a decade before the publication of *The Jungle.* (Chicago Historical Society)

Jurgis had first inspected the packing plants with Szedvilas, he had marveled while he listened to the tale of all the things that were made out of the carcasses of animals and of all the lesser industries that were maintained there; now he found that each one of these lesser industries was a separate little inferno, in its way as horrible as the killing-beds, the source and fountain of them all. The workers in each of them had their own peculiar diseases. And the wandering visitor might be skeptical about all the swindles, but he could not be skeptical about these, for the worker bore the evidence of them about on his own person—generally he had only to hold out his hand.

There were the men in the pickle rooms, for instance, where old Antanas had gotten his death; scarce a one of these had not some spot of horror on his person. Let a man so much as scrape his finger pushing a truck in the pickle rooms, and he might have a sore that would put him out of the world; all the joints in his fingers might be eaten by the acid, one by one. Of the butchers and floormen, the beef boners and trimmers, and all those who used knives, you could scarcely find a person who had the use of his thumb; time and time again the base of it had been slashed, till it was a mere lump of flesh against which the man pressed the knife to hold it. The hands of these men would be criss-crossed with cuts, until you could no longer pretend to count them or to trace them. They would have no nails—they had worn them off pulling hides; their knuckles were swollen so that their fingers spread out like a fan. There were men who worked in the cooking rooms, in the midst of steam and sickening odors, by artificial light; in these rooms the germs of tuberculosis might live for two years, but the supply was renewed every hour. There were the beef luggers, who carried two-hundred-pound quarters into the refrigerator cars, a fearful kind of work, that began at four o'clock in the morning, and that wore out the most powerful man in a few years. There were those who worked in the chilling rooms, and whose special disease was rheumatism; the time limit that a man could work in the chilling rooms was said to be five years. There were the wool pluckers, whose hands went to pieces even sooner than the hands of the pickle men; for the pelts of the sheep had to be painted with acid to loosen the wool, and then the pluckers had to pull out this wool with their bare hands, till the acid had eaten their fingers off. There were those who made the tins for the canned meat, and their hands, too, were a maze of cuts, and each cut represented a chance for blood poisoning. Some worked at the stamping machines, and it was very seldom that one could work long there at the pace that was set, and not give out and forget himself, and have a part of his hand chopped off. There were the "hoisters," as they were called, whose task it was to press the lever which lifted the dead cattle off the floor. They ran along upon a rafter, peering down through the damp and the steam, and as old Durham's architects had not built the killing room for the convenience of the hoisters, at every few feet they would have to stoop under a beam, say four feet above the one they ran on, which got them into the habit of stooping, so that in a few years they would be walking like chimpanzees. Worst of any, however, were the fertilizer men, and those who served in the cooking rooms. These people could not be shown to the visitor—for the odor of a fertilizer man would scare any ordinary visitor at a hundred yards, and as for the other men, who worked in tank rooms full of steam and in some of which there were open vats near the level of the floor, their peculiar trouble was that they fell into the vats; and when they were fished out, there was never enough of them left to be worth exhibiting—sometimes they would be overlooked for days, till all but the bones of them had gone out to the world as Durham's Pure Leaf Lard!

* * * * *

Early in the fall Jurgis set out for Chicago again. All the joy went out of tramping as soon as a man could not keep warm in the hay; and, like many thousands of others, he deluded himself with the hope that by coming early he could avoid the rush. He brought fifteen dollars with him, hidden away in one of his shoes, a sum which had been saved from the saloon keepers, not so much by his conscience, as by the fear which filled him at the thought of being out of work in the city in the wintertime.

He traveled upon the railroad with several other men, hiding in freight cars at night, and liable to be thrown off at any time, regardless of the speed of the train. When he reached the city he left the rest, for he had money and they did not, and he meant to save himself in this fight. He would bring to it all the skill that practice had brought him, and he would stand, whoever fell. On fair nights he would sleep in the park or on a truck or an empty barrel or box, and when it was rainy or cold he would stow himself upon a shelf in a ten-cent lodging-house, or pay three cents for the privileges of a "squatter" in a tenement hallway. He would eat at free lunches, five cents a meal, and never a cent more—so he might keep alive for two months and more, and in that time he would surely find a job. He would have to bid farewell to his summer cleanliness, of course, for he would come out of the first night's lodging with his clothes alive with vermin. There was no place in the city where he could wash even his face, unless he went down to the lake front—and there it would soon be all ice.

First he went to the steel mill and the harvester works, and found that his places there had been filled long ago. He was careful to keep away from the stockyards—he was a single man now, he told himself, and he meant to stay one, to have his wages for his own when he got a job. He began the long, weary round of factories and warehouses, tramping all day, from one end of the city to the other, finding everywhere from ten to a hundred men ahead of him. He watched the newspapers, too—but no longer was he to be taken in by the smooth-spoken agents. He had been told of all those tricks while "on the road."

In the end it was through a newspaper that he got a job, after nearly a month of seeking. It was a call for a hundred laborers, and though he thought it was a "fake," he went because the place was near by. He found a line of men a block long, but as a wagon chanced to come out of an alley and break the line, he saw his chance and sprang to seize a place. Men threatened him and tried to throw him out, but he cursed and made a disturbance to attract a policeman, upon which they subsided, knowing that if the latter interfered it would be to "fire" them all.

An hour or two later he entered a room and confronted a big Irishman behind a desk.

"Ever worked in Chicago before?" the man inquired; and whether it was a good angel that put it into Jurgis's mind, or an intuition of his sharpened wits, he was moved to answer, "no, sir."

"Where do you come from?"

"Kansas City, sir."

"Any references?"

"No sir. I'm just an unskilled man, I've got good arms."

"I want men for hard work—it's all underground, digging tunnels for telephones. Maybe it won't suit you."

"I'm willing, sir—anything for me. What's the pay?"

"Fifteen cents an hour."

"I'm willing, sir."

"All right; go back there and give your name."

So within half an hour he was at work, far underneath the streets of the city. The tunnel was a peculiar one for telephone wires; it was about eight feet high, and with a level floor nearly as wide. It had innumerable branches—a perfect spider-web beneath the city; Jurgis walked over half a mile with his gang to the place where they were to work. Stranger yet, the tunnel was lighted by electricity, and upon it was laid a double-tracked, narrow gauge railroad!

But Jurgis was not there to ask questions, and he did not give the matter a thought. It was nearly a year afterward that he finally learned the meaning of this whole affair. The City Council had passed a quiet and innocent little bill allowing a company to construct telephone conduits under the city streets; and upon the strength of this, a great corporation had proceeded to tunnel all Chicago with a system of railway freight subways. In the city there was a combination of employers, representing hundreds of millions of capital, and formed for the purpose of crushing the labor unions. The chief union which troubled it was the teamsters'; and when these freight tunnels were completed, connecting all the big factories and stores with the railroad depots, they would have the teamsters' union by the throat. Now and then there were rumors and murmurs in the Board of Aldermen, and once there was a committee to investigate—but each time another small fortune was paid over, and the rumors died away; until at last the city woke up with a start to find the work completed. There was a tremendous scandal, of course; it was found that the city records had been falsified and other crimes committed, and some of Chicago's big capitalists got into jail—figuratively speaking. The aldermen declared that they had had no idea of it all, in spite of the fact that the main entrance to the work had been in the rear of the saloon of one of them. . . .

In a work thus carried out, not much thought was given to the welfare of the laborers. On an average, the tunneling cost a life a day and several manglings; it was seldom, however, that more than a dozen or two men heard of any one accident. The work was all done by the new boring-machinery, with as little blasting as possible; but there would be falling rocks and crushed supports and premature explosions—and in addition all the dangers of railroading. So it was that one night, as Jurgis was on his way out with his gang, an engine and a loaded car dashed round one of the innumerable right-angle branches and struck him upon the shoulder, hurling him against the concrete wall and knocking him senseless.

When he opened his eyes again it was to the clanging of the bell of an ambulance. He was lying in it, covered by a blanket, and it was heading its way slowly through the holiday-shopping crowds. They took him to the county hospital, where a young surgeon set his arm, then he was washed and laid upon a bed in a ward with a score or two more of maimed and mangled men.

19

Taxing the Rich

Taxes have been a sore issue for most of American history. The colonists took up arms against England partly to protest obnoxious taxes. Pennsylvania farmers mounted the Whiskey Rebellion, which Washington and Hamilton ruthlessly crushed, against excise taxes on corn liquor. Tax revolts flared periodically elsewhere through the nineteenth century. Yet taxes, even in early America, were an accepted fact of life. Governments had to function, especially at the local level, and tax revenues were needed to pay for, among other things, public schools and colleges, prisons and asylums, roads and bridges, police and firefighters, public water and sanitation systems, canals and dams, the postal service, and the military, including the service academies.

Most early local taxes were based on property ownership rather than personal or business income, which was appropriate when livelihoods derived directly from land or workshop or countinghouse. The federal government got most of its tax revenue from customs duties or selected taxes, usually modest excise taxes on domestic production. Only during the Civil War, when finances were stretched to the breaking point, did Congress levy a tax on incomes, and then only for the duration of the conflict.

In the late nineteenth century, reformers again urged an income tax, in part to fund programs and services but also, by now, to reduce the swollen private fortunes that were so startling a feature of industrial America. Numerous states instituted income tax systems, as did, very modestly, the national government. Populists and other reformers, however, wanted more. They wanted a progressive, or graduated, tax system that would tax high incomes at a higher rate than those below. They also wanted a significant inheritance, or death, tax on accumulated wealth, again to reduce economic inequality. They wanted, in other words, to use the tax system to spread prosperity around and share the wealth. Congress passed a modest income tax in 1894, which the Supreme Court promptly ruled unconstitutional.

Democrats were more likely to advocate graduated income and inheritance taxes than Republicans, who drew support from the wealthier classes. But Theodore Roosevelt, the Republican governor of New York, endorsed a Democratic proposal to impose a tax on corporations in 1902, and as president his interest in taxation grew. He became a strong proponent of the steeply graduated inheritance tax and, increasingly, of the graduated income tax as well. In his 1906 message to Congress on tax policy, excerpted below, he came out for both, though TR, ever the shrewd politician, was more cautious about taxing income than inheritance. TR and other voices thus built a constituency for both a federal income tax and a graduated tax structure. In 1913 the country ratified the 16th Amendment, allowing a federal income tax. That same year Congress imposed a graduated tax of 1 to 6 percent on personal incomes of $3,000 and over. The income tax thus joined women's suffrage and prohibition as keystone achievements of the Progressive era.

Questions to Consider. What reasons did Roosevelt give for supporting a stiff inheritance tax? Why was he the first president to urge Congress to tax inheritances? To what political groups did he appear to be appealing? Do you find his arguments for taxing inheritance compelling today? What were his reasons for mentioning an income tax? Does he seem to have been as aggressive in arguing for this tax as for a tax on inheritances? What might have accounted for any differences that you detect?

Message to Congress (1906)

THEODORE ROOSEVELT

There are many kinds of taxes which can only be levied by the general government so as to produce the best results, because, among other reasons, the attempt to impose them in one particular State too often results merely in driving the corporation or individual affected to some other locality or other State. The National Government has long derived its chief revenue from a tariff on imports and from an internal or excise tax. In addition to these there is every reason why, when next our system of taxation is revised, the National Government should impose a graduated inheritance tax, and, if possible, a graduated income tax. The man of great wealth owes a peculiar obligation to the State, because he derives special advantages from the mere existence of government. Not only should he recognize this obligation in the way he leads

From James Richardson, *Messages and Papers of the Presidents* (Government Printing Office, Washington, D.C., 1909), XI: 1200–1202.

Theodore Roosevelt, hands raised for emphasis, speaking to a crowd of railroad workers, supporters, and the curious, including many perched atop surrounding structures for a better view. Roosevelt, an ardent devotee of "the strenuous life," was one of the era's most dynamic and compelling public speakers in spite of his high-pitched, sometimes squeaky voice. (New-York Historical Society)

his daily life and in the way he earns and spends his money, but it should also be recognized by the way in which he pays for the protection the State gives him. On the one hand, it is desirable that he should assume his full and proper share of the burden of taxation; on the other hand, it is quite as necessary that in this kind of taxation, where the men who vote the tax pay but little of it, there should be clear recognition of the danger of inaugurating any such system save in a spirit of entire justice and moderation. Whenever we, as a people, undertake to remodel our taxation system along the lines suggested, we must make it clear beyond peradventure that our aim is to distribute the burden of supporting the government more equitably than at present; that we intend to treat rich man and poor man on a basis of absolute equality, and that we regard it as equally fatal to true democracy to do or permit injustice to the one as to do or permit injustice to the other.

I am well aware that such a subject as this needs long and careful study in order that the people may become familiar with what is proposed to be done, may clearly see the necessity of proceeding with wisdom and self-restraint, and may make up their minds just how far they are willing to go in the matter; while only trained legislators can work out the project in necessary detail. But I feel that in the near future our national legislators should enact a law providing for a graduated inheritance tax by which a steadily increasing rate of duty should be put upon all moneys or other valuables coming by gift, bequest, or devise to any individual or corporation. It may be well to make the tax heavy in proportion as the individual benefited is remote of kin. In any event, in my judgment the pro rata of the tax should increase very heavily with the increase of the amount left to any one individual after a certain point has been reached. It is most desirable to encourage thrift and ambition, and a potent source of thrift and ambition is the desire on the part of the bread-winner to leave his children well off. This object can be attained by making the tax very small on moderate amounts of property left; because the prime object should be to put a constantly increasing burden on the inheritance of those swollen fortunes which it is certainly of no benefit to this country to perpetuate.

There can be no question of the ethical propriety of the government thus determining the conditions upon which any gift or inheritance should be received. Exactly how far the inheritance tax would, as an incident, have the effect of limiting the transmission by devise or gift of the enormous fortunes in question it is not necessary at present to discuss. It is wise that progress in this direction should be gradual. At first a permanent national inheritance tax, while it might be more substantial than any such tax has hitherto been, need not approximate, either in amount or in the extent of the increase by graduation, to what such a tax should ultimately be.

This species of tax has again and again been imposed although only temporarily, by the National Government. It was first imposed by the act of July 6, 1797, when the makers of the Constitution were alive and at the head of affairs. It was a graduated tax; though small in amount, the rate was increased with the amount left to any individual, exceptions being made in the case of certain close kin. A similar tax was again imposed by the act of July 1, 1862; a minimum sum of $1,000 in personal property being excepted from taxation, the tax then becoming progressive according to the remoteness of kin. The war-revenue act of June 13, 1898, provided for an inheritance tax on any sum exceeding the value of $10,000, the rate of the tax increasing both in accordance with the amounts left and in accordance with the legatee's remoteness of kin. The Supreme Court has held that the succession tax imposed at the time of the Civil War was not a direct tax but an impost or excise which was both constitutional and valid. More recently the court, in an opinion delivered by Mr. Justice White, which contained an exceedingly able and elaborate discussion of the powers of the Congress to impose death duties, sustained the constitutionality of the inheritance-tax feature of the war-revenue act of 1898.

In its incidents, and apart from the main purpose of raising revenue, an income tax stands on an entirely different footing from an inheritance tax; because it involves no question of the perpetuation of fortunes swollen to an unhealthy size. The question is in its essence a question of the proper adjustment of burdens to benefits. As the law now stands it is undoubtedly difficult to devise a national income tax which shall be constitutional. But whether it is absolutely impossible is another question; and if possible it is most certainly desirable. The first purely income-tax law was passed by the Congress in 1861, but the most important law dealing with the subject was that of 1894. This the court held to be unconstitutional.

The question is undoubtedly very intricate, delicate, and troublesome. The decision of the court was only reached by one majority. It is the law of the land, and of course is accepted as such and loyally obeyed by all good citizens. Nevertheless, the hesitation evidently felt by the court as a whole in coming to a conclusion, when considered together with the previous decisions on the subject, may perhaps indicate the possibility of devising a constitutional income-tax law which shall substantially accomplish the results aimed at. The difficulty of amending the Constitution is so great that only real necessity can justify a resort thereto. Every effort should be made in dealing with this subject, as with the subject of the proper control by the National Government over the use of corporate wealth in interstate business, to devise legislation which without such action shall attain the desired end; but if this fails, there will ultimately be no alternative to a constitutional amendment.

20

City Lights

Progressivism was a powerful force in turn-of-the-century America. Progressives believed in efficiency, so they fought to reform the civil service and to make government as effective and accountable as private business. They believed that capital, labor, and government should work together, so they urged the mediation of labor conflicts and the regulation of giant corporations. Believing in citizen participation, Progressives pioneered women's suffrage, the secret ballot, and the removal from office of corrupt officials by popular vote. Concerned with the suffering poor, Progressives promoted charity work, better public schools, university extension service, and better housing. They thought saloons and liquor caused trouble, so they struggled for prohibition. Most Progressives were educated, middle-class, native-born Protestants who felt uneasy around corporate greed and slum violence; they could be both self-righteous and narrow-minded. But they cared about the country. They were confident they could change things and tried energetically to do just that. As President Theodore Roosevelt once cried on their behalf, "We stand at Armageddon and do battle for the Lord."

Settlement houses were quintessential Progressive institutions. Established throughout urban America between 1880 and 1920, settlement houses—largely the handiwork of women reformers—arose to serve the vast swarm of newcomers to the country's great cities. These new "settlers" were European immigrants for the most part, but they also included recent arrivals, black and white, from the rural South. The settlement houses provided meeting halls. The staffs sponsored lectures, encouraged political participation and sometimes union activity, taught English classes, agitated for tighter health codes, and held citizenship and naturalization classes. These early social workers paid special attention to the problems of poor women and inevitably, therefore, to the problems of immigrant families.

Urban youth were a particular concern of the settlements. Settlement workers labored ceaselessly for child labor laws, more playgrounds, better schools. They worked to heal the generation gap between immigrant parents clinging to older ways and children rejecting everything old and old-fashioned, including the parents. The social workers tried to explain the new land to these children and to give them a smattering of self-improvement and urban survival skills. The following excerpt was written by Jane Addams, founder of Chicago's Hull House and in 1909 probably the country's most illustrious woman—almost certainly its most famous reformer. She did settlement work to benefit local Chicagoans. She then used local Chicagoans as case studies to demonstrate how badly the industrial system was damaging urban youth and how the system might be counteracted. This approach understandably brought great credit to the settlement houses and also great prestige to the reformers. Eventually their influence spread from neighborhood to city to state to, at last, nation.

Jane Addams was born in 1860 into a small-town middle-class Illinois family. After her graduation from college in 1881, Addams visited Europe, where she became inspired by a pioneer English settlement house that worked with the London poor. By 1889 she had founded a similar house in a ramshackle Chicago mansion. Addams attracted numerous bright, dedicated young women to work with her, including Florence Kelley, later an Illinois factory inspector, and Mary Kenny, a labor organizer. Together the three made Hull House famous. Addams's writings and speeches helped spread its reputation. *The Spirit of Youth and the City Streets* alone sold twenty thousand copies, and Addams's autobiography far more. She received the Nobel Peace Prize in 1931, four years before her death.

Questions to Consider. Why did Addams see the theater as a serious urban problem, and how did she propose to combat it? Does her distinction between baseball and theater seem valid? How did she account for the popularity of saloons among youth? What would she offer as a substitute? What role did factory labor play in the lives of the urban youth described by Addams? How did factory labor affect their behavior? Did she propose fundamental changes? Do her alternatives seem realistic? Would the problems of the theater, the saloon, and the factory have affected small-town youth, too?

The Spirit of Youth (1909)

JANE ADDAMS

This spring a group of young girls accustomed to the life of a five-cent theater, reluctantly refused an invitation to go to the country for a day's outing

From Jane Addams, *The Spirit of Youth and the City Streets* (The Macmillan Company, New York, 1909).

Jane Addams. Addams never used the words "adolescent" or "teenager." She thought the first too dry and academic; the second, slang. But it was this age group that most concerned her, as indeed it worried other adults of that period, who often wanted to pound delinquency out of the young by finger-wagging, confinement, and force. "Saint Jane" hoped to bury the bad tendencies of young people by giving their good ones a fighting chance. (Brown Brothers)

because the return on a late train would compel them to miss one evening's performance. They found it impossible to tear themselves away not only from the excitements of the theater itself but from the gaiety of the crowd of young men and girls invariably gathered outside discussing the sensational posters.

A steady English shopkeeper lately complained that unless he provided his four daughters with the money for the five-cent theaters every evening they would steal it from his till, and he feared that they might be driven to procure it in even more illicit ways. Because his entire family life had been thus disrupted he gloomily asserted that "this cheap show had ruined his 'ome and was the curse of America." This father was able to formulate the anxiety of many immigrant parents who are absolutely bewildered by the keen absorption of their children in the cheap theater. This anxiety is not, indeed, without foundation. An eminent alienist[1] of Chicago states that he has had a number of patients among neurotic children whose emotional natures have been so over-wrought by the crude appeal to which they had been so constantly subjected in the theaters, that they have become victims of hallucination and mental disorder. . . .

This testimony of a physician that the conditions are actually pathological, may at last induce us to bestir ourselves in regard to procuring a more wholesome form of public recreation. Many efforts in social amelioration have been undertaken only after such exposures; in the meantime, while the occasional child is driven distraught, a hundred children permanently injure their eyes watching the moving films, and hundreds more seriously model their conduct upon the standards set before them on this mimic stage.

Three boys, aged nine, eleven, and thirteen years, who had recently seen depicted the adventures of frontier life including the holding up of a stage coach and the lassoing of the driver, spent weeks planning to lasso, murder, and rob a neighborhood milkman, who started on his route at four o'clock in the morning. They made their headquarters in a barn and saved enough money to buy a revolver, adopting as their watchword the phrase "Dead Men Tell no Tales." . . . Fortunately for him, as the lariat was thrown the horse shied, and, although the shot was appropriately fired, the milkman's life was saved. Such a direct influence of the theater is by no means rare, even among older boys. Thirteen young lads were brought into the Municipal Court in Chicago during the first week that "Raffles, the Amateur Cracksman" was upon the stage, each one with an outfit of burglar's tools in his possession, and each one shamefacedly admitting that the gentlemanly burglar in the play had suggested to him a career of similar adventure.

In so far as the illusions of the theater succeed in giving youth the rest and recreation which comes from following a more primitive code of morality, it has a close relation to the function performed by public games. It is, of course, less valuable because the sense of participation is largely confined to the emotions and the imagination, and does not involve the entire nature. . . .

Well considered public games easily carried out in a park or athletic field, might both fill the mind with the imaginative material constantly supplied by the theater, and also afford the activity which the cramped muscles of the town dweller so sorely need. Even the unquestioned ability which the theater possesses to bring men together into a common mood and to afford

1. **Alienist:** psychiatrist.—*Eds.*

them a mutual topic of conversation, is better accomplished with the one national game which we already possess, and might be infinitely extended through the organization of other public games.

The theater even now by no means competes with the baseball league games which are attended by thousands of men and boys who, during the entire summer, discuss the respective standing of each nine and the relative merits of every player. During the noon hour all the employees of a city factory gather in the nearest vacant lot to cheer their own home team in its practice for the next game with the nine of a neighboring manufacturing establishment and on a Saturday afternoon the entire male population of the city betakes itself to the baseball field; the ordinary means of transportation are supplemented by gay stage-coaches and huge automobiles, noisy with blowing horns and decked with gay pennants. The enormous crowd of cheering men and boys are talkative, good-natured, full of the holiday spirit, and absolutely released from the grind of life. They are lifted out of their individual affairs and so fused together that a man cannot tell whether it is his own shout or another's that fills his ears; whether it is his own coat or another's that he is wildly waving to celebrate a victory. He does not call the stranger who sits next to him his "brother" but he unconsciously embraces him in an overwhelming outburst of kindly feeling when the favorite player makes a home run. Does not this contain a suggestion of the undoubted power of public recreation to bring together all classes of a community in the modern city unhappily so full of devices for keeping men apart? . . .

We are only beginning to understand what might be done through the festival, the street procession, the band of marching musicians, orchestral music in public squares or parks, with the magic power they all possess to formulate the sense of companionship and solidarity. . . .

As it is possible to establish a connection between the lack of public reaction and the vicious excitements and trivial amusements which become their substitutes, so it may be illuminating to trace the connection between the monotony and dullness of factory work and the petty immoralities which are often the youth's protest against them.

There are many city neighborhoods in which practically every young person who has attained the age of fourteen years enters a factory. When the work itself offers nothing of interest, and when no public provision is made for recreation, the situation becomes almost insupportable to the youth whose ancestors have been rough-working and hard-playing peasants.

In such neighborhoods the joy of youth is well nigh extinguished; and in that long procession of factory workers, each morning and evening, the young walk almost as wearily and listlessly as the old. Young people working in modern factories situated in cities still dominated by the ideals of Puritanism face a combination which tends almost irresistibly to overwhelm the spirit of youth. When the Puritan repression of pleasure was in the ascendant in America the people it dealt with lived on farms and villages where, although youthful pleasures might be frowned upon and crushed out, the young people still had a chance to find self-expression in their work. Plowing the field and spinning the flax could be carried on with a certain joyousness and vigor which the organization of modern industry too often precludes. Present industry based upon the inventions of the nineteenth century has little connection with the old patterns in which men have worked for generations. The modern factory calls for an expenditure of nervous energy almost more than it demands muscular effort, or at least machinery so far performs the work of the massive muscles, that greater stress is laid upon fine and exact movements necessarily involving nervous strain. But these movements are exactly of the type to which the muscles of a growing boy least readily respond, quite as the admonition to be accurate and faithful is that which appeals the least to his big primitive emotions. . . .

In vast regions of the city which are completely dominated by the factory, it is as if the development of industry had outrun all the educational and social arrangements.

The revolt of youth against uniformity and the necessity of following careful directions laid down by some one else, many times results in such nervous irritability that the youth, in spite of all sorts of prudential reasons, "throws up his job," if only to get outside the factory walls into the freer street, just as the narrowness of the school inclosure induces many a boy to jump the fence.

When the boy is on the street, however, and is "standing around on the corner" with the gang to which he mysteriously attaches himself, he finds the difficulties of direct untrammeled action almost as great there as they were in the factory, but for an entirely different set of reasons. The necessity so strongly felt in the factory for an outlet to his sudden and furious bursts of energy, his overmastering desire to prove that he could do things "without being bossed all the time," finds little chance for expression, for he discovers that in whatever really active pursuit he tries to engage, he is promptly suppressed by the police. . . .

The unjustifiable lack of educational supervision during the first years of factory work makes it quite impossible for the modern educator to offer any real assistance to young people during that trying transitional period between school and industry. The young people themselves who fail to conform can do little but rebel against the entire situation.

There are many touching stories by which this might be illustrated. One of them comes from a large steel mill of a boy of fifteen whose business it was to throw a lever when a small tank became filled with molten metal. During the few moments when the tank was filling it was his foolish custom to catch the reflection of the metal upon a piece of looking-glass, and to throw the bit of light into the eyes of his fellow workmen. Although an exasperated foreman had twice dispossessed him of his mirror, with a third fragment he was one day flicking the gloom of the shop when the neglected tank overflowed, almost instantly burning off both his legs. Boys working in the stock yards, during their moments of wrestling and rough play, often slash each other painfully with the short knives which they use in their work, but in spite of this the play impulse is too irrepressible to be denied. . . .

The discovery of the labor power of youth was to our age like the discovery of a new natural resource, although it was merely incidental to the invention of modern machinery and the consequent subdivision of labor. In utilizing it thus ruthlessly we are not only in danger of quenching the divine fire of youth, but we are imperiling industry itself when we venture to ignore these very sources of beauty, of variety and of suggestion.

21

The War for Democracy

Woodrow Wilson won the presidency in 1912 on behalf of a "new freedom," a program involving lower tariffs, banking reform, antitrust legislation, and, in foreign policy, the repudiation of Theodore Roosevelt's gunboat diplomacy. Even after sending troops to various Caribbean countries and to Mexico, Wilson claimed that his main concern was to promote peace and democracy in the world. When World War I erupted in Europe, Wilson saw the war as the result of imperialistic rivalries ("a war with which we have nothing to do") and urged, despite personal sympathy with Great Britain, that the United States stay neutral so as to influence the peace negotiations. Wilson won reelection in 1916 largely on a promise to keep the country out of war. But a combination of pro-British propaganda in American newspapers and German submarine attacks on American ships proved formidable, and in April 1917, Wilson finally requested a declaration of war in the following address to Congress. The sweeping, visionary arguments of this remarkable speech shaped not only America's expectations about the war itself but also attitudes about the proper U.S. role in international affairs for years to come.

Born in 1856 in Virginia, Woodrow Wilson grew up in the South; his father was a Presbyterian minister. He attended Princeton and Johns Hopkins, where he earned a doctorate, and began to write and teach in the field of constitutional government and politics. He gained national stature while president of Princeton from 1902 until 1910; he became the Democratic governor of New Jersey in 1911 and, two years later, president of the United States. Wilson's main objective at the peace conference after World War I was to create a League of Nations to help keep the peace. In 1919 during an intensive speechmaking campaign to arouse public support for the League, Wilson suffered a debilitating stroke. He died in Washington, D.C., in 1924.

Questions to Consider. Note, in reading the following message, that although Woodrow Wilson believed in the unique and superior character of American institutions, he was willing to enter into alliances with European powers. What were the four principal grounds on which Wilson was willing to reverse the American diplomatic tradition? Which of these did he seem to take most seriously? Were there other American interests that he might have stressed but did not? What reasons might Wilson have had for stressing so strongly America's attachment to Germany's people as opposed to its government? Might Wilson's arguments and rhetoric have served to prolong rather than to shorten the war?

Address to Congress (1917)

WOODROW WILSON

I have called the Congress into extraordinary session because there are serious, very serious choices of policy to be made, and made immediately, which it was neither right nor constitutionally permissible that I should assume the responsibility of making.

On the third of February last I officially laid before you the extraordinary announcement of the Imperial German Government that on and after the first day of February it was its purpose to put aside all restraints of law or of humanity and use its submarines to sink every vessel that sought to approach either the ports of Great Britain and Ireland or the western coasts of Europe or any of the ports controlled by the enemies of Germany within the Mediterranean. . . .

I was for a little while unable to believe that such things would in fact be done by any government that had hitherto subscribed to the humane practices of civilized nations. International law had its origin in the attempt to set up some law which would be respected and observed upon the seas, where no nation had right of dominion and where lay the free highways of the world. . . . This minimum of right the German Government has swept aside under the plea of retaliation and necessity and because it had no weapons which it could use at sea except these which it is impossible to employ as it is employing them without throwing to the winds all scruples of humanity or of respect for all understandings that were supposed to underlie the intercourse of the world. I am not now thinking of the loss of property involved, immense and serious as that is, but only of the wanton and wholesale destruction of the lives of noncombatants, men, women, and children, engaged in pursuits which have always, even in the darkest periods of modern history, been deemed innocent and legitimate. Property can be paid for; the lives of peaceful and

From *The New York Times,* April 3, 1917.

innocent people cannot be. The present German submarine warfare against commerce is a warfare against mankind.

It is a war against all nations. American ships have been sunk, American lives taken, in ways which it has stirred us very deeply to learn of, but the ships and people of other neutral and friendly nations have been sunk and overwhelmed in the waters in the way. There has been no discrimination. The challenge is to all mankind. Each nation must decide for itself how it will meet it. The choice we make for ourselves must be made with a moderation of counsel and a temperateness of judgement befitting our character and our motives as a nation. We must put excited feeling away. Our motive will not be revenge or the victorious assertion of the physical might of the nation, but only the vindication of right, of human right, of which we are only a single champion. . . .

With a profound sense of the solemn and even tragical character of the step I am taking and of the grave responsibilities which it involves, but in unhesitating obedience to what I deem my constitutional duty, I advise that the Congress declare the recent course of the Imperial German Government to be in fact nothing less than war against the government and people of the United States; that it formally accept the status of belligerent which has thus been thrust upon it; and that it take immediate steps not only to put the country in a more thorough state of defense but also to exert all its power and employ all its resources to bring the Government of the German Empire to terms and end the war. . . .

We have no quarrel with the German people. We have no feeling towards them but one of sympathy and friendship. It was not upon their impulse that their government acted in entering this war. It was not with their previous knowledge or approval. It was a war determined upon as wars used to be determined upon in the old, unhappy days when peoples were nowhere consulted by their rulers and wars were provoked and waged in the interest of dynasties or of little groups of ambitious men who were accustomed to use their fellow men as pawns and tools. . . .

We are accepting this challenge of hostile purpose because we know that in such a Government, following such methods, we can never have a friend; and that in the presence of its organized power, always lying in wait to accomplish we know not what purpose, there can be no assured security for the democratic Governments of the world. We are now about to accept gauge of battle with this natural foe to liberty and shall, if necessary, spend the whole force of the nation to check and nullify its pretensions and its power. We are glad, now that we see the facts with no veil of false pretense about them, to fight thus for the ultimate peace of the world and for the liberation of its peoples, the German peoples included: for the rights of nations great and small and the privilege of men everywhere to choose their way of life and of obedience. The world must be made safe for democracy. Its peace must be planted upon the tested foundations of political liberty. We have no selfish ends to serve. We desire no conquest, no dominion. We seek no indemnities for ourselves, no material compensation for the sacrifices we shall freely make. We are but one of the champions of the rights of mankind. We shall be satisfied when those rights have been made as secure as the faith and the freedom of nations can make them. . . .

It will be all the easier for us to conduct ourselves as belligerents in a high spirit of right and fairness because we act without animus, not in enmity towards a people or with the desire to bring any injury or disadvantage upon them, but only in armed opposition to an irresponsible government which has thrown aside all considerations of humanity and of right and is running amuck. We are, let me say again, the sincere friends of the German people, and shall desire nothing so much as the early reestablishment of intimate relations of mutual advantage between us,—however hard it may be for them, for the time being, to believe that this is spoken from our hearts. We have borne with their present Government through all these bitter months because of that friendship,—exercising a patience and forbearance which would otherwise have been impossible. We shall, happily, still have an opportunity to prove that friendship in our daily attitude and actions towards the millions of men and women of German birth and native sympathy who live amongst us and share our life, and we shall be proud to prove it towards all who are in fact loyal to their neighbors and to the Government in the hour of test. They are, most of them, as true and loyal Americans as if they had never known any other fealty of allegiance. They will be prompt to stand with us in rebuking and restraining the few who may be of a different mind and purpose. If there should be disloyalty, it will be dealt with with a firm hand of stern repression; but, if it lifts its head at all, it will lift it only here and there and without countenance except from a lawless and malignant few.

It is a distressing and oppressive duty, Gentlemen of the Congress, which I have performed in thus addressing you. There are, it may be, many months of fiery trial and sacrifice ahead of us. It is a fearful thing to lead this great peaceful people into war, into the most terrible and disastrous of all wars, civilization itself seeming to be in the balance. But the right is more precious than peace, and we shall fight for the things which we have always carried nearest our hearts,—for democracy, for the right of those who submit to authority to have a voice in their own Governments, for the rights and liberties of small nations, for a universal dominion of right by such a concert of free peoples as shall bring peace and safety to all nations and make the world itself at last free. To such a task we can dedicate our lives and our fortunes, everything that we have, with the pride of those who know that the day has come when America is privileged to spend her blood and her might for the principles that gave her birth and happiness and the peace which she has treasured. God helping her, she can do no other.

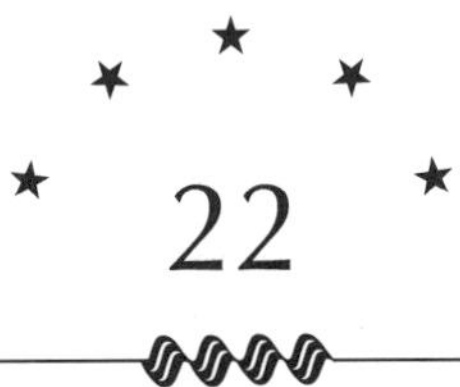

22

Skeptics

Many Americans found great glory in World War I. After all, the doughboys, as the American infantrymen were called, had turned the tide against Germany, and John ("Black Jack") Pershing, commander of the U.S. forces, emerged from the conflict a national hero. But the human price had been stiff: 100,000 Americans dead and 200,000 wounded. American casualties in World War I were low compared with European casualties (almost 2 million Germans and 1 million British died) or with U.S. losses in the Civil War (600,000) or in World War II (400,000). But the American losses were hardly insignificant, particularly since the country was in the war for only eighteen months and mobilized only about 4 million men. Much of the dying occurred in the appalling conditions of the Argonne Forest, where years of trenching and shelling had created a veritable wasteland of death.

Justifying such remarkable carnage would have taken remarkable results—something on the order of the new international order that Woodrow Wilson had promised. But this, of course, the president had not been able to deliver, not even his own country's membership in the League of Nations. So the skepticism that had attended U.S. entry into the war persisted, engendering a somber, even cynical mood beneath the boisterous patriotic surface. One source of this dark mood was the *Chicago Tribune,* which was the most influential newspaper in the Midwest and contained persistent editorials criticizing Wilsonian interventionism. The *Tribune* editorial of November 13, 1921, reprinted below, is in response to a wave of recrimination, social unrest, and small-scale military skirmishes in Europe and also the growing European calls for U.S. financial aid. This editorial is an expression of characteristic midwestern Republican views on the foolishness of idealism, the evils of European politics, and the folly of war.

A variant of these views also pervaded the major fiction of the period. Many writers of the early twentieth century were probably predisposed to skepticism about the war effort because they felt alienated and estranged from "bourgeois" America, with its perpetual striving for status and possessions, and some had pacifist leanings even before the United States entered World War I in 1917. Actual participation in the war confirmed the pacifist inclinations of several writers. Such books as E. E. Cummings's *The Enormous Room,* John Dos Passos's *Three Soldiers,* William Faulkner's *Soldier's Pay,* and Ernest Hemingway's *A Farewell to Arms* depicted the war as murderous and meaningless. Hemingway worked the war most deeply into his fiction. The excerpts below come from *In Our Time,* a collection of stories both about the war and about life in upstate Michigan strung together with brief mood-setting paragraphs; all the paragraphs reprinted here are this kind of paragraph, each with its own characters and locale. Hemingway wrote in a spare, detached style that was widely imitated in the postwar years and won him almost as much acclaim as his plots and characters. The disillusionment that pervaded his work was imitated, too, so much so that finally it seemed almost incredible that the United States could have participated in the war. Americans who sought an explanation for U.S. entry in World War I increasingly found some mixture of self-righteousness, bumbling stupidity, and the machinations of the arms dealers, and resolved never to go to war again—and did not until Pearl Harbor.

The editor and publisher of the *Chicago Tribune* when the editorial below was published was Robert R. McCormick, a graduate of Yale University and Northwestern University's law school and nephew of Cyrus H. McCormick of mechanical reaper fame. Forty-one years old in 1921, Robert McCormick had already held political office in Chicago and served as both a *Tribune* war correspondent and an artillery officer in France. Under McCormick's direction the *Tribune* company had a fivefold increase in newspaper circulation and also had acquired vast nonnewspaper business holdings. McCormick died in Illinois in 1955, with his formidable suspicions of idealists and Europeans still intact. His fellow Chicagoan, Ernest Hemingway, was born in 1899 into a middle-class family. Having skipped college to become a newspaper reporter, he spent the war years with a volunteer ambulance unit in Italy and after the war joined the growing colony of expatriate Americans in Paris. Hemingway received the Nobel Prize for Literature in 1954. He died at his home in Ketchum, Idaho, in 1961.

Questions to Consider. The 1921 *Tribune* editorial painted a gloomy picture of European conditions three years after the end of the war. Does the editorial seem to express surprise at this state of affairs? What or whom did the writer hold most responsible? Had the war, then, been utterly futile and valueless? What actions did the writer advise the United States to take, or not to take? With whom was the editorial arguing? In the Hemingway paragraphs, does the dominant mood seem to be anger, pity, or sarcasm? Are there any common features in these Hemingway scenes? Why might people of the 1920s have found them startling, even shocking? Do they still have shock power?

On the western front. American machine gunners searching out pockets of resistance in the German defenses during the costly U.S. offensive of summer 1918. (National Archives)

Unregenerate Europe (1921)

THE CHICAGO TRIBUNE

It is natural that pacifists and excited humanitarians should stress the evil consequences of the world war at this time. It is equally natural that foreign statesmen and public agencies should join them in keeping this phase of the European situation [of famine and insurrections] before us. It gives a tremendous momentum to the pacifist propaganda, and it relieves the governments and peoples of Europe of a large part of their responsibility for the present condition of their affairs.

But the American mind should clear itself on this point. No one will deny that the war is responsible directly for a vast wastage of life and property.

© Copyrighted Chicago Tribune Company. All rights reserved. Used with permission.

But what needs recognition and emphasis at this moment . . . is that had common sense and self-control governed the policies of the governments and the sentiments of the peoples of Europe their affairs would not be tottering now on the rim of chaos.

On the contrary, were there wisdom and courage in the statesmanship of Europe, were there the same selfless devotion in chancelleries and parliaments as was exhibited on the battlefield, Europe would have been today well on the way to recovery.

The expenditures of the war and the intensification of long existing animosities and jealousies undoubtedly have complicated the problems of statecraft and of government. Undoubtedly the temporary depletion of man power and the temporary exhaustion of body and spirit among the war worn peoples were a burden which recovery has had to assume. Undoubtedly the wastage of wealth and diversion of productive agencies were a handicap to expeditious restoration.

But that these are chiefly responsible for the present state of Europe we do not admit and the future judgment of history, we are confident, will deny.

It is chiefly the folly which has been persistently demonstrated by governments and people since the war that is responsible for Europe's condition today. It is because the moment hostilities ceased and the enemy was disarmed, victors and vanquished turned their backs on the healing and constructive principles they had solemnly asserted from time to time when matters were going against them at the battle front, that the European nations almost without exception have been going down hill. There never in history has been a more perfect illustration of the ancient sarcasm: "When the devil is sick, the devil a monk would be; when the devil is well, the devil a monk is he."

If we wish to know why Europe is in the present state, we cannot do better than to draw a parallel between the assertions of purpose and principle of the allies and "associated" powers in 1916, '17, and '18, and what has actually happened since Nov. 11, 1918.

The war was a gigantic folly and waste. No one will deny that. But it was not so foolish nor so wasteful as the peace which has followed it. The European governments, those who come at our invitation and those who remain away, would have us believe they are mere victims of the war. They say nothing of what the war did for them. We might remind them that they profited as well as lost by the war. Many of them were freed from age long tyranny. They got rid of kaisers and saber clattering aristocracies. They were given freedom, and their present state shows how little they have known how to profit by it. They have been given new territories and new resources, and they have shown how little they deserve their good fortune. The last three years in Europe have been given not to sane efforts to heal wounds, remove hostilities, develop cooperation for the common economic restoration which is essential to the life of each. On the contrary, they have been marked by new wars and destruction, by new animosities and rivalries, by a refusal to face facts, make necessary sacrifices and compromises for financial and economic recovery, by greedy grabbing of territory and new adventures in the very imperialism which brought about the war.

It is well for Americans and their representatives to keep this in mind. The appeal to America's disinterestedness is unfairly fortified by the assumption that Europe is the innocent victim of one egotist's or one nation's ruthless ambition. We can take due account of the disastrous effects of the Prussian effort at dominance, but that should not overshadow the stubborn errors which began over again on the very threshold of peace, and which have made the peace more destructive than the war. When the European governments and peoples are ready to make a real peace, which cannot arrive until they give over the policies and attitudes that produced the world war, America will then not fail to give generous aid. But America would be foolish to contribute to the support of present methods or give any encouragement to the spirit which now prevails in the old world.

In Our Time (1925)

ERNEST HEMINGWAY

Minarets stuck up in the rain out of Adrianople [Turkey] across the mud flats. The carts were jammed for thirty miles along the Karagatch road. Water buffalo and cattle were hauling carts through the mud. There was no end and no beginning. Just carts loaded with everything they owned. The old men and women, soaked through, walked along keeping the cattle moving. The Maritza [River] was running yellow almost up to the bridge. Carts were jammed solid on the bridge with camels bobbing along through them. Greek cavalry herded along the procession. The women and children were in the carts, crouched with mattresses, mirrors, sewing machines, bundles. There was a woman having a baby with a young girl holding a blanket over her and crying. Scared sick looking at it. It rained all through the evacuation.

*

We were in a garden in Mons [Belgium]. Young Buckley came in with his patrol from across the river. The first German I saw climbed up over the garden wall. We waited till he got one leg over and then potted him. He had so much equipment on and looked awfully surprised and fell down into the garden. Then three more came over further down the wall. We shot them. They all came just like that.

Reprinted with permission of Scribner, an imprint of Simon & Schuster, Inc., from *In Our Time* by Ernest Hemingway. Copyright 1925 by Charles Scribner's Sons. Copyright renewed 1953 by Ernest Hemingway.

*

It was a frightfully hot day. We'd jammed an absolutely perfect barricade across the bridge. It was simply priceless. A big old wrought-iron grating from the front of a house. Too heavy to lift and you could shoot through it and they would have to climb over it. It was absolutely topping. They tried to get over it, and we potted them from forty yards. They rushed it, and officers came out alone and worked on it. It was an absolutely perfect obstacle. Their officers were very fine. We were frightfully put out when we heard the flank had gone, and we had to fall back.

*

They shot the six cabinet ministers at half-past six in the morning against the wall of a hospital. There were pools of water in the courtyard. There were wet dead leaves on the paving of the courtyard. It rained hard. All the shutters of the hospital were nailed shut. One of the ministers was sick with typhoid. Two soldiers carried him downstairs and out into the rain. They tried to hold him up against the wall but he sat down in a puddle of water. The other five stood very quietly against the wall. Finally the officer told the soldiers it was no good trying to make him stand up. When they fired the first volley he was sitting down in the water with his head on his knees.

*

Nick sat against the wall of the church where they had dragged him to be clear of machine gun fire in the street. Both legs stuck out awkwardly. He had been hit in the spine. His face was sweaty and dirty. The sun shone on his face. The day was very hot. Rinaldi, big backed, his equipment sprawling, lay face downward against the wall. Nick looked straight ahead brilliantly. The pink wall of the house opposite had fallen out from the roof, and an iron bedstead hung twisted toward the street. Two Austrian dead lay in the rubble in the shade of the house. Up the street were other dead. Things were getting forward in the town. It was going well. Stretcher bearers would be along any time now. Nick turned his head and looked down at Rinaldi. "Senta Rinaldo; Senta. You and me we've made a separate peace." Rinaldi lay still in the sun, breathing with difficulty. "We're not patriots." Nick turned his head away, smiling sweatily. Rinaldi was a disappointing audience.

*

While the bombardment was knocking the trench to pieces at Fossalta [Italy], he lay very flat and sweated and prayed, "Oh Jesus Christ get me out of here. Dear Jesus, please get me out. Christ, please, please, please, Christ. If you'll only keep me from getting killed I'll do anything you say. I believe in you and I'll tell everybody in the world that you are the only thing that matters. Please, please, dear Jesus." The shelling moved further up the line. We went to work on the trench and in the morning the sun came up and the day was hot and muggy and cheerful and quiet. The next night back at Mestre he did not tell the girl he went upstairs with at the Villa Rossa about Jesus. And he never told anybody.

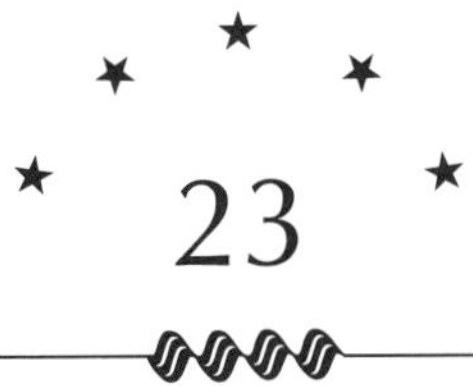

23

SALESMANSHIP

In the conclusion of *The Great Gatsby,* F. Scott Fitzgerald summed up the dissipation, extravagance, and spiritual sterility of the post–World War I generation:

> They were careless people, Tom and Daisy—they smashed up things and creatures and then retreated back into their money or their vast carelessness, or whatever it was that kept them together, and let other people clean up the mess they had made. . . .
>
> Gatsby believed in the green light, the orgiastic future that year by year recedes before us. It eluded us then, but that's no matter—tomorrow we will run faster, stretch out our arms farther. . . . And one fine morning—

Other great novelists and poets wrote about the "sad young men" and women of the Jazz Age, and though each looked at life through a unique lens, they shared a similar disenchantment with society's obsession with business, money, and material success. "The business of America is business," Calvin Coolidge declared, but he struck a responsive chord in the citizenry with that statement and was an extremely popular president.

Obsession with business was all but "orgiastic" in the 1920s. Beginning in 1922 the United States experienced an era of tremendous economic expansion and unprecedented prosperity. The country's industrial output more than doubled, per capita income increased by one-third, and there was almost no inflation. The use of labor-saving devices such as refrigerators, vacuum cleaners, and washing machines became widespread, and millions of Americans purchased automobiles on readily available credit. The United States had become a "consumer culture."

Nevertheless, production levels were so high that consumers were unable to buy all the products that industry produced, and new markets had to be created. It was in this climate that the advertising industry came of age. Among the most successful "ad men" of the era was Bruce Barton, chairman of the board of the New York advertising agency Batten, Barton, Durstine & Osborne, and author of an immensely popular book, part of which is reproduced below. In *The Man Nobody Knows,* Barton portrayed Jesus Christ as a salesman—

not an ordinary salesman, but the world's greatest salesman—and exhorted his readers to profit by his example. Barton wrote:

> Only strong magnetic men inspire great enthusiasm and build great organizations. Yet Jesus built the greatest organization of all. . . . He picked up twelve men from the bottom ranks of business and forged them into an organization that conquered the world.

The story of the carpenter from Nazareth, Barton added, is "the story of the founder of modern business."

Barton was hardly alone in his sentiments. A contemporary observed:

> The sanest religion is business. Any relationship that forces a man to follow the Golden Rule rightfully belongs amid the ceremonials of the church. A great business enterprise includes and presupposes this relationship.

Meanwhile, by the time he died in 1925, Russell H. Conwell, a Baptist minister, had delivered his lecture, "Acres of Diamonds," more than six thousand times and had touched millions of readers. "Money is power, and you ought to be reasonably ambitious to have it," he preached. "If you can honestly attain unto riches . . . it is your Christian and godly duty to do so."

Barton would have agreed. After all, as the head of a successful ad agency and the author of eight books with titles like *More Power to You* and *It's a Good Old World,* he had accumulated a small fortune. Having served as congressman from Tennessee, he died in 1967 at age eighty-one.

Questions to Consider. Is the author respectful of Jesus? Billy Sunday was a popular evangelist of the time. A church historian noted that "accompanying his contortions, furniture smashing, and partial undressing was an unbroken torrent of words. What the church needed . . . was fighting men of God, not 'hog-jowled, weasel-eyed, sponge-columned, mushy-fisted, jelly-spined, pussy-footing, four-flushing, Charlotte-russe Christians.'" Do you see a relationship between the approach of "vaudeville evangelists" like Sunday and the sales philosophy of Bruce Barton?

The Man Nobody Knows (1925)

BRUCE BARTON

Jesus was, as we say, many-sided, and every man sees the side of His nature which appeals most to himself.

The doctor thinks of the great Physician whose touch never failed, who by the genius that remains a mystery to man preceded modern science in a knowledge of the relation of the spirit to health, a knowledge still incomplete. The preacher studies the Sermon on the Mount and marvels that truths so profound should be expressed in words so clear and simple. The politically active man remembers best His courage in opposing the most powerful elements in His community and is awed by His capacity to speak honestly without loss of loyalty. Lawyers have written in praise of His pleading at His trial; and the literary critics of every age have cheerfully acknowledged His mastery as a storyteller.

Each man, it is plain, understands that part of His universal genius which with his own abilities and skills he can most nearly approach. I am not a doctor or lawyer or critic but an advertising man. That means that I am and have been concerned with the ways in which words, design and color may carry conviction to people, with the art-science of bringing others to your point of view.

I propose in this chapter to consider some words and deeds of Jesus which persuaded and still persuade men of the wisdom and justice in His teaching. So I have, I hope, seen Jesus as a man who lived and worked, and not as the symbol conventionally displayed.

Let us begin by asking why He could command public attention and why, in contrast, His churches have not done so well. The answer is twofold. His mission was to teach men. But before even He could teach, He must get men to listen. He was never trite; He had no single method. The Gospels show clearly that no one could predict what He would say or do; His actions and words were always new, arresting, challenging and meaningful to the men among whom He lived. . . .

He was known by His service, not by His sermons; this is the noteworthy fact. His preaching seems in the light of such events almost incidental. On only one occasion did He deliver a long discourse, and that was probably interrupted often by questions and debates. He did not come to establish a theology but to lead a good life. Living more healthfully than any of His contemporaries, He spread health wherever He went. Thinking more daringly, more divinely, than anyone before Him, He expressed Himself in words of great beauty. His sermons, if they may be called sermons, were chiefly explanatory of His service. He healed a lame man, gave sight to a blind man, fed the hungry, cheered the poor; and by these works He was known.

The church, which hopes to spread widely the news of good work, often receives little attention. Yet it is much more fruitful in such good works than the uninformed suspect. . . .

These are Jesus' works, done in Jesus' name. If He lived again now, He would be known by His service, not merely by His sermons. One thing is certain: He would not neglect the market place. Few of His sermons were delivered in synagogues. For the most part He was in the crowded places—the Temple court, the city squares, the centers where goods were bought and sold. I emphasized this fact once to a group of preachers.

Reprinted with the permission of Simon & Schuster, Inc., from *The Man Nobody Knows* by Bruce Barton. Copyright 1925 by Bobbs-Merrill, renewed 1952 by Bruce Barton.

"You mean that we ought to do street preaching!" one of them exclaimed. . . .

No. Few ideas gain currency unless they may be presented simultaneously to hundreds of thousands. Magazines, newspapers, and radio networks are now the street in Capernaum. Here our goods are sold; here voices are raised to win our loyalty to ideas, to causes—to faiths. That the voice of Jesus should be still in our market place is an omission which He could soon find a way to correct. . . .

Benjamin Franklin in his autobiography tells the process which he went through in acquiring an effective style. He would read a passage from some great master of English, then lay the book aside and attempt to reproduce the thought in his own words. Comparing his version with the original, he discovered wherein he had obscured the thought or wasted words or failed to drive straight to the point. Every man who wishes to know a little more of Jesus should study the parables in the same fashion, schooling himself in their language and learning the elements of their power.

1. First of all they are marvelously condensed. . . .

Jesus had no introductions. A single sentence grips attention; three or four more tell the story; one or two more and both the thought and its application are clear. And this is true of ideas that reformed the moral structure of the world! When He wanted a new disciple, He said simply "Follow me." . . .

Two men spoke on the battleground of Gettysburg nearly a century ago. The first delivered an oration of more than two hours in length; not one person in ten who reads this page can even recall his name; certainly not one in a thousand can quote a single sentence from his masterly effort. The second speaker uttered two hundred and fifty words, and those words, Lincoln's Gettysburg Address, are a part of the mental endowment of almost every American. . . .

Jesus hated prosy dullness. He praised the Centurion who was anxious not to waste His time; the only prayer which He publicly commended was uttered by a poor publican who merely cried out, "God, be merciful to me a sinner." A seven-word prayer, and Jesus called it a good one. A sixty-six word prayer, He said, contained all that men needed to say or God to hear. What would be His verdict on most of our prayers and our speeches and our writing?

2. His language was marvelously simple—a second great essential. There is hardly a sentence in His teaching which a child cannot understand. His illustrations were all drawn from the commonest experiences of life: "a sower went forth to sow"; "a certain man had two sons"; "a man built his house on the sands"; "the kingdom of heaven is like a grain of mustard seed." . . .

Jesus used few qualifying words and no long ones. We referred a minute ago to those three literary masterpieces. The Lord's Prayer, The Twenty-third Psalm, The Gettysburg Address. Recall their phraseology:

Our Father which art in Heaven, hallowed be thy name

The Lord is my shepherd; I shall not want

Four score and seven years ago

Not a single three-syllable word; hardly any two-syllable words. All the greatest things in human life are one-syllable things—love, joy, hope, home, child, wife, trust, faith, God—and the great pieces of writing, generally speaking, use the small word in place of the large if meaning permits.

3. Sincerity illuminates strongly every word, every sentence He uttered; sincerity is the third essential. Many wealthy men have purchased newspapers with the idea of advancing their personal fortunes or bringing about some political action in which they have a private interest. Such newspapers almost invariably fail. No matter how much money is spent on them, no matter how zealously the secret of their ownership is guarded, readers eventually become conscious that something is wrong. They come to feel that the voice of the editor is not his own.

It was the way Jesus looked at men, and the life He led among them, that gave His words transforming power. What He was and what He said were one and the same thing. Nobody could stand at His side for even a minute without being persuaded that here was a man who loved people and considered even the humblest of them worthy of the best He had to give. There is no presupposition more deadening to a writer than the idea that he can "write down" to his readers. . . .

Persuasion depends on respect for the listeners, and in Jesus great respect coupled with great love.

4. Finally Jesus knew that any idea may have to be repeated. . . .

It has been said that "reputation is repetition." No important truth can be impressed on the minds of any large number of people by being said only once. The thoughts which Jesus had to give the world were revolutionary, but they were few in number. "God is your father," He said, "caring more for the welfare of every one of you than any human father can possibly care for his children. His Kingdom is happiness! His rule is love." This is what He had to teach, and He knew the necessity of driving it home from every possible angle. So in one of His stories God is the Shepherd searching the wilds for one wandering sheep; in another the Father welcoming home a prodigal boy; in another a King who forgives his debtors large amounts and expects them to be forgiving in turn—many stories but the same big Idea.

Because the stories were unforgettable, the idea lived and is today one of the most powerful influences on human action and thought. To be sure the work is far from complete. The idea that God is the Father of all men—not merely of a specially selected few—has still to reach some areas and to establish its dominance in society. More or less unconsciously a lot of us share the feeling of the French nobleman in Saint Simon's immortal story, who was sure that God would "think twice before damning a person of his quality." . . .

Whoever feels an impulse to make his own life count in the grand process of human betterment can have no surer guide for his activities than Jesus. Let him learn the lesson of the parables: that in teaching people you first capture their interest; that your service rather than your sermons must be your claim on their attention; that what you say must be simple and brief and above all *sincere.*

The "White Angel Breadline" in San Francisco, 1933. (The Oakland Museum)

CHAPTER FOUR

Crisis and Hope

24

AMERICAN EARTHQUAKE

American industrialization meant not only surging production but also periodic business "busts"—in the 1870s, the 1890s, 1907, and 1919–21. In each of these cases, prices, profits, and employment all plunged and remained low until the economy's basic strength pushed them again to higher levels. But no previous bust matched the Great Depression, which descended on the nation in the early 1930s. From 1929, when Herbert Hoover became the third consecutive Republican president since World War I, until 1933, when Franklin D. Roosevelt, a Democrat, succeeded him, the economy all but collapsed. Stocks and bonds lost three-fourths of their value, bank failures increased from five hundred to four thousand a year, farm income fell by half, and unemployment rose from 4 percent to almost 25 percent.

It was this last figure that most stunned and terrified ordinary Americans. There had been unemployment before, but never so much or for so long. And this joblessness was not limited to minorities or factory workers, as so often had been the case. The ranks of the destitute now included hundreds of thousands of white-collar workers, small businesspeople, and sharecroppers. Most disturbing of all, millions of women were now jobless and impoverished; many were homeless, with nowhere to turn. The country found it disquieting in the extreme.

People were aware of the massive human suffering of the Great Depression both because it was so widespread and because it was reported with such immediacy and attention to stark detail. Great fiction appeared, from Jack Conroy's *The Disinherited* at the beginning of the period to *The Grapes of Wrath,* John Steinbeck's epic of displaced Okies, at its end. Gripping photography and murals and innovative drama and poetry, glittering with unprecedented concreteness of detail, all depicted facets of the American ordeal. Journalism followed a similar path. Meridel LeSueur's article on Minnesota women, excerpted below, appeared in *New Masses,* a lively, irreverent Communist party literary journal that attracted and published much excellent social writing. In this case, the editors—staunch Stalinists—praised LeSueur's writing but also reproached her for defeatism and lack of "true revolutionary spirit."

Meridel LeSueur was born in 1900 in Iowa. Her grandfather was a Protestant fundamentalist temperance zealot; her father helped found the Industrial Workers of the World. After high school LeSueur attended the American Academy of Dramatic Art and worked in Hollywood as an actress and stuntwoman in the 1920s. During the 1930s she lived with her two children in Minneapolis while writing what a critic called "luminous short stories" as well as articles on farmers and the unemployed, especially women. Hailed in the 1930s as a major writer, she was blacklisted during the 1940s as a Communist sympathizer and lived by writing children's books and women's articles under a pseudonym. One of the first writers to examine the lives of poor women, her literary career revived during the 1970s with the emergence of feminism. Between 1971 and 1985 twelve of her books, new and old, appeared.

Questions to Consider. Who were the poor women LeSueur described in "Women on the Breadlines"? What did they have in common besides their poverty? Were they equally poor? Were their aspirations the same? How did their gender affect their condition and behavior during the Great Depression? How did they relate to one another, to authority figures, and to men? In later years conservatives would attack LeSueur for her radicalism. Can the reasons for these attacks be seen in this article? When Stalinists of the 1930s attacked her for being too negative and defeatist, were the attacks justified?

Women on the Breadlines (1932)

MERIDEL LESUEUR

I am sitting in the city free employment bureau. It's the woman's section. We have been sitting here now for four hours. We sit here every day, waiting for a job. There are no jobs. Most of us have had no breakfast. Some have had scant rations for over a year. Hunger makes a human being lapse into a state of lethargy, especially city hunger. Is there any place else in the world where a human being is supposed to go hungry amidst plenty without an outcry, without protest, where only the boldest steal or kill for bread, and the timid crawl the streets, hunger like the beak of a terrible bird at the vitals?

We sit looking at the floor. No one dares think of the coming winter. There are only a few more days of summer. Everyone is anxious to get work to lay

From *New Masses* (January 1932), 5–7.

"Migrant Mother," a Dorothea Lange portrait of Florence Thompson, age 32, a Cherokee from Oklahoma in a California migrant labor camp. One of the foremost photographers of her time, Lange captured the pathos of the 1930s on film as brilliantly as Meridel LeSueur captured it in prose. (Library of Congress)

up something for that long siege of bitter cold. But there is no work. Sitting in the room we all know it. That is why we don't talk much. We look at the floor dreading to see that knowledge in each other's eyes. There is a kind of humiliation in it. We look away from each other. We look at the floor. It's too terrible to see this animal terror in each other's eyes.

So we sit hour after hour, day after day, waiting for a job to come in. There are many women for a single job. A thin sharp woman sits inside the wire cage looking at a book. For four hours we have watched her looking at that book. She has a hard little eye. In the small bare room there are half a dozen women sitting on the benches waiting. Many come and go. Our faces are all familiar to each other, for we wait here everyday.

This is a domestic employment bureau. Most of the women who come here are middle-aged, some have families, some have raised their families and are now alone, some have men who are out of work. Hard times and the man leaves to hunt for work. He doesn't find it. He drifts on. The woman probably doesn't hear from him for a long time. She expects it. She isn't surprised. She struggles alone to feed the many mouths. Sometimes she gets help from the charities. If she's clever she can get herself a good living from the charities, if she's naturally a lick-spittle, naturally a little docile and cunning. If she's proud then she starves silently, leaving her children to find work, coming home after a day's searching to wrestle with her house, her children.

Some such story is written on the faces of all these women. There are young girls too, fresh from the country. Some are made brazen too soon by the city. There is a great exodus of girls from the farms into the city now. Thousands of farms have been vacated completely in Minnesota. The girls are trying to get work. The prettier ones can get jobs in the stores when there are any, or waiting on table, but these jobs are only for the attractive and the adroit, the others, the real peasants, have a more difficult time. . . .

A young girl who went around with Ellen [a poor, attractive young woman] tells about seeing her last evening back of a cafe downtown outside the kitchen door, kicking, showing her legs so that the cook came out and gave her some food and some men gathered in the alley and threw small coin on the ground for a look at her legs. And the girl says enviously that Ellen had a swell breakfast and treated her to one too, that cost two dollars.

A scrub woman whose hips are bent forward from stooping with hands gnarled like water soaked branches clicks her tongue in disgust. No one saves their money, she says, a little money and these foolish young things buy a hat, a dollar for breakfast, a bright scarf. And they do. If you've ever been without money, or food, something very strange happens when you get a bit of money, a kind of madness. You don't care. You can't remember that you had no money before, that the money will be gone. You can remember nothing but that there is the money for which you have been suffering. Now here it is. A lust takes hold of you. You see food in the windows. In imagination you eat hugely; you taste a thousand meals. You look in windows. Colours are brighter; you buy something to dress up in. An excitement takes hold of you. You know it is suicide but you can't help it. You must have food, dainty, splendid food and a bright hat so once again you feel blithe, rid of that ratty gnawing shame.

"I guess she'll go on the street now," a thin woman says faintly and no one takes the trouble to comment further. Like every commodity now the body is difficult to sell and the girls say you're lucky if you get fifty cents. . . .

It's one of the great mysteries of the city where women go when they are out of work and hungry. There are not many women in the bread line. There are no flop houses for women as there are for men, where a bed can be had for a quarter or less. You don't see women lying on the floor at the mission in the free flops. They obviously don't sleep in the jungle or under newspapers in the park. There is no law I suppose against their being in these places but the fact is they rarely are.

Yet there must be as many women out of jobs in cities and suffering extreme poverty as there are men. What happens to them? Where do they go? Try to get into the Y.W. without any money or looking down at heel. Charities take care of very few and only those that are called "deserving." The lone girl is under suspicion by the virgin women who dispense charity.

I've lived in cities for many months broke, without help, too timid to get in bread lines. I've known many women to live like this until they simply faint on the street from privations, without saying a word to anyone. A woman will shut herself up in a room until it is taken away from her, and eat a cracker a day and be as quiet as a mouse so there are no social statistics concerning her. . . .

Sometimes a girl facing the night without shelter will approach a man for lodging. A woman always asks a man for help. Rarely another woman. I have known girls to sleep in men's rooms for the night, on a pallet without molestation, and given breakfast in the morning. . . .

Mrs. Grey, sitting across from me is a living spokesman for the futility of labour. She is a warning. Her hands are scarred with labour. Her body is a great puckered scar. She has given birth to six children, buried three, supported them all alive and dead, bearing them, burying them, feeding them. Bred in hunger they have been spare, susceptible to disease. For seven years she tried to save her boy's arm from amputation, diseased from tuberculosis of the bone. It is almost too suffocating to think of that long close horror of years of child bearing, child feeding, rearing, with the bare suffering of providing a meal and shelter.

Now she is fifty. Her children, economically insecure, are drifters. She never hears of them. She doesn't know if they are alive. She doesn't know if she is alive. Such subtleties of suffering are not for her. For her the brutality of hunger and cold, the bare bone of life. That is enough. These will occupy a life. Not until these are done away with can those subtle feelings that make a human being be indulged.

She is lucky to have five dollars ahead of her. That is her security. She has a tumour that she will die of. She is thin as a worn dime with her tumour sticking out of her side. She is brittle and bitter. Her face is not the face of a human being. She has born more than it is possible for a human being to bear. She is reduced to the least possible denominator of human feelings.

It is terrible to see her little bloodshot eyes like a beaten hound's, fearful in terror.

We cannot meet her eyes. When she looks at any of us we look away. She is like a woman drowning and we turn away. . . .

The young ones know though. I don't want to marry. I don't want any children. So they all say. No children. No marriage. They arm themselves alone, keep up alone. The man is helpless now. He cannot provide. If he propagates he cannot take care of his young. The means are not in his hands. So they live alone. Get what fun they can. The life risk is too horrible now. Defeat is too clearly written on it.

It is appalling to think that these women sitting so listless in the room may work as hard as it is possible for a human being to work, may labour night and day, like Mrs. Gray wash street cars from midnight to dawn and offices in the early evening, scrubbing for fourteen and fifteen hours a day, sleeping only five hours or so, doing this their whole lives, and never earn one day of security, having always before them the pit of the future. The endless labour, the bending back, the water soaked hands, earning never more than a week's wages, never having in their hands more life than that.

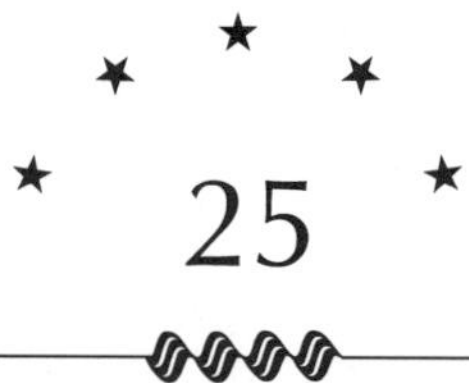

25

THE POLITICS OF UPHEAVAL

There are cycles in American presidential politics. Of the first nine presidential elections, for instance, Jefferson's Democratic Republicans won seven, the Federalists two. The Democrats also won six of the next nine elections. Then a new cycle began in which the Republicans won seven of nine elections from 1860 to 1892 (versus just two for the once-mighty Democrats) and also won seven of the next nine, with their only setbacks coming at the hands of Woodrow Wilson in 1912 and 1916. At this point, the cataclysm of the Great Depression and the charisma of Franklin D. Roosevelt returned the Democrats to dominance. They won, often by landslide margins, every election from 1932 to 1964, except for two losses to Dwight Eisenhower in the 1950s. Since then, however, they have reverted to their post–Civil War form, enabling the Nixon-Reagan-Bush GOP to post a five-to-one score through 1988.

Given the magnitude of the Great Depression and Franklin D. Roosevelt's role in triggering so massive a political realignment, his inaugural address in 1933 might appear moderate. It calls for confidence, honest labor, the protection of agriculture and land, organized relief, and a bit of economic planning. Only Roosevelt's castigation of the "money changers" and his plea for executive authority to meet the crisis seemed to prefigure the sweeping liberalism that many observers instinctively associate with the Roosevelt years. Nevertheless, the address was charged with emotion and a sense of mission. Its moderation reflected both the confusion of the times, when few people understood the nation's problems and still fewer had solutions, and the personal conservatism of the speaker, who was ultimately American capitalism's savior as well as its reformer.

Franklin Delano Roosevelt, a distant cousin of Theodore Roosevelt, was born in 1882 to a wealthy New York family. He attended exclusive schools and colleges and practiced law in New York City. He married his cousin Eleanor in 1905, entered Democratic politics—serving in the state senate from 1910 to 1913—and became assistant secretary of the navy in 1913. After running (and losing) as the Democrats' vice-presidential candidate in 1920, he contracted polio, which left him permanently crippled. Remaining active in politics, he served as governor of New York from 1928 to 1932, when he defeated Hoover for the presidency. During the 1932 campaign Roosevelt criticized Hoover for excessive government spending and an unbalanced budget. Nevertheless, after entering the White House, Roosevelt also was obliged to adopt a spending policy to help those who were starving, put people to work, and revive the economy. His New Deal stressed economic recovery as well as relief and reform. Roosevelt's programs, backed by the great Democratic majorities that he forged, mitigated many of the effects of the Great Depression, though the slump never actually ended until the advent of World War II. Roosevelt achieved reelection in 1936, 1940, and 1944, a record unequaled then and unconstitutional since 1951. He died in office in Warm Springs, Georgia, in 1945.

Questions to Consider. Why, in his first inaugural address, did Roosevelt place great emphasis on candor, honesty, and truth. Did he display these qualities himself in discussing the crisis? In what ways did he try to reassure the American people? What reasons did he give for the Great Depression? What values did he think were important for sustaining the nation in a time of trouble? What solutions did he propose for meeting the economic crisis? How did he regard his authority to act under the Constitution? How would you have reacted to his address if you had been an unemployed worker, a hard-pressed farmer, or a middle-class citizen who had lost a home through foreclosure?

First Inaugural Address (1933)

FRANKLIN D. ROOSEVELT

This is a day of national consecration, and I am certain that my fellow-Americans expect that on my induction into the Presidency I will address them with a candor and a decision which the present situation of our nation impels. This is pre-eminently the time to speak the truth, the whole truth, frankly and boldly. Nor need we shrink from honestly facing conditions in our country today. This great nation will endure as it has endured, will revive and will prosper.

So first of all let me assert my firm belief that the only thing we have to fear is fear itself—nameless, unreasoning, unjustified terror which paralyzes

From *The New York Times*, March 5, 1933.

needed efforts to convert retreat into advance. In every dark hour of our national life a leadership of frankness and vigor has met with that understanding and support of the people themselves which is essential to victory. I am convinced that you will again give that support to leadership in these critical days.

In such a spirit on my part and on yours we face our common difficulties. They concern, thank God, only material things. Values have shrunken to fantastic levels; taxes have risen; our ability to pay has fallen; government of all kinds is faced by serious curtailment of income; the means of exchange are frozen in the currents of trade; the withered leaves of industrial enterprise lie on every side; farmers find no markets for their produce; the savings of many years in thousands of families are gone.

More important, a host of unemployed citizens face the grim problem of existence, and an equally great number toil with little return. Only a foolish optimist can deny the dark realities of the moment.

Yet our distress comes from no failure of substance. We are stricken by no plague of locusts. Compared with the perils which our forefathers conquered because they believed and were not afraid, we have still much to be thankful for. Nature still offers her bounty and human efforts have multiplied it. Plenty is at our doorstep, but a generous use of it languishes in the very sight of the supply. Primarily, this is because the rulers of the exchange of mankind's goods have failed through their own stubbornness and their own incompetence, have admitted their failure and abdicated. Practices of the unscrupulous money changers stand indicted in the court of public opinion, rejected by the hearts and minds of men.

True, they have tried, but their efforts have been cast in the pattern of an outworn tradition. Faced by failure of credit, they have proposed only the lending of more money. Stripped of the lure of profit by which to induce our people to follow their false leadership, they have resorted to exhortations, pleading tearfully for restored confidence. They know only the rules of a generation of self-seekers. They have no vision, and when there is no vision the people perish.

The money changers have fled from their high seats in the temple of our civilization. We may now restore that temple to the ancient truths. The measure of the restoration lies in the extent to which we apply social values more noble than mere monetary profit.

Happiness lies not in the mere possession of money; it lies in the joy of achievement, in the thrill of creative effort. The joy and moral stimulation of work no longer must be forgotten in the mad chase of evanescent profits. These dark days will be worth all they cost us if they teach us that our true destiny is not to be ministered unto but to minister to ourselves and to our fellow-men.

Recognition of the falsity of material wealth as the standard of success goes hand in hand with the abandonment of the false belief that public office and high political position are to be valued only by the standards of pride of place and personal profit; and there must be an end to a conduct in banking and in business which too often has given to a sacred trust the likeness of callous and selfish wrongdoing. Small wonder that confidence languishes, for it thrives only on honesty, on honor, on the sacredness of obligations, on faithful protection, on unselfish performance. Without them it cannot live.

Restoration calls, however, not for changes in ethics alone. This nation asks for action, and action now.

Our greatest primary task is to put people to work. This is no unsolvable problem if we face it wisely and courageously. It can be accomplished in part by direct recruiting by the Government itself, treating the task as we would treat the emergency of war, but at the same time, through this employment, accomplishing greatly needed projects to stimulate and reorganize the use of our natural resources.

Hand in hand with this, we must frankly recognize the overbalance of population in our industrial centers and, by engaging on a national scale in the redistribution, endeavor to provide a better use of the land for those best fitted for the land. The task can be helped by definite efforts to raise the values of agricultural products and with this the power to purchase the output of our cities. It can be helped by preventing realistically the tragedy of the growing loss, through foreclosure, of our small homes and our farms. It can be helped by insistence that the Federal, State and local governments act forthwith on the demand that their cost be drastically reduced. It can be helped by the unifying of relief activities which today are often scattered, uneconomical and unequal. It can be helped by national planning for a supervision of all forms of transportation and of communications and other utilities which have a definitely public character. There are many ways in which it can be helped, but it can never be helped merely by talking about it. We must act, and act quickly. . . .

This I propose to offer, pledging that the larger purposes will bind upon us all as a sacred obligation with a unity of duty hitherto evoked only in the time of armed strife.

With this pledge taken, I assume unhesitatingly the leadership of this great army of our people, dedicated to a disciplined attack upon our common problems.

Action in this image and to this end is feasible under the form of government which we have inherited from our ancestors. Our Constitution is so simple and practical that it is possible always to meet extraordinary needs by changes in emphasis and arrangement without loss of essential form. That is why our constitutional system has proved itself the most superbly enduring political mechanism the modern world has produced. It has met every stress of vast expansion of territory, of foreign wars, of bitter internal strife, of world relations.

It is to be hoped that the normal balance of executive and legislative authority may be wholly adequate to meet the unprecedented task before us.

But it may be that an unprecedented demand and need for undelayed action may call for temporary departure from that normal balance of public procedure.

I am prepared under my constitutional duty to recommend the measures that a stricken nation in the midst of a stricken world may require. These measures, or such other measures as the Congress may build out of its experience and wisdom, I shall seek, within my constitutional authority, to bring to speedy adoption.

But in the event that the Congress shall fail to take one of these two courses, and in the event that the national emergency is still critical, I shall not evade the clear course of duty that will then confront me. I shall ask the Congress for the one remaining instrument to meet the crisis—broad Executive power to wage a war against the emergency as great as the power that would be given me if we were in fact invaded by a foreign foe.

For the trust reposed in me I will return the courage and the devotion that befit the time. I can do no less. . . .

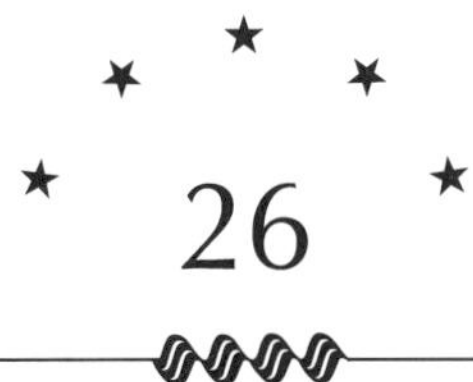

Organizing the Masses

Economic conditions in the 1930s had a tremendous impact on American labor. The Great Depression wreaked havoc with the lives of working people. By 1932, New York had a million jobless and Chicago another 600,000; 50 percent of Cleveland's workforce was unemployed, as was 60 percent of Akron's and 80 percent of Toledo's. Even those who still had jobs saw their wages and hours decline dramatically, and things did not greatly improve as the decade wore on.

The New Deal gave labor unions an opportunity to replenish their membership, which had plummeted to half of its World War I strength. The chief piece of legislation affecting unions was the Labor Relations Act of 1935, which established a national board to keep employers from interfering with labor organizers or union members and to supervise union elections. Thus encouraged, leaders of several large unions bolted the conservative American Federation of Labor (AFL) to form the Committee for Industrial Organization, which soon became the Congress of Industrial Organizations (CIO). The AFL emphasized craft unions (which were made up of workers in a given trade); the CIO insisted that industrial unions (which included all industrial workers, skilled and unskilled, in an industry) were essential in the great mass-production industries in which labor previously had been unorganized. In 1936 and 1937 the CIO, led by John L. Lewis, president of the United Mine Workers, mounted successful, though bloody, organizing campaigns to establish unions in the steel, rubber, electrical, automobile, and other basic industries. The AFL soon responded with organizing drives of its own. Thus, total union membership had tripled by 1940. The New Deal facilitated the rise of Big Labor as it did the welfare state, all the while preserving the country's basic economic system.

John L. Lewis, the forceful CIO leader, was born near Lucas, Iowa, in 1880 to a Welsh immigrant family. Leaving school after the seventh grade, Lewis worked briefly with his father in the coal fields and then wandered across the West for several years before returning to the mines in about 1905. He soon became active in union affairs and in 1920 was elected president of the United Mine Workers. Although he was originally associated with the AFL, Lewis spearheaded the formation of the CIO after the passage of the Labor Relations Act of 1935 and presided vigorously and dramatically for the next few years over the violent struggle for industrial unionism. In the 1940s he repeatedly quarreled with leaders of the CIO, the AFL, and the federal government, called several bitter coal strikes, and was twice held in contempt of court for ignoring antistrike injunctions. He nonetheless remained a revered labor spokesman. He was president of the United Mine Workers until 1960 and chairman of its retirement fund until his death in Washington, D.C., in 1969.

Questions to Consider. John L. Lewis had great gifts as an orator. ("He can use his voice like a policeman's billy," said one commentator, "or like a monk at orisons.") His physical appearance was also striking—he had a mass of reddish hair, bushy eyebrows, and piercing blue eyes. But his effectiveness as a speaker depended on his choice of words. In the 1936 radio speech reprinted below, he was trying to justify the CIO to an American public still not particularly friendly to organized labor. Do you think his style of speech was likely to win the understanding and sympathy of middle-class Americans? How "radical" was the position taken in his speech? How did he link the CIO to traditional American values and institutions? How extensive, according to Lewis, was resistance to the CIO's organizing drive in the big unorganized industries of the country? How did he implicate the federal government in this resistance? In what ways did he distinguish the CIO's philosophy from that of "alien" doctrines like Communism? What did he have to say about politics?

The Steelworkers Organization Campaign (1936)

JOHN L. LEWIS

Out of the agony and travail of economic America, the Committee for Industrial Organization was born. To millions of Americans, exploited without stint by corporate industry and socially debased beyond the understanding of the fortunate, its coming was as welcome as the dawn to the night watcher. To a lesser group of Americans, infinitely more fortunately situated, blessed with larger quantities of the world's goods and insolent in their assumption of privilege, its coming was heralded as a

From *John L. Lewis and the International Union, United Mine Workers of America: The Story from 1917 to 1952* (United Mine Workers of America, Washington, D.C., 1952), 43–49. Reprinted by permission of the United Mine Workers of America.

Strike pickets. During the winter of 1936–1937 the Congress of Industrial Organizations climaxed its drive to unionize America's basic industries with a series of strikes that caused conflict in some communities and tensions in many others. In this artwork, workers picket for bargaining rights and higher wages in late 1937. A year later, total union membership had zoomed to almost 8 million. Workers were responding to CIO organizers who sang, "You'll win. What I mean. . . . Take it easy. . . . but take it!" (*We Demand!,* by Joe Jones; The Butler Institute of American Art)

harbinger of ill, sinister of purpose, of unclean methods and nonvirtuous objectives.

The workers of the nation were tired of waiting for corporate industry to right their economic wrongs, to alleviate their social agony and to grant them their political rights. Despairing of fair treatment, they resolved to do something for themselves. They, therefore, have organized a new labor movement, conceived within the principles of the national Bill of Rights and committed to the proposition that the workers are free to assemble in their own forums, voice their own grievances, declare their own hopes, and contract on even terms with modern industry, for the sale of their only material possession—their labor.

The Committee for Industrial Organization has a numerical enrollment of 3,718,000 members. It has thirty-two affiliated national and international unions. Of this number, eleven unions account for 2,765,000 members. This group is organized in the textile, auto, garment, lumber, rubber, electrical manufacturing, power, steel, coal and transport industries. The remaining membership exists in the maritime, oil production and refining, shipbuilding, leather, chemical, retail, meat packing, vegetable canning, metalliferous mining, miscellaneous manufacturing, agricultural labor, and service and miscellaneous industries. Some 200 thousand workers are organized into 506 chartered local unions not yet attached to a national industrial union. Much of this progress was made in the face of violent and deadly opposition which reached its climax in the slaughter of workers paralleling the massacres of Ludlow [Colorado, 1914] and Homestead [Pennsylvania, 1892].

In the steel industry, the corporations generally have accepted collective bargaining and negotiated wage agreements with the Committee for Industrial Organization. Eighty-five per cent of the industry is thus under contract and a peaceful relationship exists between the management and the workers. Written wage contracts have been negotiated with 399 steel companies covering 510 thousand men. One thousand thirty-one local lodges in 700 communities have been organized.

Five of the corporations in the steel industry elected to resist collective bargaining and undertook to destroy the steel workers' union. These companies filled their plants with industrial spies, assembled depots of guns and gas bombs, established barricades, controlled their communities with armed thugs, leased the police power of cities and mobilized the military power of a state to guard them against the intrusion of collective bargaining within their plants.

During this strike, eighteen steel workers were either shot to death or had their brains clubbed out by police or armed thugs in the pay of the steel companies. In Chicago, Mayor [Edward V.] Kelly's police force was successful in killing ten strikers before they could escape the fury of the police, shooting eight of them in the back. One hundred sixty strikers were maimed and injured by police clubs, riot guns and gas bombs and were hospitalized.

Hundreds of strikers were arrested, jailed, treated with brutality while incarcerated and harassed by succeeding litigation. None but strikers were murdered, gassed, injured, jailed or maltreated. No one had to die except the workers who were standing for the right guaranteed them by the Congress and written in the law.

The infamous Governor [Martin L.] Davey of Ohio, successful in the last election because of his reiterated promises of fair treatment to labor, used the military power of the commonwealth on the side of the Republic Steel Co. and the Youngstown Sheet and Tube Co. Nearly half of the staggering military expenditure incident to the crushing of this strike in Ohio was borne by the federal government through the allocation of financial aid to the military establishment of the state.

The steel workers have now buried their dead, while the widows weep and watch their orphaned children become objects of public charity. The murder of these unarmed men has never been publicly rebuked by any authoritative officer of the state or federal government. Some of them, in extenuation, plead lack of jurisdiction, but murder as a crime against the moral code can always be rebuked without regard to the niceties of legalistic jurisdiction by those who profess to be the keepers of the public conscience.

Shortly after Kelly's police force in Chicago had indulged in their bloody orgy, Kelly came to Washington looking for political patronage. That patronage was forthcoming and Kelly must believe that the killing of the strikers is no liability in partisan politics.

The men in the steel industry who sacrificed their all were not merely aiding their fellows at home but were adding strength to the cause of their comrades in all industry. Labor was marching toward the goal of industrial democracy and contributing constructively toward a more rational arrangement of our domestic economy.

Labor does not seek industrial strife. It wants peace, but a peace with justice. In the long struggle for labor's rights, it has been patient and forebearing. Sabotage and destructive syndicalism have had no part in the American labor movement. Workers have kept faith in American institutions. Most of the conflicts which have occurred have been when labor's right to live has been challenged and denied.

Fascist organizations have been launched and financed under the shabby pretext that the CIO movement is communistic. The real breeders of discontent and alien doctrines of government and philosophies subversive of good citizenship are such as these who take the law into their own hands.

No tin-hat brigade of goose-stepping vigilantes or Bible-babbling mob of blackguarding and corporation-paid scoundrels will prevent the onward march of labor, or divert its purpose to play its natural and rational part in the development of the economic, political and social life of our nation.

Unionization, as opposed to Communism, presupposes the relation of employment; it is based upon the wage system and it recognizes fully and unreservedly the institution of private property and the right to investment profit.

The organized workers of America, free in their industrial life, conscious partners in production, secure in their homes and enjoying a decent standard of living, will prove the finest bulwark against the intrusion of alien doctrines of government.

Do those who have hatched this foolish cry of Communism in the CIO fear the increased influence will be cast on the side of shorter hours, a better system of distributed employment, better homes for the underprivileged, social security for the aged, a fairer distribution of the national income?

Certainly labor wants a fairer share in the national income. Assuredly labor wants a larger participation in increased productivity efficiency. Obviously the population is entitled to participate in the fruits of the genius of our men of achievement in the field of the material sciences.

Under the banner of the Committee for Industrial Organization, American labor is on the march. Its objectives today are those it had in the beginning: to strive for the unionization of our unorganized millions of workers and for the acceptance of collective bargaining as a recognized American institution.

The objectives of this movement are not political in a partisan sense. Yet it is true that a political party which seeks the support of labor and makes pledges of good faith to labor must, in equity and good conscience, keep that faith and redeem those pledges.

The spectacle of august and dignified members of the Congress, servants of the people and agents of the republic, skulking in hallways and closets, hiding their faces in a party caucus to prevent a quorum from acting upon a labor measure, is one that emphasizes the perfidy of politicians and blasts the confidence of labor's millions in politicians' promises and statesmen's vows.

Labor next year cannot avoid the necessity of a political assay of the work and deeds of its so-called friends and its political beneficiaries. It must determine who are its friends in the arena of politics as elsewhere. It feels that its cause is just and that its friends should not view its struggle with neutral detachment or intone constant criticism of its activities.

Those who chant their praises of democracy, but who lose no chance to drive their knives into labor's defenseless back, must feel the weight of labor's woe even as its open adversaries must ever feel the thrust of labor's power.

Labor, like Israel, has many sorrows. Its women weep for their fallen and they lament for the future of the children of the race. It ill behooves one who has supped at labor's table and who has been sheltered in labor's house to curse with equal fervor and fine impartiality both labor and its adversaries when they become locked in deadly embrace.

War Aims

Circumstances change, said Franklin D. Roosevelt, and so did he as president, from (in other words) "Mr. New Deal" facing the dangers of the Great Depression in the 1930s to "Mr. Win-the-War" facing the dangers of the Axis Powers in the 1940s. Historians have sometimes seen the coming of war as a discontinuity in his administration.

But the break was not so sharp as it might have been. One thread providing continuity was that Roosevelt was never disinterested in world affairs, even during the most urgent days of the Depression. As the Nazi threat to France and England and the Japanese threat to China grew in the late 1930s, so did Roosevelt's determination to help—if he could do so without declaring war. Another thread was that Roosevelt perceived the looming conflict partly in ideological terms—as a struggle, with the forces of authoritarianism and social reaction pitted against the forces of democracy and social progress. To some extent, Roosevelt's view of the conflict resembled Woodrow Wilson's goal in World War I of making the world "safe for democracy." It also followed logically from the nature of the enemy, which most people regarded as nothing but a coalition of racist, militaristic tyrants. Opposing such an enemy meant, by extension, opposing what the enemy stood for.

In his "Four Freedoms" address, delivered to Congress and broadcast to the public in January 1941—prior to America's formal entry into the war—Roosevelt went beyond Woodrow Wilson in his statement of war goals. In this speech, as in others he delivered over the next four years, the president made it clear that he considered this war to be not just about freedom of speech, press, and religion, as his predecessors might have it. This was also a war about freedom from want, the philosophy underlying many of the New Deal programs. And it was about freedom from fear, a sentiment that had filled his first inaugural address eight years before. At least in this 1941 statement, "Mr. Win-the-War" continued to be "Mr. New Deal."

Questions to Consider. Isolationist, antiwar feelings were still very strong in the country in early 1941. How did Roosevelt try at the beginning of his speech to neutralize antiwar sentiment? At what point in the address did he introduce what might be considered progressive political ideas of the kind that characterized the New Deal? According to Roosevelt, what were the foundations of "a healthy and strong democracy"? Would all Americans have agreed with his list of democratic "foundations"? Why did the president demand individual sacrifice and warn people not to try to get rich from his programs? Of the "four freedoms" Roosevelt eventually enumerated, which do you think would have been most popular in the 1940s?

The Four Freedoms (1941)

FRANKLIN D. ROOSEVELT

I address you, the Members of the Seventy-seventh Congress, at a moment unprecedented in the history of the Union. I use the word "unprecedented," because at no previous time has American security been as seriously threatened from without as it is today. . . .

Every realist knows that the democratic way of life is at this moment being directly assailed in every part of the world—assailed either by arms, or by secret spreading of poisonous propaganda by those who seek to destroy unity and promote discord in nations still at peace.

During sixteen months this assault has blotted out the whole pattern of democratic life in an appalling number of independent nations, great and small. The assailants are still on the march, threatening other nations, great and small.

Therefore, as your President, performing my constitutional duty to "give to the Congress information on the state of the Union," I find it necessary to report that the future and the safety of our country and of our democracy are overwhelmingly involved in events far beyond our borders.

Armed defense of democratic existence is now being gallantly waged in four continents. If that defense fails, all the population and all the resources of Europe, Asia, Africa, and Australasia will be dominated by the conquerors. The total of those populations and their resources greatly exceeds the sum total of the population and resources of the whole of the Western Hemisphere—many times over. . . .

No realistic American can expect from a dictator's peace international generosity, or return of true independence, or world disarmament, or freedom of expression, or freedom of religion—or even good business.

From *The New York Times,* January 7, 1941.

Such a peace would bring no security for us or for our neighbors. Those who would give up essential liberty to purchase a little temporary safety deserve neither liberty nor safety. . . .

There is much loose talk of our immunity from immediate and direct invasion from across the seas. Obviously, as long as the British Navy retains its power, no such danger exists. Even if there were no British Navy, it is not probable that any enemy would be stupid enough to attack us by landing troops in the United States from across thousands of miles of ocean, until it had acquired strategic bases from which to operate.

But we learn much from the lessons of the past years in Europe—particularly the lesson of Norway, whose essential seaports were captured by treachery and surprise built up over a series of years. . . .

As long as the aggressor nations maintain the offensive, they, not we, will choose the time and the place and the method of their attack. . . .

Let us say to the democracies, "We Americans are vitally concerned in your defense of freedom. We are putting forth our energies, our resources, and our organizing powers to give you the strength to regain and maintain a free world. We shall send you, in ever-increasing numbers, ships, planes, tanks, guns. This is our purpose and our pledge."

In fulfillment of this purpose we will not be intimidated by the threats of dictators that they will regard as a breach of international law and as an act of war our aid to the democracies which dare to resist their aggression. Such aid is not an act of war, even if a dictator should unilaterally proclaim it so to be.

When the dictators are ready to make war upon us, they will not wait for an act of war on our part. They did not wait for Norway or Belgium or The Netherlands to commit an act of war.

Their only interest is in a new one-way international law, which lacks mutuality in its observance and, therefore, becomes an instrument of oppression. . . .

As men do not live by bread alone, they do not fight by armaments alone. Those who man our defenses, and those behind them who build our defenses, must have the stamina and courage which come from an unshakable belief in the manner of life which they are defending. The mighty action which we are calling for cannot be based on a disregard of all things worth fighting for.

There is nothing mysterious about the foundations of a healthy and strong democracy. The basic things expected by our people of their political and economic systems are simple.

They are:

Equality of opportunity for youth and for others.
Jobs for those who can work.
Security for those who need it.
The ending of special privilege for the few.

The preservation of civil liberties for all.

The enjoyment of the fruits of scientific progress in a wider and constantly rising standard of living.

These are the simple and basic things that must never be lost sight of in the turmoil and unbelievable complexity of our modern world. The inner and abiding strength of our economic and political systems is dependent upon the degree to which they fulfill these expectations. . . .

I have called for personal sacrifice. I am assured of the willingness of almost all Americans to respond to that call.

A part of the sacrifice means the payment of more money in taxes. . . .

No person should try, or be allowed to get rich out of this program. . . .

In the future days, which we seek to make secure, we look forward to a world founded upon four essential human freedoms.

The first is freedom of speech and expression, everywhere in the world.

The second is freedom of every person to worship God in his own way, everywhere in the world.

The third is freedom from want, which, translated into world terms, means economic understandings which will secure to every nation a healthy peacetime life for its inhabitants, everywhere in the world.

The fourth is freedom from fear—which, translated into world terms, means a worldwide reduction of armaments to such a point and in such a through fashion that no nation will be in a position to commit an act of physical aggression against any neighbor—anywhere in the world.

That is no vision of a distant millennium. It is a definite basis for a kind of world attainable in our own time and not the so-called new order of tyranny which the dictators seek to impose. That kind of world is the very antithesis of the kind created with the crash of a bomb.

To that new order we oppose the greater conception—the moral order. A good society is able to face schemes of world domination and foreign revolutions alike without fear.

Since the beginning of our American history we have been engaged in change—in a perpetual peaceful revolution—a revolution which goes on steadily, quietly adjusting itself to changing conditions—without the concentration camp or the quicklime in the ditch. The world order which we seek is the cooperation of free countries, working together in a friendly, civilized society.

This Nation has placed its destiny in the hands and heads and hearts of its millions of free men and women; and its faith in freedom under the guidance of God. Freedom means the supremacy of human rights everywhere. Our support goes to those who struggle to gain those rights or keep them. Our strength is in our unity of purpose.

To that high concept there can be no end save victory.

Day of Infamy

The United States did not completely isolate itself from other nations after the disillusionment of World War I. During the 1920s the U.S. government negotiated arms-limitations pacts, sought to preserve the Open Door in China, encouraged massive bank loans to a war-ravaged Europe, and maintained troops in Latin America. Yet throughout the 1920s and into the 1930s the United States held steady on two key matters. It refused to enter military or defense alliances with any nation and to spend heavily on armies and armaments. During the 1930s the American public was probably more opposed to war than at any other time in U.S. history.

The rise of aggressive governments in Nazi Germany, Fascist Italy and Imperial Japan gradually changed America's sense of detachment. But the shift to involvement was slow. Not until German forces subdued France in 1940 did President Franklin Roosevelt promise "everything short of war" to a beleaguered England. Roosevelt asked Congress for a declaration of war only when Japan, which saw America's presence in the Pacific as a threat to its own ambitions there, conducted devastating attacks on the American fleet and naval base at Pearl Harbor, Hawaii, and on the Philippines on December 7, 1941. The president's emphasis on the surprise element in this "day of infamy" and on the need henceforth to guard against "treachery" presaged not only the vast wartime military build-up to come but also the maintenance of a large military establishment after the war was over. Roosevelt's address in 1941 thus shaped America's perceptions of its international position just as Woodrow Wilson's had in 1917, though in a profoundly different direction.

Questions to Consider. Several questions arise from a reading of Roosevelt's announcement of war. How comparable was the sinking of American ships by Japanese airplanes in 1941 to the sinking of American ships by German submarines in 1917? Did this difference in the nature of the weaponry add to the impact of Roosevelt's announcement? Note, too, that Roosevelt did not attach a lengthy declaration of large goals for humanity to his message, as Wilson had done. Why not? Did the facts actually "speak for themselves," as Roosevelt stated? How could the president assert that the American people had "already formed their opinion"? Did the notions of American exceptionalism and the redemption of humanity sneak into the message despite its brevity?

Address to Congress (1941)

FRANKLIN D. ROOSEVELT

Yesterday, December 7, 1941—a date which will live in infamy—the United States of America was suddenly and deliberately attacked by naval and air forces of the Empire of Japan.

The United States was at peace with that nation and, at the solicitation of Japan, was still in conversation with its Government and its Emperor looking toward the maintenance of peace in the Pacific. Indeed, one hour after Japanese air squadrons had commenced bombing in Oahu, the Japanese Ambassador to the United States and his colleague delivered to the Secretary of State a formal reply to a recent American message. While this reply stated that it seemed useless to continue the existing diplomatic negotiations, it contained no threat or hint of war or armed attack.

It will be recorded that the distance of Hawaii from Japan makes it obvious that the attack was deliberately planned many days or even weeks ago. During the intervening time the Japanese Government has deliberately sought to deceive the United States by false statements and expressions of hope for continued peace.

The attack yesterday on the Hawaiian Islands has caused severe damage to American naval and military forces. Very many American lives have been lost. In addition American ships have been reported torpedoed on the high seas between San Francisco and Honolulu.

Yesterday the Japanese Government also launched an attack against Malaya. Last night Japanese forces attacked Hong Kong. Last night Japanese forces attacked Guam. Last night Japanese forces attacked the Philippine Islands. Last night the Japanese attacked Wake Island. This morning the Japanese attacked Midway Island.

Japan has, therefore, undertaken a surprise offensive extending throughout the Pacific area. The facts of yesterday speak for themselves. The people

From *The New York Times,* December 9, 1941.

Magazine of USS Shaw explodes. This, one of the most remarkable combat photographs of all time, was taken at the exact moment the destroyer blew up during the Japanese attack on Pearl Harbor. (Brown Brothers)

of the United States have already formed their opinions and well understand the implications to the very life and safety of our nation.

As Commander-in-Chief of the Army and Navy, I have directed that all measures be taken for our defense.

Always will we remember the character of the onslaught against us.

No matter how long it may take us to overcome this premeditated invasion, the American people in their righteous might will win through to absolute victory.

I believe I interpret the will of the Congress and of the people when I assert that we will not only defend ourselves to the uttermost but will make very certain that this form of treachery shall never endanger us again.

Hostilities exist. There is no blinking at the fact that our people, our territory and our interests are in grave danger.

With confidence in our armed forces—with the unbounded determination of our people—we will gain the inevitable triumph—so help us God.

I ask that the Congress declare that since the unprovoked and dastardly attack by Japan on Sunday, December seventh, a state of war has existed between the United States and the Japanese Empire.

Hiroshima, Japan, two years after the dropping of the atomic bomb. After three years and $2 billion invested in secret research and production, the United States exploded the first atomic device at Alamogordo, New Mexico, on July 16, 1945. A scientist who was there said it was as if "the earth had opened and the skies had split or like the moment of creation when God said, 'Let there be light.'" Although the catastrophic power of the weapon was clear, President Truman never really considered not using it. The latest estimates indicate that a quarter of a million people died in the atomic attacks on Hiroshima and Nagasaki. (Corbis-Bettmann)

ten nurses out of more than two hundred. The sole uninjured doctor on the Red Cross Hospital staff was Dr. Sasaki. After the explosion, he hurried to a storeroom to fetch bandages. This room, like everything he had seen as he ran through the hospital, was chaotic—bottles of medicines thrown off shelves and broken, salves spattered on the walls, instruments strewn everywhere. He grabbed up some bandages and an unbroken bottle of mercurochrome, hurried back to the chief surgeon, and bandaged his cuts. Then he went out into the corridor and began patching up the wounded patients and the doctors and nurses there. He blundered so without his glasses that he took a pair off the face of a wounded nurse, and although they only approximately compensated for the errors of his vision, they were better than nothing. (He was to depend on them for more than a month.)

Dr. Sasaki worked without method, taking those who were nearest him first, and he noticed soon that the corridor seemed to be getting more and more crowded. Mixed in with the abrasions and lacerations which most people in the hospital had suffered, he began to find dreadful burns. He realized then that casualties were pouring in from outdoors. There were so many that he began to pass up the lightly wounded; he decided that all he could hope to do was to stop people from bleeding to death. Before long, patients lay and crouched on the floors of the wards and the laboratories and all the other rooms, and in the corridors, and on the stairs, and in the front hall, and under the portecochère, and on the stone front steps, and in the driveway and courtyard, and for blocks each way in the streets outside. Wounded people supported maimed people; disfigured families leaned together. Many people were vomiting. A tremendous number of schoolgirls—some of those who had been taken from their classrooms to work outdoors, cleaning fire lanes—crept into the hospital. In a city of two hundred and forty-five thousand, nearly a hundred thousand people had been killed or doomed at one blow; a hundred thousand more were hurt. At least ten thousand of the wounded made their way to the best hospital in town, which was altogether unequal to such a trampling, since it had only six hundred beds, and they had all been occupied. The people in the suffocating crowd inside the hospital wept and cried, for Dr. Sasaki to hear, "*Sensei!* Doctor!" and the less seriously wounded came and pulled at his sleeve and begged him to go to the aid of the worse wounded. Tugged here and there in his stockinged feet, bewildered by the numbers, staggered by so much raw flesh, Dr. Sasaki lost all sense of the profession and stopped working as a skillful surgeon and a sympathetic man; he became an automaton, mechanically wiping, daubing, winding, wiping, daubing, winding. . . .

The morning, again, was hot. Father Kleinsorge went to fetch water for the wounded in a bottle and a teapot he had borrowed. He had heard that it was possible to get fresh tap water outside Asano Park. Going through the rock gardens, he had to climb over and crawl under the trunks of fallen pine trees; he found he was weak. There were many dead in the gardens. At a beautiful moon bridge, he passed a naked, living woman who seemed to have been burned from head to toe and was red all over. Near the entrance to the park, an Army doctor was working, but the only medicine he had was iodine, which he painted over cuts, bruises, slimy burns, everything—and by now everything he painted had pus on it. Outside the gate of the park, Father Kleinsorge found a faucet that still worked—part of the plumbing of a vanished house—and he filled his vessels and returned. When he had given the wounded the water, he made a second trip. This time, the woman by the bridge was dead. On his way back with the water, he got lost on a detour around a fallen tree, and as he looked for his way through the woods, he heard a voice ask from the underbrush, "Have you anything to drink?" He saw a uniform. Thinking there was just one soldier, he approached with the water. When he had penetrated the bushes, he saw there were about twenty men, and they were all in exactly the same nightmarish state: their faces were wholly burned, their eyesockets were hollow, the fluid from their melted eyes had run down their cheeks. (They must have had their faces upturned when the bomb went off; perhaps they were anti-aircraft personnel.) Their mouths were mere swollen, pus-covered wounds, which they could not bear to stretch enough to admit the spout of the teapot. So Father Kleinsorge got a large piece of grass and drew out the stem so as to make a straw, and gave them all water to drink that way. One of them said, "I can't see anything." Father Kleinsorge answered, as cheerfully as he could, "There's a doctor at the entrance to the park. He's busy now, but he'll come soon and fix your eyes, I hope." . . .

Early that day, August 7th, the Japanese radio broadcast for the first time a succinct announcement that very few, if any, of the people most concerned with its content, the survivors in Hiroshima, happened to hear: "Hiroshima suffered considerable damage as the result of an attack by a few B-29s. It is believed that a new type of bomb was used. The details are being investigated." Nor is it probable that any of the survivors happened to be tuned in on a short-wave rebroadcast of an extraordinary announcement by the president of the United States, which identified the new bomb as atomic: "That bomb had more power than twenty thousand tons of TNT. It had more than two thousand times the blast power of the British Grand Slam, which is the largest bomb ever yet used in the history of warfare." Those victims who were able to worry at all about what had happened thought of it and discussed it in more primitive, childish terms—gasoline sprinkled from an airplane, maybe, or some combustible gas, or a big cluster of incendiaries, or the work of parachutists; but, even if they had known the truth, most of them were too busy or too weary or too badly hurt to care that they were the objects of the first great experiment in the use of atomic power, which (as the voices on the short wave shouted) no country except the United States, with its industrial know-how, its willingness to throw two billion gold dollars into an important wartime gamble, could possibly have developed. . . .

Dr. Sasaki and his colleagues at the Red Cross Hospital watched the unprecedented disease unfold and at last evolved a theory about its nature. It had, they decided, three stages. The first stage had been all over before the doctors even knew they were dealing with a new sickness; it was the direct reaction to the bombardment of the body, at the moment when the bomb went off, by neutrons, beta particles, and gamma rays. The apparently uninjured people who had died so mysteriously in the first few hours or days had succumbed in this first stage. It killed ninety-five per cent of the people within a half-mile of the center, and many thousands who were farther away. The doctors realized in retrospect that even though most of these dead had also suffered from burns and blast effects, they had absorbed enough radiation to kill them. The rays simply destroyed body cells—caused their nuclei to degenerate and broke their walls. Many people who did not die right away came down with nausea, headache, diarrhea, malaise, and fever, which lasted several days. Doctors could not be certain whether some of these symptoms were the result of radiation or nervous shock. The second stage set in ten or fifteen days after the bombing. Its first symptom was falling hair. Diarrhea and fever, which in some cases went as high as 106, came next. Twenty-five to thirty days after the explosion, blood disorders appeared: gums bled, the white-blood-cell count dropped sharply, and *petechiae* [eruptions] appeared on the skin and mucous membranes. The drop in the number of white blood corpuscles reduced the patient's capacity to resist infection, so open wounds were unusually slow in healing and many of the sick developed sore throats and mouths. The two key symptoms, on which the doctors came to base their prognosis, were fever and the lowered white-corpuscle count. If fever remained steady and high, the patient's chances for survival were poor. The white count almost always dropped below four thousand; a patient whose count fell below one thousand had little hope of living. Toward the end of the second stage, if the patient survived, anemia, or a drop in the red blood count, also set in. The third stage was the reaction that came when the body struggled to compensate for its ills—when, for instance, the white count not only returned to normal but increased to much higher than normal levels. In this stage, many patients died of complications, such as infections in the chest cavity. Most burns healed with deep layers of pink, rubbery scar tissue, known as keloid tumors. The duration of the disease varied, depending on the patient's constitution and the amount of radiation he had received. Some victims recovered in a week; with others the disease dragged on for months.

As the symptoms revealed themselves, it became clear that many of them resembled the effects of overdoses of X-ray, and the doctors based their therapy on that likeness. They gave victims liver extract, blood transfusions, and vitimins, especially B_1. The shortage of supplies and instruments hampered them. Allied doctors who came in after the surrender found plasma and penicillin very effective. Since the blood disorders were, in the long run, the predominant factor in the disease, some of the Japanese doctors evolved a theory as to the seat of the delayed sickness. They thought that perhaps gamma rays, entering the body at the time of the explosion, made the phosphorus in the victims' bones radioactive, and that they in turn emitted beta particles, which, though they could not penetrate far through flesh, could enter the bone marrow, where blood is manufactured, and gradually tear it down. Whatever its source, the disease had some baffling quirks. Not all the patients exhibited all the main symptoms. People who suffered flash burns were protected, to a considerable extent, from radiation sickness. Those who had lain quietly for days or even hours after the bombing were much less liable to get sick than those who had been active. Gray hair seldom fell out. And, as if nature were protecting man against his own ingenuity, the reproductive processes were affected for a time; men became sterile, women had miscarriages, menstruation stopped. . . .

A surprising number of the people of Hiroshima remained more or less indifferent about the ethics of using the bomb. Possibly they were too terrified by it to want to think about it at all. Many citizens of Hiroshima, however, continued to feel a hatred for Americans which nothing could possibly erase. "I see," Dr. Sasaki once said, "that they are holding a trial for war criminals in Tokyo just now. I think they ought to try the men who decided to use the bomb and they should hang them all."

Father Kleinsorge and the other German Jesuit priests, who as foreigners, could be expected to take a relatively detached view, often discussed the ethics of using the bomb. One of them, Father Siemes, who was out at Nagatsuka [Hiroshima suburb] at the time of the attack, wrote in a report to the Holy See in Rome: "Some of us consider the bomb in the same category as poison gas and were against its use on a civilian population. Others were of the opinion that in total war, as carried on in Japan, there was no difference between civilians and soldiers, and that the bomb itself was an effective force tending to end the bloodshed, warning Japan to surrender and thus to avoid total destruction. It seems logical that he who supports total war in principle cannot complain of a war against civilians. The crux of the matter is whether total war in its present form is justifiable, even when it serves a just purpose. Does it not have material and spiritual evil as its consequences which far exceed whatever good might result? When will our moralists give us a clear answer to this question?"

An anti-Vietnam riot. Confrontations during the Vietnam era were often emotional and violent. (Corbis-Bettmann)

CHAPTER FIVE

Protracted Conflict

30. CONTAINMENT

The Sources of Soviet Conduct (1947)
GEORGE F. KENNAN

31. REBUILDING EUROPE

Report on the Plan for European Recovery (1948)
GEORGE C. MARSHALL

32. SEEING REDS

Lincoln Day Address (1950)
JOSEPH R. MCCARTHY

Declaration of Conscience (1950)
MARGARET CHASE SMITH

33. A QUESTION OF COMMAND

Address on Korea and MacArthur (1951)
HARRY S TRUMAN

34. THE MILITARY-INDUSTRIAL COMPLEX

Farewell Address (1961)
DWIGHT D. EISENHOWER

35. THE DEFENSE OF FREEDOM

Inaugural Address (1961)
JOHN F. KENNEDY

36. BLANK CHECK

Message to Congress on the Gulf of Tonkin (1964)
LYNDON B. JOHNSON

37. AGONY IN ASIA

A Time to Break Silence (1967)
MARTIN LUTHER KING, JR.

30

CONTAINMENT

When Germany invaded Poland in September 1939, Britain and France came to Poland's aid, and World War II began. But the surrender of Germany in May 1945 did not mean a free and independent Poland. Instead, when the war ended, the Soviet Union took over most of eastern Europe, including Poland, and installed regimes of its own choosing, backed by military force. The Russians had suffered severely in both World War I and World War II from invasions from the West and were determined to surround themselves with a ring of friendly states after the war. But American policy makers, shocked by the ruthlessness with which the Russians had accomplished their purpose, interpreted Soviet policy as expansionist rather than defensive in nature and began to fear that the Soviet Union had designs on western Europe as well. The United States therefore sponsored economic aid (the Marshall Plan) as well as military aid (the Truman Doctrine) to nations in Europe that seemed threatened by Soviet aggression; it also persuaded the nations of western Europe to organize the North Atlantic Treaty Organization (NATO). Thus was born the cold war between the Soviet Union and the United States.

In July 1947 an article entitled "The Sources of Soviet Conduct" appeared in *Foreign Affairs,* an influential journal published in New York. The author, identified only as "X," was later revealed to be George F. Kennan, head of the policy-planning staff of the State Department, so the article may have reflected official American views on Soviet foreign policy. Pointing out that the Soviet Union based its policies on a firm belief in the "innate antagonism between capitalism and socialism," Kennan warned that the Russians were going to be difficult to deal with for a long time. He added that the Kremlin was "under no ideological compulsion to accomplish its purposes in a hurry" and that the only wise course for the United States to follow was that of "a long-term, patient but firm and vigilant containment of Russian expansionist tendencies." Kennan's article, which is excerpted below, shaped as well as reflected American policy.

George F. Kennan was born in Milwaukee, Wisconsin, in 1904. After graduating from Princeton University in 1925, he joined the foreign service, in which he specialized in Russian affairs while serving in minor European posts. In 1933 he went to Moscow, when the United States extended diplomatic recognition to the Soviet Union and opened an embassy there. Kennan served elsewhere in the late 1930s, but he returned to the Soviet Union during World War II and was appointed U.S. ambassador there in 1952. Kennan continued to write extensively on Russian and American diplomacy even after leaving the foreign service in the late 1950s. He came to deplore the excessively military application of the containment doctrine he had outlined in 1947, and in his later books and articles he made various proposals for demilitarization and disengagement that might diminish cold war tensions and lessen the chances of nuclear war.

Questions to Consider. In assigning responsibility for the cold war to a combination of Marxist ideology, the Kremlin's desire for power, and the world Communist movement, Kennan was also arguing, of course, that the West was largely defensive and even innocent. What evidence from twentieth-century history might be introduced to counter this argument? Kennan argued, similarly, that the Soviet threat was likely to last, practically speaking, forever. Given his views on Soviet objectives, were social or political changes conceivable that might alter these objectives or the Soviet capacity to pursue them? Did changes of this type in fact occur? Again, Kennan's article outlined his notions of Soviet society clearly enough. What assumptions, according to the evidence of the article, was Kennan making about American society? Finally, Kennan wrote his essay to mold American policy. One can imagine, however, various policies flowing from this analysis: an effort to roll back Russian power in Europe, an armed "garrison" state in the United States, intense economic or propaganda competition, and even a preemptive nuclear strike. Which of these did Kennan himself hope to see?

The Sources of Soviet Conduct (1947)

GEORGE F. KENNAN

The political personality of Soviet power as we know it today is the product of ideology and circumstances: ideology inherited by the present Soviet leaders from the movement in which they had their political origin, and

From *Foreign Affairs* (July 1947), 25: 566–582. Reprinted by permission of *Foreign Affairs,* July 1947. Copyright 1947 by the Council on Foreign Relations, Inc.

A Berlin concert hall under repair. The U.S. Congress approved the first $5 billion for the European Recovery Program (as the Marshall Plan was officially called) in 1948 with the stipulation that most of the funds would go to purchase American-made products. Goods began to arrive in Europe soon afterward. Much of the early aid went for agricultural assistance and housing construction to stave off the malnutrition and homelessness that had haunted Europe after World War I. (Corbis-Bettmann)

circumstances of the power which they now have exercised for nearly three decades in Russia. . . .

Marxian ideology, in its Russian-Communist projection, has always been in process of subtle evolution. The materials on which it bases itself are extensive and complex. But the outstanding features of Communist thought as it existed in 1916 may perhaps be summarized as follows: (a) that the central factor in the life of man, the fact which determines the character of public life and the "physiognomy of society," is the system by which material goods are produced and exchanged; (b) that the capitalist system of production is a nefarious one which inevitably leads to the exploitation of the working class by the capital-owning class and is incapable of developing adequately the economic resources of society or of distributing fairly the material goods produced by human labor; (c) that capitalism contains the seeds of its own destruction and must, in view of the inability of the capital-owning class to adjust itself to economic change, result eventually and inescapably in a revolutionary transfer of power to the working class; and (d) that imperialism, the final phase of capitalism, leads directly to war and revolution.

The rest may be outlined in Lenin's own words: "Unevenness of economic and political development is the inflexible law of capitalism. It follows from this that the victory of Socialism may come originally in a few capitalist countries or even in a single capitalist country. The victorious proletariat of that country, having expropriated the capitalists and having organized Socialist production at home, would rise against the remaining capitalist world, drawing to itself in the process the oppressed classes of other countries." It must be noted that there was no assumption that capitalism would perish without proletarian revolution. A final push was needed from a revolutionary proletariat movement in order to tip over the tottering structure. But it was regarded as inevitable that sooner or later that push be given. . . .

Now the outstanding circumstance concerning the Soviet regime is that down to the present day this process of political consolidation has never been completed and the men in the Kremlin have continued to be predominantly absorbed with the struggle to secure and make absolute the power which they seized in November 1917. They have endeavored to secure it primarily against forces at home, within Soviet society itself. But they have also endeavored to secure it against the outside world. For ideology, as we have seen, taught them that the outside world was hostile and that it was their duty eventually to overthrow the political forces beyond their borders. The powerful hands of Russian history and tradition reached up to sustain them in this feeling. . . .

Now it lies in the nature of the mental world of the Soviet leaders, as well as in the character of their ideology, that no opposition to them can be officially recognized as having any merit or justification whatsoever. Such opposition can flow, in theory, only from the hostile and incorrigible forces of dying capitalism. As long as remnants of capitalism were officially recognized as existing in Russia, it was possible to place on them, as an internal element, part of the blame for the maintenance of a dictatorial form of society. But as these remnants were liquidated, little by little, this justification fell away; and when it was indicated officially that they had been finally destroyed, it disappeared altogether. And this fact created one of the most basic of the compulsions which came to act upon the Soviet regime: since capitalism no longer existed in Russia and since it could not be admitted that there could be serious or widespread opposition to the Kremlin springing spontaneously from the liberated masses under its authority, it became necessary to justify the retention of the dictatorship by stressing the menace of capitalism abroad. . . .

As things stand today, the rulers can no longer dream of parting with these organs and suppression. The quest for absolute power, pursued now for nearly three decades with a ruthlessness unparalleled (in scope at least) in modern times, has again produced internally as it did externally, its own reaction. The excesses of the police apparatus have fanned the potential opposition to the regime into something far greater and more dangerous than it could have been before those excesses began. . . .

So much for the historical background. What does it spell in terms of the political personality of Soviet power as we know it today?

Of the original ideology, nothing has been officially junked. Belief is maintained in the basic badness of capitalism, in the inevitability of its destruction, in the obligation of the proletariat to assist in that destruction and to take power into its own hands. But stress has come to be laid primarily on those concepts which relate most specifically to the Soviet regime itself: to its position as the sole truly Socialist regime in a dark and misguided world, and to the relationships of power within it. . . .

This means that we are going to continue for a long time to find the Russians difficult to deal with. It does not mean that they should be considered as embarked upon a do-or-die program to overthrow our society by a given date. The theory of the inevitability of the eventual fall of capitalism has the fortunate connotation that there is no hurry about it. The forces of progress can take their time in preparing the final *coup de grace*. Meanwhile, what is vital is that the "Socialist fatherland"—that oasis of power which has been already won for Socialism in the person of the Soviet Union—should be cherished and defended by all good Communists at home and abroad, its fortunes promoted, its enemies badgered and confounded. The promotion of premature, "adventuristic" revolutionary projects abroad which might embarrass Soviet power in any way would be an inexcusable, even a counter-revolutionary act. The cause of Socialism is the support and promotion of Soviet power, as defined in Moscow.

But we have seen that the Kremlin is under no ideological compulsion to accomplish its purposes in a hurry. Like the Church, it is dealing in ideological concepts which are of long-term validity, and it can afford to be patient. It has no right to risk the existing achievements of the revolution for the sake of vain baubles of the future. The very teachings of Lenin himself require great caution and flexibility in the pursuit of Communist purposes. Again, these precepts are fortified by the lessons of Russian history: of centuries of obscure battles between nomadic forces over the stretches of a vast unfortified plain. Here caution, circumspection, flexibility and deception are the valuable qualities; and their value finds natural appreciation in the Russian or the oriental mind. Thus the Kremlin has no compunction about retreating in the face of superior force. And being under the compulsion of no timetable, it does not get panicky under the necessity for such a retreat. Its political action is a fluid stream which moves constantly, wherever it is permitted to move, toward a given goal. Its main concern is to make sure that it has filled every nook and cranny available to it in the basin of world power. But if it finds unassailable barriers in its path, it accepts these philosophically and accommodates itself to them. . . .

These considerations make Soviet diplomacy at once easier and more difficult to deal with than the diplomacy of individual aggressive leaders like Napoleon and Hitler. On the one hand it is more sensitive to contrary force, more ready to yield on individual sectors of the diplomatic front when that force is felt to be too strong, and thus more rational in the logic and rhetoric of power. On the other hand it cannot be easily defeated or discouraged by a single victory on the part of its opponents. And the patient persistence by which it is animated means that it can be effectively countered not by sporadic acts which represent the momentary whims of democratic opinion but only by intelligent long-range policies on the part of Russia's adversaries—policies no less steady in their purpose, and no less variegated and resourceful in their application, than those of the Soviet Union itself.

In these circumstances it is clear that the main element of any United States policy toward the Soviet Union must be that of a long-term, patient but firm and vigilant containment of Russian expansive tendencies. It is important to note, however, that such a policy has nothing to do with outward histrionics: with threats or blustering or superfluous gestures of outward "toughness." While the Kremlin is basically flexible in its reaction to political realities, it is by no means unamenable to considerations of prestige. Like almost any other government, it can be placed by tactless and threatening gestures in a position where it cannot afford to yield even though this might be dictated by its sense of realism. The Russian leaders are keen judges of human psychology, and as such they are highly conscious that loss of temper and of self-control is never a source of strength in political affairs. They are quick to exploit such evidence of weakness. For these reasons, it is a *sine qua non* of successful dealing with Russia that the foreign government in question should remain at all times cool and collected and that its demands on Russian policy should be put forward in such a manner as to leave the way open for a compliance not too detrimental to Russian prestige. . . .

But in actuality the possibilities for American policy are by no means limited to holding the line and hoping for the best. It is entirely possible for the United States to influence by its actions the internal developments, both within Russia and throughout the international Communist movement, by which Russian policy is largely determined. This is not only a question of the modest measure of informational activity which this government can conduct in the Soviet Union and elsewhere, although that, too, is important. It is rather a question of the degree to which the United States can create among the peoples of the world generally the impression of a country which knows what it wants, which is coping successfully with the problems of its internal life and with the responsibilities of a World Power, and which has a spiritual vitality capable of holding its own among the major ideological currents of the time. . . .

By the same token, exhibitions of indecision, disunity and internal disintegration within this country have an exhilarating effect on the whole Communist movement. At each evidence of these tendencies, a thrill of hope and excitement goes through the Communist world; a new jauntiness can be noted in the Moscow tread; now groups of foreign supporters climb on to what they can only view as the band wagon of international politics; and Russian pressure increases all along the line in international affairs.

It would be an exaggeration to say that American behavior unassisted and alone could exercise a power of life and death over the Communist movement and bring about the early fall of Soviet power in Russia. But the United States has it in its power to increase enormously the strains under which Soviet policy must operate, to force upon the Kremlin a far greater degree of moderation and circumspection than it has had to observe in recent years, and in this way to promote tendencies which must eventually find their outlet in either the breakup or the gradual mellowing of Soviet power.

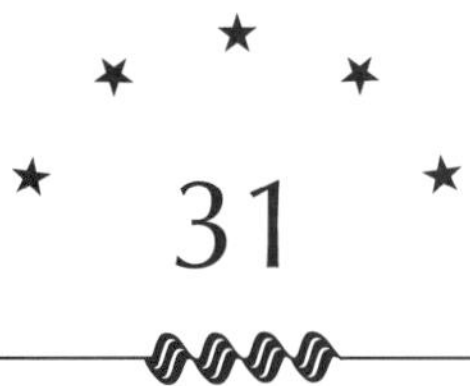

31

Rebuilding Europe

Franklin D. Roosevelt fought World War II for internationalist ideals. Concerned to preserve and extend democracy, Roosevelt was equally determined to help create a new international order in which the United States would play a major role, as it had not after World War I. Roosevelt was therefore profoundly committed to the establishment of the United Nations, which he helped bring into being during the war and whose U.N. Relief and Rehabilitation Administration (largely supported by the United States) distributed millions of dollars of aid to war-torn regions of the world. He was also committed to using America's industrial resources to help the Allied countries wage total war, which he effected through the immense U.S. Lend-Lease program of wartime and postwar economic and military assistance.

Roosevelt died before the war ended, and both Lend-Lease and UNRRA ceased functioning in 1947. Yet Roosevelt's legacy of generous internationalism endured into the Truman administration, particularly as regards Europe, which American policymakers considered vital to U.S. interests. And postwar Europe was in fact in serious trouble, unable to rebuild or even feed itself, threatened, it seemed, by an adversarial Soviet Union, and facing economic collapse and political upheaval.

In 1947 the State Department urged President Truman to coordinate and expand the remaining U.S. aid efforts and use them to promote real revival rather than mere relief. In June Secretary of State George C. Marshall delivered an address at Harvard University outlining a major U.S. economic recovery program for Europe. Non-Communist Europe responded immediately and positively. Marshall's 1948 testimony before the Senate Committee on Foreign Relations, excerpted below, sketched the broad outlines of the European Recovery Program. Truman signed the measure into law in April 1948.

Aid began to flow almost immediately—over $12 billion over the next three years. The "Marshall Plan," as it came to be called, fed people, put coal and oil in furnaces, rebuilt factories and city services, furthered the economic integration of Europe, and laid the groundwork for the social democracy that characterized western Europe for the next half-century. The farsightedness of the Plan stemmed partly from the fact that the Americans were rebuilding an industrialized Europe that would eventually compete with them. But they helped anyway, believing that a prosperous and stable Europe would be good for the United States. Moreover, since the Plan required the Europeans to spend the assistance on American products, it boosted the U.S. economy as well. It may be that except for World War II itself, the Marshall Plan was the single most successful large-scale diplomatic initiative in American history.

George C. Marshall was born in Uniontown, Pennsylvania, in 1880. Marshall graduated from Virginia Military Institute in 1901, became an army officer, served in the Philippines, attended the army's General Staff School, and filled high staff posts during World War I. In 1939 Roosevelt appointed Marshall army chief of staff, responsible for organizing, training, supplying, and deploying U.S. troops. He held this post until 1945, becoming, in many eyes, the greatest chief of staff of any nation in World War II. Marshall served President Truman as secretary of state from 1947 to 1949 and as secretary of defense early in the Korean conflict. In 1953 he received the Nobel Prize for Peace for his work on European recovery. He died in Washington in 1959.

Questions to Consider. What were the general purposes of the European Recovery Program as outlined by Marshall? What arguments did he advance in favor of his plan? What objections did he anticipate, and how did he answer each one?

Report on the Plan for European Recovery (1948)

GEORGE C. MARSHALL

On December 19 the President placed before you the recommendations of the executive branch of the Government for a program of United States assistance to European economic recovery.

This program will cost our country billions of dollars. It will impose a burden on the American taxpayer. It will require sacrifices today in order that we may enjoy security and peace tomorrow. Should the Congress approve the program for European recovery, as I urgently recommend, we Americans will have made a historic decision of our peacetime history. . . .

So long as hunger, poverty, desperation, and resulting chaos threaten the great concentrations of people in western Europe—some 270,000,000—there

From *Hearings before the Committee on Foreign Relations,* U.S. Senate, 80th Cong., 2d Sess., 1948, on United States Assistance to European Economic Recovery, part 1, 1–10.

will steadily develop social unease and political confusion on every side. Left to their own resources there will be, I believe, no escape from economic distress so intense, social discontents so violent, political confusion so widespread, and hopes of the future so shattered that the historic base of western civilization, of which we are by belief and inheritance an integral part, will take on a new forum in the image of the tyranny that we fought to destroy in Germany. The vacuum which the war created in western Europe will be filled by the forces of which wars are made. Our national security will be seriously threatened. We shall in effect live in an armed camp, regulated and controlled. But if we furnish effective aid to support the now visible reviving hope of Europe, the prospect should speedily change. The foundation of political vitality is economic recovery. Durable peace requires the restoration of western European vitality.

We have engaged in a great war. We poured out our resources to win that war. We fought it to make real peace possible. Though the war has ended peace has not commenced. We must not fail to complete that which we commenced.

The peoples of western Europe have demonstrated their will to achieve a genuine recovery by entering into a great cooperative effort. Within the limits of their resources they formally undertake to establish the basis for the peace which we all seek, but they cannot succeed without American assistance. Dollars will not save the world, but the world today cannot be saved without dollars. . . .

I believe that this measure has received as concentrated study as has ever gone into the preparation of any proposal made to the Congress. The best minds in numerous related fields have worked for months on this vast and complicated subject. In addition, the best economic and political brains of 16 European nations have given us in an amazingly short time their analyses and conclusions.

The problem we face is enormously complex. It affects not only our country and Europe, but almost every other part of the globe. . . .

I will confine my remarks to the three basic questions involved: First, "Why does Europe need help?" Second, "How much help is needed?" And third, "How should help be given?"

The "why": Europe is still emerging from the devastation and dislocation of the most destructive war in history. Within its own resources Europe cannot achieve within a reasonable time economic stability. The war more or less destroyed the mechanism whereby Europe supported itself in the past and the initial rebuilding of that mechanism requires outside assistance under existing circumstances.

The western European participating countries, with a present population almost twice our own, constitute an interdependent area containing some of the most highly industrialized nations of the world. As a group, they are one of the two major workshops of the world. Production has become more and more specialized, and depends in large part on the processing of raw materials, largely imported from abroad, into finished goods and the furnishing of services to other areas. These goods and services have been sold throughout the world and the proceeds therefrom paid for the necessary imports.

The war smashed the vast and delicate mechanism by which European countries made their living. It was the war which destroyed coal mines and deprived the workshop of sufficient mechanical energy. It was the war which destroyed steel mills and thus cut down the workshop's material for fabrication. It was the war which destroyed transportation lines and equipment and thus made the ability to move goods and people inadequate. It was the war which destroyed livestock herds, made fertilizers unobtainable and thus reduced soil fertility. It was the war which destroyed merchant fleets and thus cut off accustomed income from carrying the world's goods. It was the war which destroyed or caused the loss of so much of foreign investments and the income which it has produced. It was the war which bled inventories and working capital out of existence. It was the war which shattered business relationships and markets and the sources of raw materials. The war disrupted the flow of vital raw materials from southeast Asia, thereby breaking the pattern of multilateral trade which formerly provided, directly or indirectly, large dollar earnings for western Europe. In the postwar period artificial and forcible reorientation to the Soviet Union of eastern European trade had deprived western Europe of sources of foodstuff and raw material from that area. Here and there the present European situation has been aggravated by unsound or destructive policies pursued in one or another country, but the basic dislocations find their source directly in the war.

The inability of the European workshop to get food and raw materials required to produce the exports necessary to get the purchasing power for food and raw materials is the worst of the many vicious circles that beset the European peoples. Not withstanding the fact that industrial output, except in western Germany, has almost regained its prewar volume, under the changed conditions this is not nearly enough. The loss of European investments abroad, the destruction of merchant fleets, and the disappearance of other sources of income, together with increases in populations to be sustained, make necessary an increase in production far above prewar levels, even sufficient for a living standard considerably below prewar standards.

This is the essence of the economic problem of Europe. This problem would exist even though it were not complicated by the ideological struggles in Europe between those who want to live as freemen and those small groups who aspire to dominate by the method of police states. The solution would be much easier, of course, if all the nations of Europe were cooperating. But they are not. Far from cooperating, the Soviet Union and the Communist parties have proclaimed their determined opposition to a plan for European economic recovery. Economic distress is to be employed to further political ends.

There are many who accept the picture that I have just drawn but who raise a further question: "Why must the United States carry so great a load in helping Europe?" The answer is simple. The United States is the only country in the world today which has the economic power and productivity to furnish the needed assistance.

I wish now to turn to the other questions which we must answer. These are "how much" aid is required and "how" should that aid be given. . . .

The objective of the European recovery program submitted for your consideration is to achieve lasting economic recovery for western Europe; recovery in the sense that after our aid has terminated, the European countries will be able to maintain themselves by their own efforts on a sound economic basis. . . .

The total estimated cost of the program is now put at somewhere between 15.1 to 17.8 billions. But this will depend on developments each year, the progress made, and unforeseeable variations in the weather as it affects crops. The over-all cost is not capable of precise determination so far in advance. . . .

The proposed program does involve some sacrifice on the part of the American people, but it should be kept in mind that the burden of the program diminishes rapidly after the first 15 months. Considerations of the cost must be related to the momentous objective, on the one hand, and to the probable price of the alternatives. The $6,800,000,000 proposed for the first 15 months is less than a single month's charge of the war. A world of continuing uneasy half-peace will create demands for constantly mounting expenditures for defense. This program should be viewed as an investment in peace. In those terms, the cost is low.

The third main consideration which, I feel, should be borne in mind in connection with this measure is that relating to conditions or terms upon which American assistance will be extended. It is the obvious duty of this government to insure insofar as possible that the aid extended should be effectively used to promote recovery and not diverted to other purposes, whatever their nature. This aspect of the program is perhaps the most delicate and difficult and one which will require the exercise of a mature judgment and intelligent understanding of the nature of the problem faced by the European governments and of our particular position of leadership in this matter. We must always have in mind that we are dealing with democratic governments of sovereign nations.

We will be working with a group of nations each with a long and proud history. The peoples of these countries are highly skilled, able, and energetic and justly proud of their cultures. They have ancient traditions of self-reliance and are eager to take the lead in working out their own salvation.

We have stated in many ways that American aid will not be used to interfere with the sovereign rights of these nations and their own responsibility to work out their own salvation. I cannot emphasize too much my profound conviction that the aid we furnish must not be tied to conditions which would, in effect, destroy the whole moral justification for our cooperative assistance toward European partnership.

We are dealing with democratic governments. One of the major justifications of asking the American people to make the sacrifice necessary under this program is the vital stake that the United States has in helping to preserve democracy in Europe. As democratic governments they are responsive, like our own, to the peoples of their countries—and we would not have it otherwise. We cannot expect any democratic government to take upon itself obligations or accept conditions which run counter to the basic national sentiment of its people. This program calls for free cooperation among nations mutually respecting one another's sincerity of purpose in the common endeavor—a cooperation which we hope will long outlive the period of American assistance. . . .

What are the prospects of success of such a program for the economic recovery of a continent? It would be absurd to deny the existence of obstacles and risks. Weather and the extent of world crops are unpredictable. The possible extent of political sabotage and the effectiveness with which its true intentions are unmasked and thus made susceptible to control cannot be fully foreseen. All we can say is this program does provide the means for success and if we maintain the will for success I believe that success will be achieved.

To be quite clear, this unprecedented endeavor of the New World to help the Old is neither sure nor easy. It is a calculated risk. But there can be no doubts as to the alternatives. The way of life that we have known is literally in balance.

Our country is now faced with a momentous decision. If we decide that the United States is unable or unwilling effectively to assist in the reconstruction of western Europe, we must accept the consequences of its collapse into the dictatorship of police states.

I said a moment ago that this program does provide the means for success, and if we maintain the will for success, I believe that success will be achieved.

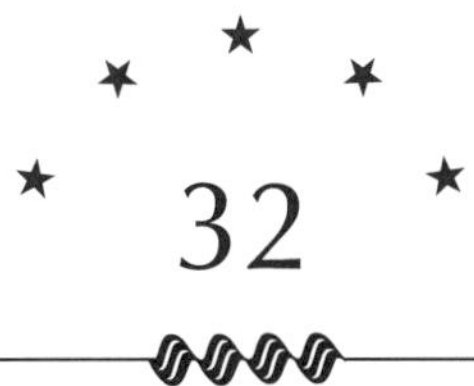

Seeing Reds

In 1946 Joseph R. McCarthy defeated Progressive Senator Robert M. La Follette, Jr., in the Republican primary in Wisconsin and went on to win election to the U.S. Senate that fall. During the primary contest he was supported by Wisconsin Communists who were infuriated by La Follette's pre–Pearl Harbor anti-interventionism and by his criticisms of Soviet dictator Joseph Stalin. Asked about the support the Communists were giving him against La Follette, McCarthy said airily, "The Communists have votes, too, don't they?" Four years later he became the leader of an impassioned crusade against Communism, and the word "McCarthyism" came to mean a reckless and demagogic assault on domestic dissent.

McCarthyism did not operate in a vacuum. Revelations of Communist spy activity in Canada, England, and the United States after World War II produced demands for counterespionage measures, and in 1947 President Truman inaugurated a loyalty program to ferret out Communists in government. Meanwhile, a series of "spy" cases hit the headlines: the trial and conviction of eleven Communist leaders under the Smith Act for conspiring to advocate the violent overthrow of the government; the conviction of former State Department official Alger Hiss, denounced as a Communist spy, for perjury; and the trial and execution of Julius and Ethel Rosenberg, government workers charged with passing atomic secrets to the Russians. For many Americans, the distinction between the expression of unpopular ideas and deliberate conspiratorial activity on behalf of a foreign power became increasingly blurred. In 1950, Senator McCarthy obliterated the distinction.

In a radio speech (excerpted below) given in Wheeling, West Virginia, in February 1950, McCarthy announced that he had in his hand a list of Communists in the State Department "known to the Secretary of State" and "still working and making policy." Overnight McCarthy became a national figure. Although he never showed anyone his famous "list" and was increasingly vague about the precise number of names it contained (205 or 81 or 57 or "a lot"), he came to exercise great influence in the U.S. Senate and in the nation. In July 1950, a

Senate subcommittee headed by Maryland's Millard Tydings dismissed McCarthy's charges as "a fraud and a hoax." But when Tydings, a conservative Democrat, ran for reelection that fall, McCarthy's insinuations that he was pro-Communist helped defeat him. Similar accusations helped defeat Connecticut Democrat William Benton in 1952.

Not every Republican admired Senator McCarthy or approved his tactics, even when they benefited Republican candidates. Margaret Chase Smith of Maine, the only woman in the U.S. Senate in 1950, had served with McCarthy on the Permanent Investigations Subcommittee of the Senate and had become perturbed by his lack of concern for the unfair damage the subcommittee might do to individuals' reputations. Smith became still more perturbed following McCarthy's West Virginia speech in February 1950 about Communists in the State Department. Conscious that she was a first-term senator and believing that the initial challenge to McCarthy should come from the Democrats (the majority party in the Senate), she delayed speaking her mind for some time. When the Democrats failed to rebut McCarthy's charges effectively, she determined to speak out and did so on June 1, 1950. Six other Republican senators endorsed Smith's "Declaration of Conscience," as it soon came to be called. But she was the one who made the speech, which became one of the most famous of its time.

It would take more than a statement by a handful of Senate Republicans to halt Joe McCarthy. In 1951 McCarthy charged that George C. Marshall, President Truman's former secretary of state and of defense, was part of "a conspiracy so immense and infamy so black as to dwarf any previous venture in the history of man." During the 1952 presidential campaign McCarthy talked ominously of "twenty years of treason" under the Democrats. His followers identified Roosevelt's New Deal, Truman's Fair Deal, and, indeed, all efforts for social reform since the Great Depression as Communist inspired. In 1953, as chairman of the Senate Committee on Government Operations, McCarthy launched a series of investigations of federal agencies, including the Voice of America, the International Information Agency, and the Army Signal Corps installation at Fort Monmouth, New Jersey. When the army decided to fight back, McCarthyism reached its climax in a series of televised Senate hearings in the spring of 1954. During these hearings, the Wisconsin senator's accusations and defamations of character gradually alienated all but his most devoted followers. On July 30, Republican Senator Ralph Flanders of Vermont, who had not endorsed Margaret Chase Smith's 1950 Declaration, introduced a resolution of censure. In December, the Senate voted, 67 to 32, to censure McCarthy for his behavior.

Joseph R. McCarthy was born in Grand Chute, Wisconsin, in 1908 to middle-class Roman Catholic parents. He graduated from Marquette University and entered the legal profession in Wisconsin in 1935. Originally a Democrat, he won his first political race (for a local judgeship) as a Republican in 1939. After serving as a Marine from 1942 to 1944, he became a state Republican power with his defeat of La Follette in the 1946 senatorial race. McCarthy's strongest bases of support were Wisconsin's small business owners and voters of German heritage; they reelected him in 1952 and largely continued their support even after his fall from national popularity. He died at the Bethesda Naval Hospital in Maryland in 1957.

Margaret Chase was born in 1897 in Skowhegan, Maine, where, after graduating from high school, she taught school, worked for the telephone company, and was circulation manager for a local newspaper. In 1930 she married Clyde Harold Smith, who served in Congress from 1936 to 1940. When he died in 1940, Margaret Chase Smith was elected to fill his seat, and in 1949 she became the first woman ever elected to the U.S. Senate. Following her 1950 "Declaration of Conscience," she became a target of the McCarthyites, who in 1954 ran a "proxy" candidate against her in the Maine Republican primary. Smith won by a five-to-one margin and later lodged a successful million-dollar lawsuit against two reporters who had labeled her a Communist. Liberal on race and civil liberties issues, conservative in foreign policy, Smith was one of the most senior members of the U.S. Senate and the ranking Republican on the Armed Services Committee when she finally lost a reelection bid in 1972 at age 75. She died in 1995.

Questions to Consider. Why did McCarthy launch his attack in 1950 rather than in 1949 or 1951? What area of the world most concerned him and what had happened there to give his message impact? Why did he attack from an out-of-the-way place (Wheeling, West Virginia) rather than from Washington or even his home state, Wisconsin, and why, moreover, on the radio? What reasons might McCarthy have had for singling out the State Department for attack, rather than, for example, the Department of Defense or the Department of Justice? In view of the fact that seven twentieth-century presidents and even more secretaries of state had attended just four private colleges (Yale, Harvard, Princeton, and Amherst) was there a certain logic in men such as McCarthy trying to link a Communist conspiracy with a conspiracy of "those who have had all the benefits"?

Margaret Chase Smith's Declaration began with a reference to "national suicide" and ineffectual legislative and executive leadership. Why did Smith begin a speech designed to thwart a Republican senator in this way? How did Smith define "Americanism"? Would most Americans have agreed with her in 1950? Why was it considered courageous for Smith to oppose the political tactics of "Fear, Ignorance, Bigotry, and Smear"? Did Smith believe that Communists might in fact be in the federal government? Did she believe they should remain there if discovered? What two reasons did she give for opposing McCarthy?

Lincoln Day Address (1950)

JOSEPH R. MCCARTHY

Ladies and gentlemen, tonight as we celebrate the one hundred and forty-first birthday of one of the greatest men in American history, I would like to be able to talk about what a glorious day today is in the history of the world. As we celebrate the birth of this man who with his whole heart and soul hated war, I would like to be able to speak of peace in our time, of war being outlawed, and of worldwide disarmament. These would be truly appropriate things to be able to mention as we celebrate the birthday of Abraham Lincoln.

Five years after a world war has been won, men's hearts should anticipate a long peace, and men's minds should be free from the heavy weight that comes with war. But this is not such a period—for this is not a period of peace. This is a time of the "cold war." This is a time when all the world is split into two vast, increasingly hostile armed camps—a time of a great armaments race.

Today we are engaged in a final, all-out battle between Communistic atheism and Christianity. The modern champions of Communism have selected this as the time. And, ladies and gentlemen, the chips are down—they are truly down.

Six years ago, at the time of the first conference to map out the peace—Dumbarton Oaks—there was within the Soviet orbit 180 million people. Lined up on the antitotalitarian side there were in the world roughly 1,625 million people. Today, only six years later, there are 800 million people under the absolute domination of soviet Russia—an increase of over 400 percent. On our side, the figure has shrunk to around 500 million. In other words, in less than six years the odds have changed from 9 to 1 in our favor to 8 to 5 against us. This indicates the swiftness of the tempo of Communist victories and American defeats in the cold war. As one of our outstanding historical figures once said, "When a great democracy is destroyed, it will not be because of enemies from without, but rather because of enemies from within."

From *The Congressional Record,* 81st Congress, v. 96, part 2 (February 20, 1950).

The truth of this statement is becoming terrifyingly clear as we see this country each day losing on every front. . . .

The reason why we find ourselves in a position of impotency is not because our only powerful potential enemy has sent men to invade our shores, but rather because of the traitorous actions of those who have been treated so well by this Nation. It has not been the less fortunate or members of minority groups who have been selling this Nation out, but rather those who have had all the benefits that the wealthiest nation on earth has had to offer—the finest homes, the finest college education, and the finest jobs in Government we can give.

This is glaringly true in the State Department. There the bright young men who are born with silver spoons in their mouths are the ones who have been worst. . . .

When Chiang Kai-shek was fighting our war, the State Department had in China a young man named John S. Service. His task, obviously, was not to work for the Communization of China. Strangely, however, he sent official reports back to the State Department urging that we torpedo our ally Chiang Kai-shek and stating, in effect, that Communism was the best hope for China.

Later, this man—John Service—was picked up by the Federal Bureau of Investigation for turning over to the Communists secret State Department information. Strangely, however, he was never prosecuted. However, Joseph Grew, the Under Secretary of State, who insisted on his prosecution, was forced to resign. Two days after Grew's successor, Dean Acheson, took over as Under Secretary of State, this man—John Service—who had been picked up by the FBI and who had previously urged that Communism was the best hope of China, was not only reinstated in the State Department but promoted. And finally, under Acheson, placed in charge of all placements and promotions.

Today, ladies and gentlemen, this man Service is on his way to represent the State Department and Acheson in Calcutta—by far and away the most important listening post in the Far East. . . .

This, ladies and gentlemen, gives you somewhat of a picture of the type of individuals who have been helping to shape our foreign policy. In my opinion the State Department, which is one of the most important government departments, is thoroughly infested with Communists.

I have in my hand 57 cases of individuals who would appear to be either card carrying members or certainly loyal to the Communist Party, but who nevertheless are still helping to shape our foreign policy.

One thing to remember in discussing the Communists in our Government is that we are not dealing with spies who get 30 pieces of silver to steal the blueprints of a new weapon. We are dealing with a far more sinister type of activity because it permits the enemy to guide and shape our policy. . . .

As you hear this story of high treason, I know that you are saying to yourself, "Well, why doesn't the Congress do something about it?" Actually, ladies and gentlemen, one of the important reasons for the graft, the corruption, the dishonesty, the disloyalty, the treason in high Government positions—one of the most important reasons why this continues is a lack of moral uprising on the part of the 140 million American people. In the light of history, however, this is not hard to explain.

It is the result of an emotional hangover and a temporary moral lapse which follows every war. It is the apathy to evil which people who have been subjected to the tremendous evils of war feel. As the people of the world see mass murder, the destruction of defenseless and innocent people, and all of the crime and lack of morals which go with war, they become numb and apathetic. It has always been thus after war.

However, the morals of our people have not been destroyed. They still exist. This cloak of numbness and apathy has only needed a spark to rekindle them. Happily, this spark has finally been supplied.

As you know, very recently the Secretary of State [Dean Acheson] proclaimed his loyalty to a man [Alger Hiss] guilty of what has always been considered as the most abominable of all crimes—of being a traitor to the people who gave him a position of great trust. The Secretary of State in attempting to justify his continued devotion to the man who sold out the Christian world to the atheistic world, referred to Christ's Sermon on the Mount as a justification and reason therefor, and the reaction of the American people to this would have made the heart of Abraham Lincoln happy.

When this pompous diplomat in striped pants, with a phony British accent, proclaimed to the American people that Christ on the Mount endorsed Communism, high treason, and betrayal of a sacred trust, the blasphemy was so great that it awakened the dormant indignation of the American people.

He has lighted the spark which is resulting in a moral uprising and will end only when the whole sorry mess of twisted, warped thinkers are swept from the national scene so that we may have a new birth of national honesty and decency in Government.

Declaration of Conscience (1950)

MARGARET CHASE SMITH

I would like to speak briefly and simply about a serious national condition. It is a national feeling of fear and frustration that could result in national suicide and the end of everything that we Americans hold dear. It is a condition that comes from the lack of effective leadership in either the Legislative Branch or the Executive Branch of our Government.

From *The New York Times,* June 2, 1950.

That leadership is so lacking that serious and responsible proposals are being made that national advisory commissions be appointed to provide such critically needed leadership. . . .

I speak as a Republican. I speak as a woman. I speak as a United States Senator. I speak as an American. . . .

I think that it is high time that we remembered that we have sworn to uphold and defend the Constitution. I think that it is high time that we remembered that the Constitution, as amended, speaks not only of the freedom of speech but also of trial by jury instead of trial by accusation. . . .

Those of us who shout the loudest about Americanism in making character assassinations are all too frequently those who, by our own words and acts, ignore some of the basic principles of Americanism:

The right to criticize;

The right to hold unpopular beliefs;

The right to protest;

The right of independent thought.

The exercise of these rights should not cost one single American citizen his reputation or his right to a livelihood nor should he be in danger of losing his reputation or livelihood merely because he happens to know someone who holds unpopular beliefs. Who of us doesn't? Otherwise none of us could call our souls our own. Otherwise thought control would have set in.

The American people are sick and tired of being afraid to speak their minds lest they be politically smeared as "Communists" or "Fascists" by their opponents. Freedom of speech is not what it used to be in America. It has been so abused by some that it is not exercised by others. . . .

Today our country is being psychologically divided by the confusion and the suspicions that are bred in the United States Senate to spread like cancerous tentacles of "know nothing, suspect everything" attitudes. Today we have a Democratic Administration that has developed a mania for loose spending and loose programs. History is repeating itself—and the Republican Party again has the opportunity to emerge as the champion of unity and prudence.

The record of the present Democratic Administration has provided us with sufficient campaign issues without the necessity of resorting to political smears. America is rapidly losing its position as leader of the world simply because the Democratic Administration has pitifully failed to provide effective leadership. . . .

Yet to displace it with a Republican regime embracing a philosophy that lacks political integrity or intellectual honesty would prove equally disastrous to this nation. The nation sorely needs a Republican victory. But I don't want to see the Republican Party ride to political victory on the Four Horsemen of Calumny—Fear, Ignorance, Bigotry, and Smear.

I doubt if the Republican Party could—simply because I don't believe the American people will uphold any political party that puts political exploitation above national interest. Surely we Republicans aren't that desperate for victory. . . .

As a United States Senator, I am not proud of the way in which the Senate has been made a publicity platform for irresponsible sensationalism. I am not proud of the reckless abandon in which unproved charges have been hurled from this side of the aisle. I am not proud of the obviously staged, undignified countercharges that have been attempted in retaliation from the other side of the aisle.

I don't like the way the Senate has been made a rendezvous for vilification, for selfish political gain at the sacrifice of individual reputations and national unity. I am not proud of the way we smear outsiders from the Floor of the Senate and hide behind the cloak of congressional immunity and still place ourselves beyond criticism on the Floor of the Senate.

As an American, I am shocked at the way Republicans and Democrats alike are playing directly into the Communist design of "confuse, divide, and conquer." As an American, I don't want a Democratic Administration "whitewash" or "cover-up" any more than I want a Republican smear or witch hunt.

As an American, I condemn a Republican "Fascist" just as much as I condemn a Democrat "Communist." I condemn a Democrat "Fascist" just as much as I condemn a Republican "Communist." They are equally dangerous to you and me and to our country. As an American, I want to see our nation recapture the strength and unity it once had when we fought the enemy instead of ourselves.

It is with these thoughts that I have drafted what I call a "Declaration of Conscience." I am gratified that [six Republican senators] have concurred in that declaration and have authorized me to announce their concurrence.

A QUESTION OF COMMAND

In 1950 the cold war between the United States and the Soviet Union turned suddenly hot in Korea, a peninsula abutting China near Japan. Korea had been freed from Japanese rule at the end of World War II, divided at the 38th parallel, and occupied by Russian troops in the north and American troops in the south. The Russians installed a friendly regime in North Korea and then withdrew; the United Nations, at U.S. urging, did the same in South Korea. On June 25, 1950, North Korean armies suddenly crossed the 38th parallel and launched a full-scale invasion of South Korea. President Truman, seeing the hand of China and therefore of the Soviet Union behind this move, promptly committed American troops to the defense of South Korea. He won the backing of the United Nations for his action and announced American determination to support anticommunist governments throughout East Asia. The Korean War lasted from June 1950 until the armistice of July 1953. Under United Nations auspices, sixteen nations participated in the conflict against North Korea. South Korea remained independent, but the Korean War cost the United States $22 billion and 34,000 dead.

The Korean War also prompted a major reassertion of the Constitutional primacy of civilian rule in the U.S. government. The United Nations commander in the Korean theater was General Douglas MacArthur, one of the greatest U.S. heroes of World War II and the American proconsul in charge of transforming postwar Japanese society. Against the advice of the American joint chiefs of staff, MacArthur launched a brilliant amphibious landing behind Communist lines. He then recaptured the capital city of Seoul and moved far enough into North Korea to reach the border with China.

MacArthur had gambled that China would not commit troops to the conflict; President Truman's advisers feared it would. MacArthur was wrong. Massive Chinese forces poured across the border, pushing U.N. forces back down the peninsula. Embarrassed, MacArthur publicly called for President Truman to order massive air strikes on China. The president, fearing a long and costly land war with China, refused the general's request and asked him not to argue U.S. policy in the newspapers. MacArthur again called for air attacks on China, took a swipe at the American doctrine of limited (non-nuclear and geographically restricted) war, and implied that Truman was practicing appeasement. President Truman had had enough: On April 10, 1951, he fired MacArthur for insubordination. On April 11 he gave the following radio address to the American public. MacArthur returned home to an enormous ticker-tape parade, an invitation to address a joint session of Congress, and a brief flirtation with Republican party kingpins. But Matthew Ridgway now commanded U.N. forces in Korea, Harry Truman was still president and commander in chief—and the long-established Constitutional subordination of military to civilian authority again held firm.

Harry S Truman was born on a farm near Independence, Missouri, in 1884. After graduating from high school, he worked as a farmer and a bank clerk and, during World War I, saw action in France as a captain in the field artillery. On his return from the war he entered the clothing business and in 1922 went into politics. After serving as county judge and presiding judge of Jackson County, Missouri, he was elected senator in 1934 and served in the Senate until his election as vice-president in 1944. As a senator he supported Roosevelt's New Deal policies and won a national reputation as an enemy of favoritism and waste in defense spending. His presidency from 1945 to 1953 was characterized by futile efforts to ram progressive Fair Deal legislation through a conservative Congress and, increasingly, by an anti-communist domestic and foreign policy. He is popularly remembered for his integrity, combativeness, and sense of responsibility—"The buck," he said, "stops here." Truman never made a more politically risky decision than to fire Douglas MacArthur. He died at his home in Independence, Missouri, in 1972.

Questions to Consider. Americans of Truman's era, it has been said, had two overwhelming fears: Communism and war. How did Truman attempt to balance these two fears in his 1950 address? On which side did he finally come down most strongly? American policy makers of the 1950s have been accused of exaggerating the scope and unity of international Communism. Did Truman fall into this habit? Did the confrontation with MacArthur perhaps drive Truman to overcompensate? Truman's action preserved the primacy of civilian control of war policy; why did he not defend his actions on these grounds?

General Douglas MacArthur. On June 29, 1950, the American government ordered combat troops into Korea under the command of General MacArthur. Three months later, MacArthur's forces engineered a brilliant landing behind North Korean lines and quickly overran the northern half of the country. This position proved untenable because, contrary to MacArthur's prediction, Chinese troops entered the war and pushed the Americans far into the south—one of the longest retreats in U.S. history. Here MacArthur, left, receives a decoration from President Harry S Truman—who would soon strip him of his command for insubordination. (Corbis-Bettmann)

Address on Korea and MacArthur (1951)

HARRY S TRUMAN

In the simplest terms, what we are doing in Korea is this:

We are trying to prevent a third world war.

I think most people in this country recognized that fact last June. And they warmly supported the decision of the Government to help the Republic of Korea against the Communist aggressors. Now, many persons, even

From *The New York Times*, April 12, 1951.

some who applauded our decision to defend Korea, have forgotten the basic reason for our action. . . .

The aggression against Korea is the boldest and most dangerous move the Communists have yet made.

The attack on Korea was part of a greater plan for conquering all of Asia. . . .

They want to control all Asia from the Kremlin.

This plan of conquest is in flat contradiction to what we believe. We believe that Korea belongs to the Koreans. We believe that India belongs to the Indians. We believe that all the nations of Asia should be free to work out their affairs in their own way. This is the basis of peace in the Far East and it is the basis of peace everywhere else.

The whole Communist imperialism is back of the attack on peace in the Far East. It was the Soviet Union that trained and equipped the North Koreans for aggression. The Chinese Communists massed forty-four well-trained and well-equipped divisions on the Korean frontier. These were the troops they threw into battle when the North Korean Communists were beaten.

The question we have had to face is whether the Communist plan of conquest can be stopped without general war. Our Government and other countries associated with us in the United Nations believe that the best chance of stopping it without general war is to meet the attack in Korea and defeat it there.

That is what we have been doing. It is a difficult and bitter task.

But so far it has been successful.

So far, we have prevented World War III.

So far, by fighting a limited war in Korea, we have prevented aggression from succeeding, and bringing on a general war. And the ability of the whole free world to resist Communist aggression has been greatly improved. . . .

We do not want to see the conflict in Korea extended. We are trying to prevent a world war—not to start one. The best way to do that is to make it plain that we and the other free countries will continue to resist the attack.

But you may ask why can't we take other steps to punish the aggressor. Why don't we bomb Manchuria and China itself? Why don't we assist Chinese Nationalist troops to land on the mainland of China?

If we were to do these things we would be running a very grave risk of starting a general war. If that were to happen, we would have brought about the exact situation we are trying to prevent.

If we were to do these things, we would become entangled in a vast conflict on the continent of Asia and our task would become immeasurably more difficult all over the world.

What would suit the ambitions of the Kremlin better than for our military forces to be committed to a full-scale war with Red China?

It may well be that, in spite of our best efforts, the Communists may spread the war. But it would be wrong—tragically wrong—for us to take the initiative in extending the war.

The dangers are great. Make no mistake about it. Behind the North Koreans and Chinese Communists in the front lines stand additional millions of Chinese soldiers. And behind the Chinese stand the tanks, the planes, the submarines, the soldiers, and the scheming rulers of the Soviet Union.

Our aim is to avoid the spread of the conflict. . . .

If the Communist authorities realize that they cannot defeat us in Korea, if they realize it would be foolhardy to widen the hostilities beyond Korea, then they may recognize the folly of continuing their aggression. A peaceful settlement may then be possible. The door is always open.

Then we may achieve a settlement in Korea which will not compromise the principles and purposes of the United Nations.

I have thought long and hard about this question of extending the war in Asia. I have discussed it many times with the ablest military advisers in the country. I believe with all my heart that the course we are following is the best course.

I believe that we must try to limit the war to Korea for these vital reasons: To make sure that the precious lives of our fighting men are not wasted, to see that the security of our country and the free world is not needlessly jeopardized, and to prevent a third world war.

A number of events have made it evident that General MacArthur did not agree with that policy. I have, therefore, considered it essential to relieve General MacArthur so that there would be no doubt or confusion as to the real purpose and aim of our policy.

It was with the deepest personal regret that I found myself compelled to take this action. General MacArthur is one of our greatest military commanders. But the cause of world peace is more important than any individual.

The change in commands in the Far East means no change whatever in the policy of the United States. We will carry on the fight in Korea with vigor and determination in an effort to bring the war to a speedy and successful conclusion. . . .

Real peace can be achieved through a settlement based on the following factors:

One: The fighting must stop.

Two: Concrete steps must be taken to insure that the fighting will not break out again.

Three: There must be an end to the aggression.

A settlement founded upon these elements would open the way for the unification of Korea and the withdrawal of all foreign forces.

34

The Military-Industrial Complex

During Dwight D. Eisenhower's eight years as president, the United States ended the Korean War and moved to replace expensive conventional armaments with "cheap" nuclear weapons. Moreover, though the Eisenhower administration landed troops briefly in Lebanon, sent military aid to Indochina, and helped overthrow radical governments in Iran and Guatemala, the United States managed to stay out of war in other parts of the world. There was intense cold war. But there was also peace.

Despite all the years of peace under Eisenhower, the United States in 1960 still kept 2,500,000 military personnel on active duty, poured $51 billion into the defense budget—10 percent of the entire gross national product—and threw every scientific resource into creating sophisticated weapons systems. So striking was this development that President Eisenhower, himself a former general and a probusiness Republican, felt compelled in his 1961 farewell address to warn the public against the rise of a "military-industrial complex" in the land. Since military spending never in fact receded after Eisenhower, the concept and the phrase entered permanently into the political vocabulary, thus becoming somewhat ironic Eisenhower legacies to the people.

Born in Texas in 1890, Dwight D. Eisenhower grew up in Kansas in modest circumstances. A West Point graduate of 1915, he served at various army posts in the United States and Asia and under General Douglas MacArthur during the 1930s; his abilities were also perceived by General George Marshall, and he won promotion to brigadier general in 1941. Commander of the Allied forces in western Europe, he oversaw Allied invasions of North Africa, Italy, and France during World War II, demonstrating impressive diplomatic and administrative skills, and returned to America in late 1945 as a five-star general and a vastly popular hero. It was largely these skills and this reputation, plus his disarming grin and the irresistible slogan "I like Ike," that propelled him to landslide presidential victories in 1952 and 1956. After 1961, Eisenhower eased quickly into retirement and discovered that, much like his nemesis Harry Truman, he had become one of America's beloved political figures. He died in Washington, D.C., in 1969.

Questions to Consider. Two aspects of President Eisenhower's striking address deserve special attention. First, Eisenhower was warning not only against the influence of the military and the arms industry, as represented by huge military budgets, but also against the rise of a scientific-technological elite, as symbolized by the growing control of scholarship by Washington. Of these two tendencies, which did he seem to see as the greater threat? Second, although Eisenhower said plainly that these forces—the military-industrial and the scientific technological—represented a danger to our liberties and democratic processes, he was vague about how exactly the forces did endanger them and especially about what might, in a concrete way, be done to prevent such threats. Was Eisenhower, a former general, perhaps tacitly urging that soldiers and defense contractors be restricted in their political activities—in campaign contributions, for example, or lobbying efforts—or that defense budgets be scrutinized and slimmed down with special rigor? How realistic were these hints? What connection, if any, was he making at the end of his speech between disarmament and democracy?

Farewell Address (1961)

DWIGHT D. EISENHOWER

A vital element in keeping the peace is our military establishment. Our arms must be mighty, ready for instant action, so that no potential aggressor may be tempted to risk his own destruction.

Our military organization today bears little relation to that known by any of my predecessors in peacetime, or indeed by the fighting men of World War II or Korea.

Until the latest of our world conflicts, the United States had no armaments industry. American makers of plowshares could, with time and as required, make swords as well. But now we can no longer risk emergency improvisation of national defense; we have been compelled to create a permanent armaments industry of vast proportions. Added to this, three and a half million men and women are directly engaged in the defense establishment. We annually spend on military security more than the net income of all United States corporations.

From *The New York Times,* January 18, 1961.

B-52 strategic bombers in mass production at a Boeing company plant in the state of Washington, about 1955. Military production largely built and sustained the mid-century economy of the West Coast. Aerospace was one of the three new sectors, along with petrochemicals and electronics, that built and sustained the postwar economy of the United States. (Courtesy, Boeing Defense & Space Group)

This conjunction of an immense military establishment and a large arms industry is new in the American experience. The total influence—economic, political, even spiritual—is felt in every city, every statehouse, every office of the federal government. We recognize the imperative need for this development. Yet we must not fail to comprehend its grave implications. Our toil, resources, and livelihood are all involved; so is the very structure of our society.

In the councils of government, we must guard against the acquisition of unwarranted influence, whether sought or unsought, by the military-industrial complex. The potential for the disastrous rise of misplaced power exists and will persist.

We must never let the weight of this combination endanger our liberties or democratic processes. We should take nothing for granted. Only an alert and knowledgeable citizenry can compel the proper meshing of the huge industrial and military machinery of defense with our peaceful methods and goals, so that security and liberty may prosper together.

Akin to, and largely responsible for the sweeping changes in our industrial-military posture, has been the technological revolution during recent decades.

In this revolution, research has become central; it also becomes more formalized, complex, and costly. A steadily increasing share is conducted for, by, or at the discretion of, the federal government. . . .

The prospect of domination of the nation's scholars by federal employment, project allocations, and the power of money is ever present—and is gravely to be regarded.

Yet, in holding scientific research and discovery in respect, as we should, we must also be alert to the equal and opposite danger that public policy could itself become the captive of a scientific-technological elite.

It is the task of statesmanship to mold, to balance, and to integrate these and other forces, new and old, within the principles of our democratic system—ever aiming toward the supreme goals of our free society.

Another factor in maintaining balance involves the element of time. As we peer into society's future, we—you and I, and our government—must avoid the impulse to live only for today, plundering, for our own ease and convenience, the precious resources of tomorrow. We cannot mortgage the material assets of our grandchildren without risking the loss also of their political and spiritual heritage. We want democracy to survive for all generations to come, not to become the insolvent phantom of tomorrow.

Down the long lane of the history yet to be written America knows that this world of ours, ever growing smaller, must avoid becoming a community of dreadful fear and hate, and be, instead, a proud confederation of mutual trust and respect.

Such a confederation must be one of equals. The weakest must come to the conference table with the same confidence as do we, protected as we are by our moral, economic, and military strength. That table, though scarred by many past frustrations, cannot be abandoned for the certain agony of the battlefield.

Disarmament, with mutual honor and confidence, is a continuing imperative. Together we must learn how to compose differences, not with arms, but with intellect and decent purpose. Because this need is so sharp and apparent I confess that I lay down my official responsibilities in this field with a definite sense of disappointment. As one who has witnessed the horror and the lingering sadness of war—as one who knows that another war could utterly destroy this civilization which has been so slowly and painfully built over thousands of years—I wish I could say tonight that a lasting peace is in sight.

Happily, I can say that war has been avoided. Steady progress toward our ultimate goal has been made. But, so much remains to be done. As a private citizen, I shall never cease to do what little I can to help the world advance along that road. . . .

35

The Defense of Freedom

Although the New Frontier of President John F. Kennedy had a significant domestic component centering on civil rights and social welfare programs, Kennedy's primary emphasis, as his inaugural address, reprinted below, makes clear, was on the development of a vigorous foreign policy. Kennedy perceived the Soviet threat in much the same way that Richard M. Nixon, his Republican opponent, had perceived it during the 1960 presidential campaign: as ubiquitous and unremitting and therefore to be countered at every turn. But Kennedy's views held significant differences from the policy pursued by the Eisenhower administration.

Kennedy was more willing than Eisenhower to increase defense spending; he was also more skeptical about the value of responding to revolutions in the Third World by threatening thermonuclear war. Departing from the policies of his predecessor, Kennedy moved toward a doctrine of "flexible response" that stressed conventional forces over atomic weapons and emphasized international propaganda and public relations over armaments. At once idealistic and demanding, like the 1961 inaugural address itself, Kennedy's views led to the signing of treaties with the Soviet Union that banned atmospheric nuclear testing and to the establishment of emergency communications between the White House and the Kremlin. But these same views also led to the sending of more and more military personnel to South Vietnam, to prevent Ho Chi Minh, the Communist leader of North Vietnam, from unifying Vietnam under his rule.

John F. Kennedy was born in 1917 to a wealthy Irish-American family. After graduating with honors from Harvard in 1940, he served for a time as secretary to his father, who was then U.S. ambassador to Great Britain. *Why England Slept*—his best-selling book on British military policies during the 1930s—was published in 1940. During World War II he served in the U.S. Navy and won the Navy and Marine Corps Medal for his heroism. After the war he entered politics in Massachusetts, winning election to the House of Representatives in 1946 and to the Senate in 1952. His book *Profiles in Courage,* published in 1956, won the Pulitzer Prize, and in 1960 he narrowly bested Richard Nixon in a contest for the presidency. The youngest man and the only Roman Catholic ever elected president, Kennedy projected an image of intelligence, vitality, and sophistication. Worldwide mourning occurred after he was assassinated in Dallas, Texas, on November 22, 1963.

Questions to Consider. Some historians have argued that in this address Kennedy formally shifted the focus of the cold war from Europe to the nonaligned or economically underdeveloped part of the world. Do you agree or disagree? If you agree, do you also believe there was a connection between this shift and Kennedy's emphasis on feeding and clothing the world—on winning by doing good? Was there also a connection between this shift and Kennedy's preference for invoking human rights instead of democracy? Historians have also read the address as an unprecedented fusion of "adversarialism" with "universalism." Again, do you agree or disagree? Was this fusion connected with Kennedy's sense of facing an "hour of maximum danger" in which Americans might have to "pay any price" for liberty?

Inaugural Address (1961)

JOHN F. KENNEDY

We observe today not a victory of party but a celebration of freedom—symbolizing an end as well as a beginning—signifying renewal as well as change. For I have sworn before you and Almighty God the same solemn oath our forbears prescribed nearly a century and three-quarters ago.

The world is very different now. For man holds in his mortal hands the power to abolish all forms of human poverty and all forms of human life. And yet the same revolutionary beliefs for which our forbears fought are still at issue around the globe—the belief that the rights of man come not from the generosity of the state but from the hand of God.

We dare not forget today that we are the heirs of that first revolution. Let the word go forth from this time and place, to friend and foe alike, that the torch has been passed to a new generation of Americans—born in this century, tempered by war, disciplined by a hard and bitter peace, proud of our ancient heritage—and unwilling to witness or permit the slow undoing of those human rights to which this nation has always been committed, and to which we are committed today at home and around the world.

From *The New York Times,* January 21, 1961.

John F. Kennedy. Kennedy, with his wife Jacqueline sitting at his side, during the presidential inauguration, 1961. (© 1960 Paul Schutzer/LIFE Magazine, Time Warner, Inc.)

Let every nation know, whether it wishes us well or ill, that we shall pay any price, bear any burden, meet any hardship, support any friend, oppose any foe to assure the survival and the success of liberty.

This much we pledge—and more.

To those old allies whose cultural and spiritual origins we share, we pledge the loyalty of faithful friends. United, there is little we cannot do in a host of co-operative ventures. Divided, there is little we can do—for we dare not meet a powerful challenge at odds and split asunder.

To those new states whom we welcome to the ranks of the free, we pledge our word that one form of colonial control shall not have passed away merely to be replaced by a far more iron tyranny. We shall not always expect to find them supporting our view. But we shall always hope to find them strongly supporting their own freedom—and to remember that, in the past, those who foolishly sought power by riding the back of the tiger ended up inside.

To those people in the huts and villages of half the globe struggling to break the bonds of mass misery, we pledge our best efforts to help them help themselves, for whatever period is required—not because the Communists may be doing it, not because we seek their votes, but because it is right. If a free society cannot help the many who are poor, it cannot save the few who are rich.

To our sister republics south of our border, we offer a special pledge—to convert our good words into good deeds—in a new alliance for progress—to assist free men and free governments in casting off the chains of poverty. But this peaceful revolution of hope cannot become the prey of hostile powers. Let all our neighbors know that we shall join with them to oppose aggression or subversion anywhere in the Americas. And let every other power know that this hemisphere intends to remain the master of its own house.

To that world assembly of sovereign states, the United Nations, our last best hope in an age where the instruments of war have far outpaced the instruments of peace, we renew our pledge of support—to prevent it from becoming merely a forum for invective—to strengthen its shield of the new and the weak—and to enlarge the area in which its writ may run.

Finally, to those nations who would make themselves our adversary, we offer not a pledge but a request: that both sides begin anew the quest for peace, before the dark powers of destruction unleashed by science engulf all humanity in planned or accidental self-destruction.

We dare not tempt them with weakness. For only when our arms are sufficient beyond doubt can we be certain beyond doubt that they will never be employed.

But neither can two great and powerful groups of nations take comfort from our present course—both sides overburdened by the cost of modern weapons, both rigidly alarmed by the steady spread of the deadly atom, yet both racing to alter that uncertain balance of terror that stays the hand of mankind's final war.

So let us begin anew—remembering on both sides that civility is not a sign of weakness, and sincerity is always subject to proof. Let us never negotiate out of fear. But let us never fear to negotiate.

Let both sides explore what problems unite us instead of belaboring those problems which divide us.

Let both sides, for the first time, formulate serious and precise proposals for the inspection and control of arms—and bring the absolute power to destroy other nations under the absolute control of all nations.

Let both sides seek to invoke the wonders of science instead of its terror. Together let us explore the stars, conquer the deserts, eradicate disease, tap the ocean depths, and encourage the arts and commerce.

Let both sides unite to heed in all corners of the earth the command of Isaiah—to "undo the heavy burdens . . . [and] let the oppressed go free."

And if a beachhead of co-operation may push back the jungle of suspicion, let both sides join in creating a new endeavor, not a new balance of power, but a new world of law, where the strong are just and the weak secure and the peace preserved.

All this will not be finished in the first one hundred days. Nor will it be finished in the first one thousand days, nor in the life of this administration, nor even perhaps in our lifetime on this planet. But let us begin.

In your hands, my fellow citizens, more than mine, will rest the final success or failure of our course. Since this country was founded, each generation of Americans has been summoned to give testimony to its national loyalty. The graves of young Americans who answered the call to service surround the globe.

Now the trumpet summons us again—not as a call to bear arms, though arms we need—not as a call to battle, though embattled we are—but a call to bear the burden of a long twilight struggle, year in and year out, "rejoicing in hope, patient in tribulation"—a struggle against the common enemies of man: tyranny, poverty, disease, and war itself.

Can we forge against these enemies a grand and global alliance, North and South, East and West, that can assure a more fruitful life for all mankind? Will you join in that historic effort?

In the long history of the world, only a few generations have been granted the role of defending freedom in its hour of maximum danger. I do not shrink from this responsibility—I welcome it. I do not believe that any of us would exchange places with any other people or any other generation. The energy, the faith, the devotion which we bring to this endeavor will light our country and all who serve it—and the glow from that fire can truly light the world.

And so, my fellow Americans: ask not what your country can do for you—ask what you can do for your country.

My fellow citizens of the world: ask not what America will do for you, but what together we can do for the freedom of man.

Finally, whether you are citizens of America or citizens of the world, ask of us here the same high standards of strength and sacrifice which we ask of you. With a good conscience our only sure reward, with history the final judge of deeds, let us go forth to lead the land we love, asking His blessing and His help, but knowing that here on earth God's work must truly be our own.

36

Blank Check

American involvement in Vietnam began modestly enough with a promise in 1945 to help France restore colonial rule there. The United States backed France because Ho Chi Minh, the leader of the struggle for Vietnamese independence, was a Communist. American policy makers were more impressed by Ho's Communism than by his nationalism; they viewed him as a tool of the Kremlin, although he had the backing of many non-Communists in Indochina who wanted freedom from French control. In 1954, Ho's forces defeated the French, and the French decided to withdraw from Vietnam. At this point the United States stepped in, backed a partition of Vietnam, and gave aid to the South Vietnamese government in Saigon. American policy continued to be based on the belief that Communism in Vietnam was inspired by China or the Soviet Union, if not both. If Vietnam went Communist, Washington warned, other countries in Asia might topple like so many dominoes, and Communist influence in the world would grow at the expense of America's.

U.S. military personnel entered the Vietnamese conflict between North and South under presidents Eisenhower and Kennedy. American bombers began raiding North Vietnam in 1965, after the reelection of Kennedy's successor, Lyndon B. Johnson. By 1969, American troops in South Vietnam numbered around 550,000, and American planes had dropped more bombs in Vietnam than had been dropped on Germany and Japan during World War II. Yet the Vietcong (the South Vietnamese insurgents), aided by North Vietnamese military units, seemed stronger than ever. International opinion had now turned against the United States.

A key episode in Lyndon Johnson's escalation came with the so-called Tonkin Gulf incident. On August 2, 1964, the U.S.S. *Maddox,* an American destroyer supporting South Vietnamese commando raids against North Vietnam, came under attack by enemy patrol boats. The attackers suffered heavy damage; the *Maddox* was unharmed. Two days later the *Maddox* and another U.S. destroyer again moved into North Vietnamese waters. Although the weather was bad, sonar equipment indicated enemy torpedoes. When the captain of the *Maddox* later questioned members of his crew, no one could recall any enemy attacks, and subsequent investigations of the incident likewise turned up no evidence of hostile fire. The American destroyers nevertheless reportedly leveled heavy fire against North Vietnamese patrol boats. President Johnson, despite the questionable evidence and without admitting that U.S. ships were supporting raids against the North, ordered air strikes on North Vietnamese naval bases and announced on television that he was retaliating for "unprovoked" attacks. U.S. planes would now, he said, bomb North Vietnam.

On August 5, Johnson, in the address excerpted below, asked Congress to give him authority to repel "any armed attack against the forces of the United States and to prevent further aggression." The resolution passed the House by 466 to 0 and passed the Senate by 88 to 2. The resolution, as Johnson eventually argued, was tantamount to a declaration of war—which Congress has not voted against any country since December 1941. Under its auspices, the president authorized not only the carpet-bombing of North Vietnam but the American buildup to over a half-million combat troops. Its effect in 1964 was to preempt criticism from Republican presidential candidate Barry Goldwater, a hawk on foreign policy, help raise Johnson's approval rating in the polls from 42 percent to 72 percent, and contribute to a major victory in that fall's election.

Born in the poor hill country of central Texas in 1908, Lyndon Johnson worked his way through Southwest Texas State Teachers College in San Marcos and went to Washington as assistant to a local congressman in 1931. An intensely ambitious and ardent New Deal Democrat, Johnson began his political career with his election to fill a congressional vacancy in 1937. He was elected to the U.S. Senate in 1948. Unmatched at arranging the compromises and distributing the favors and money on which congressional politics rested, he became Senate minority leader in 1953 and majority leader in 1955, when the Democrats regained control of the Senate. As the vice-presidential nominee in 1960, he helped John F. Kennedy carry enough Southern states to become president; he became president himself upon Kennedy's assassination in 1963. As president, Johnson helped enact the most sweeping civil rights legislation of the century, but he also dramatically escalated a fundamentally unpopular war. Faced with widespread opposition to his policies, he declined to run for reelection in 1968. He died in San Antonio in 1973.

Questions to Consider. On what grounds did Johnson defend the American presence in Vietnam? How did he deal with the problematic nature of the evidence of North Vietnamese attacks on U.S. ships? Johnson wanted authorization not only for limited retaliation over this specific incident but to attack North Vietnam on a large scale over a long period of time. How did he move in this address from the particular incident to the general goal? What parts of the speech might have been especially effective in undercutting Barry Goldwater's criticism of the Democrats as "soft on Communism"? Was Johnson demanding, in effect, a declaration of war? If so, why didn't he ask for that?

Message to Congress on the Gulf of Tonkin (1964)

LYNDON B. JOHNSON

Last night I announced to the American people that the North Vietnamese regime had conducted further deliberate attacks against U.S. naval vessels operating in international waters, and that I had therefore directed air action against gun boats and supporting facilities used in these hostile operations. This air action has now been carried out with substantial damage to the boats and facilities. Two U.S. aircraft were lost in the action.

After consultation with the leaders of both parties in the Congress, I further announced a decision to ask the Congress for a Resolution expressing the unity and determination of the United States in supporting freedom and in protecting peace in Southeast Asia.

These latest actions of the North Vietnamese regime have given a new and grave turn to the already serious situation in Southeast Asia. Our commitments in that area are well known to the Congress. They were first made in 1954 by President Eisenhower. They were further defined in the Southeast Asia Collective Defense Treaty approved by the Senate in February 1955.

This Treaty with its accompanying protocol obligates the United States and other members to act in accordance with their Constitutional processes to meet Communist aggression against any of the parties or protocol states.

Our policy in Southeast Asia has been consistent and unchanged since 1954. I summarized it on June 2 in four simple propositions:

1. *America keeps her word.* Here as elsewhere, we must and shall honor our commitments.

2. *The issue is the future of Southeast Asia as a whole.* A threat to any nation in that region is a threat to all, and a threat to us.

3. *Our purpose is peace.* We have no military, political or territorial ambitions in the area.

From *The New York Times,* August 6, 1964.

4. *This is not just a jungle war, but a struggle for freedom on every front of human activity.* Our military and economic assistance to South Vietnam and Laos in particular has the purpose of helping these countries to repel aggression and strengthen their independence.

The threat to the free nations of Southeast Asia has long been clear. The North Vietnamese regime has constantly sought to take over South Vietnam and Laos. This Communist regime has violated the Geneva Accords for Vietnam. It has systematically conducted a campaign of subversion, which includes the direction, training, and supply of personnel and arms for the conduct of guerrilla warfare in South Vietnamese territory. In Laos, the North Vietnamese regime has maintained military forces, used Laotian territory for infiltration into South Vietnam, and most recently carried out combat operations—all in direct violation of the Geneva Agreements of 1962.

In recent months, the actions of the North Vietnamese regime have become steadily more threatening. In May, following new acts of Communist aggression in Laos, the United States undertook reconnaissance flights over Laotian territory, at the request of the Government of Laos. These flights had the essential mission of determining the situation in territory where Communist forces were preventing inspection by the International Control Commission. When the Communists attacked these aircraft, I responded by furnishing escort fighters with instructions to fire when fired upon. Thus, these latest North Vietnamese attacks on our naval vessels are not the first direct attack on armed forces of the United States.

As President of the United States I have concluded that I should now ask the Congress, on its part, to join in affirming the national determination that all such attacks will be met, and that the U.S. will continue in its basic policy of assisting the free nations of the area to defend their freedom.

As I have repeatedly made clear, the United States intends no rashness, and seeks no wider war. We must make it clear to all that the United States is united in its determination to bring about the end of Communist subversion and aggression in the area. We seek the full and effective restoration of the international agreements signed in Geneva in 1954, with respect to South Vietnam, and again in Geneva in 1962, with respect to Laos.

I recommend a Resolution expressing the support of the Congress for all necessary action to protect our armed forces and to assist nations covered by the SEATO Treaty. At the same time, I assure the Congress that we shall continue readily to explore any avenues of political solution that will effectively guarantee the removal of Communist subversion and the preservation of the independence of the nations of the area.

The Resolution could well be based upon similar resolutions enacted by the Congress in the past—to meet the threat to Formosa in 1955, to meet the threat to the Middle East in 1957, and to meet the threat in Cuba in 1962. It could state in the simplest terms the resolve and support of the Congress for action to deal appropriately with attacks against our armed forces and to defend freedom and preserve peace in southeast Asia in accordance with the obligations of the United States under the southeast Asia Treaty. I urge the Congress to enact such a Resolution promptly and thus to give convincing evidence to the aggressive Communist nations, and to the world as a whole, that our policy in southeast Asia will be carried forward—and that the peace and security of the area will be preserved.

The events of this week would in any event have made the passage of a Congressional Resolution essential. But there is an additional reason for doing so at a time when we are entering on three months of political campaigning. Hostile nations must understand that in such a period the United States will continue to protect its national interests, and that in these matters there is no division among us.

37

AGONY IN ASIA

The escalation of American involvement in Vietnam provoked perhaps the greatest wartime opposition in American history. By the end of 1965, the first draft card burnings had occurred. Students in major universities throughout the country had organized "teach-ins" (named after the civil rights "sit-ins") to discuss the nature of the war and had held the first antiwar march on Washington. By 1967, protest rallies were drawing hundreds of thousands, and evasion of the draft among middle-class students was widespread. Some of the country's most prominent leaders, including the Reverend Martin Luther King, Jr., were vehemently criticizing the Johnson administration for its Vietnam policy. The speech reprinted below, which King delivered at Riverside Church in New York City, stresses the links between international violence and domestic violence, war spending and social poverty, and the suppression of independence movements abroad and minority aspirations at home.

Martin Luther King's stance had special force because of his stature as an advocate of peace and human rights. Born in Atlanta, Georgia, in 1929, the son of a Baptist clergyman, King entered college at the age of fifteen. He eventually received a doctorate in theology from Boston University. In 1954 he was called to the ministry of a church in Montgomery, Alabama, and in 1955 he became a leader in the successful effort to integrate the local bus system. Calling on this experience and on his philosophy of nonviolence, King was soon promoting demonstrations against segregation throughout the South. In August 1963 he spoke to 250,000 people in the nation's capital on behalf of black voting rights, the first so-called March on Washington and a model for later antiwar protests. In 1964 he won the Nobel Peace Prize. In April 1968, having broken with the Johnson administration over the Vietnam War and on the eve of a vast "Poor People's Campaign" for economic justice, King was assassinated in Memphis, Tennessee. The death of the apostle of nonviolence triggered massive race riots in the nation's cities. His funeral attracted 150,000 mourners. The inscription on his tombstone, taken from his 1963 Washington speech, reads: "Free at Last, Free at Last, Thank God Almighty, I'm Free at Last."

Questions to Consider. Of the seven reasons King gave for deciding to "break silence" over Vietnam, which—as measurable by the rank and emphasis he gave them and by his rhetorical style—seem to have mattered most to him? Note how King inveighed first against racial injustice, then against violence, and finally against both issues. Was he right to link the two so closely? Would any perceptive critic of injustice have done so, or did this reflect King's particular way of seeing things and his personal experience in the civil rights movement? Many historians believe this speech marked a sharp political shift by King away from the struggle for civil rights and toward a broader struggle for economic justice and social transformation. Is there evidence for this interpretation in the speech? Why do you suppose King waited until 1967 to launch a public attack on American policy in Vietnam? Why was he careful to call his silence, rather than his attack, a "betrayal"?

A Time to Break Silence (1967)

MARTIN LUTHER KING, JR.

I come to this magnificent house of worship tonight because my conscience leaves me no other choice. I join with you in this meeting because I am in deepest agreement with the aims and work of the organization which has brought us together: Clergy and Laymen Concerned About Vietnam. The recent statement of your executive committee are the sentiments of my own heart and I found myself in full accord when I read its opening lines: "A time comes when silence is betrayal." That time has come for us in relation to Vietnam. . . .

Over the past two years, as I have moved to break the betrayal of my own silences and to speak from the burnings of my own heart, as I have called for radical departures from the destruction of Vietnam, many persons have questioned me about the wisdom of my path. At the heart of their concerns this query has often loomed large and loud: Why are you speaking about the war, Dr. King? Why are you joining the voices of dissent? Peace and civil rights don't mix, they say. Aren't you hurting the cause of your people, they ask? And when I hear them, though I often understand the source of their

Reprinted by arrangement with The Heirs to the Estate of Martin Luther King, Jr., c/o Writers House, Inc., as agent for the proprietor. Copyright renewed 1995 by The Estate of Martin Luther King, Jr.

Wartime remembrance. Another soldier returns from Vietnam. (© 1969 Constantine Manos/Magnum Photos)

concern, I am nevertheless greatly saddened, for such questions mean that the inquirers have not really known me, my commitment or my calling. Indeed, their questions suggest that they do not know the world in which they live.

In the light of such tragic misunderstanding, I deem it of signal importance to try to state clearly, and I trust concisely, why I believe that the path from Dexter Avenue Baptist Church—the church in Montgomery, Alabama, where I began my pastorate—leads clearly to this sanctuary tonight. . . .

Since I am a preacher by trade, I suppose it is not surprising that I have seven major reasons for bringing Vietnam into the field of my moral vision. There is at the outset a very obvious and almost facile connection between the war in Vietnam and the struggle I, and others, have been waging in America. A few years ago there was a shining moment in that struggle. It seemed as if there was a real promise of hope for the poor—both black and white—through the Poverty Program. There were experiments, hopes, new beginnings. Then came the build-up in Vietnam and I watched the program broken and eviscerated as if it were some idle political plaything of a society gone mad on war, and I knew that America would never invest the necessary funds or energies in rehabilitation of its poor so long as adventures like Vietnam continued to draw men and skills and money like some demonic destructive suction tube. So I was increasingly compelled to see the war as an enemy of the poor and to attack it as such.

Perhaps the more tragic recognition of reality took place when it became clear to me that the war was doing far more than devastating the hopes of the poor at home. It was sending their sons and their brothers and their husbands to fight and to die in extraordinarily high proportions relative to the rest of the population. We were taking the black young men who had been crippled by our society and sending them 8,000 miles away to guarantee liberties in Southeast Asia which they had not found in Southwest Georgia and East Harlem. So we have been repeatedly faced with the cruel irony of watching negro and white boys on TV screens as they kill and die together for a nation that has been unable to seat them together in the same schools. So we watch them in brutal solidarity burning the huts of a poor village, but we realize that they would never live on the same block in Detroit. I could not be silent in the face of such cruel manipulation of the poor.

My third reason moves to an even deeper level of awareness, for it grows out of my experience in the ghettos of the north over the last three years—especially the last three summers. As I have walked among the desperate, rejected and angry young men I have told them that Molotov cocktails and rifles would not solve their problems. I have tried to offer them my deepest compassion while maintaining my conviction that social change comes most meaningfully through nonviolent action. But they asked—and rightly so—what about Vietnam? They asked if our own nation wasn't using massive doses of violence to solve its problems, to bring about the changes it wanted. Their questions hit home, and I knew that I could never again raise my voice against the violence of the oppressed in the ghettos without having first spoken clearly to the greatest purveyor of violence in the world today—my own government. For the sake of those boys, for the sake of this government, for the sake of the hundreds of thousands trembling under our violence, I cannot be silent.

For those who ask the question, "Aren't you a Civil Rights leader?" and thereby mean to exclude me from the movement for peace, I have this further answer. In 1957 when a group of us formed the Southern Christian Leadership Conference, we chose as our motto: "To save the soul of America." We were convinced that we could not limit our vision to certain rights for black people, but instead affirmed the conviction that America would never be free or saved from itself unless the descendants of its slaves were loosed completely from the shackles they still wear. In a way we were agreeing with Langston Hughes, that black bard of Harlem, who had written earlier:

> *O, yes*
> *I say it plain,*
> *America never was America to me,*
> *And yet I swear this oath—*
> *America will be!*[1]

Now, it should be incandescently clear that no one who has any concern for the integrity and life of America today can ignore the present war. If America's soul becomes totally poisoned, part of the autopsy must read Vietnam. It can never be saved so long as it destroys the deepest hopes of men the world over. So it is that those of us who are yet determined that America will be are led down the path of protest and dissent, working for the health of our land.

As if the weight of such a commitment to the life and health of America were not enough, another burden of responsibility was placed upon me in 1964; and I cannot forget that the Nobel Prize for Peace was also a commission—a commission to work harder than I had ever worked before for "the brotherhood of man." This is a calling that takes me beyond national allegiances, but even if it were not present I would yet have to live with the meaning of my commitment to the ministry of Jesus Christ. To me the relationship of this ministry to the making of peace is so obvious that I sometimes marvel at those who ask me why I am speaking against the war. Could it be that they do not know that the good news was meant for all men—for Communists and capitalists, for their children and ours, for black and for white, for revolutionary and conservative? Have they forgotten that my ministry is in obedience to the one who loved his enemies so fully that he died for them? What can I say to the "Viet Cong" or to Castro or to Mao as a faithful minister of this one? Can I threaten them with death or must I not share with them my life?

Finally, as I try to delineate for you and for myself the road that leads from Montgomery to this place I would have offered all that was most valid if I simply said that I must be true to my conviction that I share with all men

1. From *Collected Poems* by Langston Hughes. Copyright © 1994 by the Estate of Langston Hughes. Reprinted by permission of Alfred A. Knopf, Inc.

the calling to be a son of the Living God. Beyond the calling of race or nation or creed is this vocation of sonship and brotherhood, and because I believe that the Father is deeply concerned especially for his suffering and helpless and outcast children, I come tonight to speak for them. . . .

And as I ponder the madness of Vietnam and search within myself for ways to understand and respond to compassion my mind goes constantly to the people of that peninsula. I speak now not of the soldiers of each side, not of the junta in Saigon, but simply of the people who have been living under the curse of war for almost three continuous decades now. I think of them too because it is clear to me that there will be no meaningful solution there until some attempt is made to know them and hear their broken cries. . . .

They languish under our bombs and consider us—not their fellow Vietnamese—the real enemy. They move sadly and apathetically as we herd them off the land of their fathers into concentration camps where minimal social needs are rarely met. They know they must move or be destroyed by our bombs. So they go—primarily women and children and the aged.

They watch as we poison their water, as we kill a million acres of their crops. They must weep as the bulldozers roar through their areas preparing to destroy the precious trees. They wander into the hospitals, with at least twenty casualties from American firepower for one "Viet Cong"-inflicted injury. So far we may have killed a million of them—mostly children. They wander into the towns and see thousands of the children, homeless, without clothes, running in packs on the streets like animals. They see the children degraded by our soldiers as they beg for food. They see the children selling their sisters to our soldiers, soliciting for their mothers.

What do the peasants think as we ally ourselves with the landlords and as we refuse to put any action into our many words concerning land reform? What do they think as we test out our latest weapons on them, just as the Germans tested out new medicine and new tortures in the concentration camps of Europe? Where are the roots of the independent Vietnam we claim to be building? Is it among these voiceless ones?

We have destroyed their two most cherished institutions: the family and the village. We have destroyed their land and their crops. We have cooperated in the crushing of the nation's only non-communist revolutionary political force—the unified Buddhist Church. We have supported the enemies of the peasants of Saigon. We have corrupted their women and children and killed their men. What liberators! . . .

At this point I should make it clear that while I have tried in these last few minutes to give a voice to the voiceless on Vietnam and to understand the arguments of those who are called enemy, I am as deeply concerned about our own troops there as anything else. For it occurs to me that what we are submitting them to in Vietnam is not simply the brutalizing process that goes on in any war where armies face each other and seek to destroy. We are adding cynicism to the process of death, for they must know after a short period there that none of the things we claim to be fighting for are really involved. Before long they must know that their government has sent them into a struggle among Vietnamese, and the more sophisticated surely realize that we are on the side of the wealthy and the secure while we create a hell for the poor.

Somehow this madness must cease. We must stop now. I speak as a child of God and brother to the suffering poor of Vietnam. I speak for those whose land is being laid waste, whose homes are being destroyed, whose culture is being subverted. I speak for the poor of America who are paying the double price of smashed hopes at home and death and corruption in Vietnam. I speak as a citizen of the world, for the world as it stands aghast at the path we have taken. I speak as an American to the leaders of my own nation. The great initiative in this war is ours. The initiative to stop it must be ours. . . .

In 1957 a sensitive American official overseas said that it seemed to him that our nation was on the wrong side of a world revolution. During the past ten years we have seen emerge a pattern of suppression which now has justified the presence of U.S. military "advisers" in Venezuela. This need to maintain social stability for our investments accounts for the counterrevolutionary action of American forces in Guatemala. It tells why American helicopters are being used against guerrillas in Colombia and why American napalm and green beret forces have already been active against rebels in Peru. It is with such activity in mind that the words of the late John F. Kennedy come back to haunt us. Five years ago he said, "Those who make peaceful revolution impossible will make violent revolution inevitable."

Increasingly, by choice or by accident, this is the role our nation has taken—the role of those who make peaceful revolution impossible by refusing to give up the privileges and the pleasures that come from the immense profits of overseas investment.

I am convinced that if we are to get on the right side of the world revolution, we as a nation must undergo a radical revolution of values. We must rapidly begin the shift from a "thing-oriented" society to a "person-oriented" society. When machines and computers, profit motives and property rights are considered more important than people, the giant triplets of racism, materialism, and militarism are incapable of being conquered.

A true revolution of values will soon cause us to question the fairness and justice of many of our past and present policies. On the one hand we are called to play the Good Samaritan on life's roadside; but that will be only an initial act. One day we must come to see that the whole Jericho Road must be transformed so that men and women will not be constantly beaten and robbed as they make their journey on Life's highway. True compassion is more than flinging a coin to a beggar; it is not haphazard and superficial. It comes to see that an edifice which produces beggars needs restructuring. A true revolution of values will soon look uneasily on the glaring contrast of poverty and wealth. With righteous indignation, it will look across the seas and see individual capitalists of the West investing huge sums of money in

Asia, Africa and South America, only to take the profits out with no concern for the social betterment of the countries, and say: "This is not just." It will look at our alliance with the landed gentry of Latin America and say: "This is not just." The Western arrogance of feeling that it has everything to teach others and nothing to learn from them is not just. A true revolution of values will lay hands on the world order and say of war: "This way of settling differences is not just."

Now let us begin. Now let us rededicate ourselves to the long and bitter—but beautiful—struggle for a new world. This is the calling of the sons of God, and our brothers wait eagerly for our response. Shall we say the odds are too great? Shall we tell them the struggle is too hard? Will our message be that the forces of American life militate against their arrival as full men, and we send our deepest regrets? Or will there be another message, of longing, of hope, of solidarity with their yearnings, of commitment to their cause, whatever the cost? The choice is ours, and though we might prefer it otherwise we must choose in this crucial moment of human history.

Martin Luther King, Jr., in prayer with Ralph Abernathy (behind King's left shoulder) and other supporters of the Southern Christian Leadership Conference. (Corbis-Bettmann)

CHAPTER SIX

Movements for Change

Desegregation Begins

Racial segregation was a fact of life everywhere in the South until the middle of this century. Organizations such as the National Association for the Advancement of Colored People (NAACP) and the Congress of Racial Equality (CORE) fought hard against segregation and its handmaiden, disfranchisement of blacks. But in 1896 the Supreme Court had ruled in *Plessy* v. *Ferguson* that separate facilities for blacks and whites were legal, and there seemed little recourse from this decree, especially given the unsympathetic racial views of the national government in this period. Only in 1947 did some tentative preliminary change come with the integration of major-league baseball for commercial reasons, the integration of the armed forces by presidential order, and the integration of Southern law schools by a Supreme Court decision that year arguing that such schools were inherently unequal because they denied opportunities to those excluded.

Then, in 1954, in an NAACP lawsuit entitled *Brown* v. *The Board of Education of Topeka,* the Supreme Court extended its reasoning from law schools to the entire segregated school system, thereby reversing the "separate-but-equal" doctrine some sixty years after its adoption. Written by Chief Justice Earl Warren on behalf of a unanimous Court, at first this momentous decision, reprinted below, was met with bitter resentment and resistance from most Southern whites. Yet it marked the beginning of the end for legally segregated schools in the nation. Together with the massive civil rights movement led by Martin Luther King, Jr., and others, it outlawed all segregated public facilities, whether buses, beaches, lunch counters, voting booths, or schools.

Earl Warren was born in Los Angeles in 1891. After he was graduated from the University of California at Berkeley, he practiced law in the San Francisco area until joining the army during World War I. In the 1920s Warren embarked on a successful political career in California, serving as district attorney, state attorney general, and governor. His only electoral defeat came as Republican vice-presidential candidate in 1948. When President Eisenhower appointed him chief justice in 1953, Warren was considered a rather traditional Republican moderate. His leadership of the Court, however, brought an unexpected burst of judicial activism that strengthened not only minority rights but also the rights of voters, trial defendants, and witnesses before congressional committees. Warren resigned from the Court in 1969 and died in Washington in 1974.

Questions to Consider. Compare Earl Warren's assumptions and reasoning in this case with those of Henry Billings Brown in *Plessy* v. *Ferguson* (1896). Note, for example, that Warren virtually disregarded what Brown had believed to be so crucial—the actual differences between the races. Note, too, that Warren read very large public purposes into the bountiful commitment of local governments to public education: good citizenship, values, training, and social adjustment. Were these two factors—colorblindness and purposeful public education—enough to account for the Court's 1954 decision? If so, why did Warren introduce psychological studies into his argument? Was it merely a reflection of the findings of modern social science? Or was it because Brown had already reasoned from psychological effects in *Plessy*? In what other areas besides education might modern courts attempt to use the equal protection clause of the Fourteenth Amendment as construed by the Warren Court?

Brown v. *The Board of Education of Topeka* (1954)

EARL WARREN

These cases come to us from the States of Kansas, South Carolina, Virginia, and Delaware. They are premised on different facts and different local conditions, but a common legal question justifies their consideration together in this consolidated opinion.

In approaching this problem, we cannot turn the clock back to 1868 when the Amendment was adopted, or even to 1896 when *Plessy* v. *Ferguson* was written. We must consider public education in the light of its full development and its present place in American life throughout the Nation. Only in this way can it be determined if segregation in public schools deprives these plaintiffs of the equal protection of the laws.

Today, education is perhaps the most important function of state and local governments. Compulsory school attendance laws and the great

From *Brown* v. *The Board of Education of Topeka,* 347 U.S. 483 (1954).

Elizabeth Eckford approaching Little Rock's Central High School during the integration crisis of 1957. The crowd began to curse and yell, "Lynch her! Lynch her!" A national guardsman blocked her entrance into the school with his rifle. Faced with this, Eckford retreated back down the street away from the mob. But a week later, under the protection of U.S. Army troops, she finally attended, and integrated, Central High School. (Francis Miller/LIFE Magazine, © Time Warner, Inc.)

expenditures for education both demonstrate our recognition of the importance of education to our democratic society. It is required in the performance of our most basic public responsibilities, even service in the armed forces. It is the very foundation of good citizenship. Today it is a principal instrument in awakening the child to cultural values, in preparing him for later professional training, and in helping him to adjust normally to his environment. In these days, it is doubtful that any child may reasonably be expected to succeed in life if he is denied the opportunity of an education. Such an opportunity, where the state has undertaken to provide it, is a right which must be made available to all on equal terms.

We come then to the question presented: Does segregation of children in public schools solely on the basis of race, even though the physical facilities and other "tangible" factors may be equal, deprive the children of the minority group of equal educational opportunities? We believe that it does.

In *Sweatt* v. *Painter*, . . . in finding that a segregated law school for Negroes could not provide them equal educational opportunities, this Court relied in large part on "those qualities which are incapable of objective measurement but which make for greatness in a law school." In *McLaurin* v. *Oklahoma State Regents*, . . . the Court, in requiring that a Negro admitted to a white graduate school be treated like all other students, again resorted to intangible considerations: ". . . his ability to study, to engage in discussions and exchange views with other students, and, in general, to learn his profession." Such considerations apply with added force to children in grade and high schools. To separate them from others of similar age and qualifications solely because of their race generates a feeling of inferiority as to their status in the community that may affect their hearts and minds in a way unlikely ever to be undone. The effect of this separation on their educational opportunities was well stated by a finding in the Kansas case by a court which nevertheless felt compelled to rule against the Negro plaintiffs:

> Segregation of white and colored children in public schools has a detrimental effect upon the colored children. The impact is greater when it has the sanction of the law; for the policy of separating the races is usually interpreted as denoting the inferiority of the Negro group. A sense of inferiority affects the motivation of a child to learn. Segregation with the sanction of the law, therefore, has a tendency to retard the educational and mental development of Negro children and to deprive them of some of the benefits they would receive in a racially integrated school system.

Whatever may have been the extent of psychological knowledge at the time of *Plessy* v. *Ferguson*, this finding is amply supported by modern authority. Any language in *Plessy* v. *Ferguson* contrary to this finding is rejected.

We conclude that in the field of public education the doctrine of "separate but equal" has no place. Separate educational facilities are inherently unequal. Therefore, we hold that the plaintiffs and others similarly situated for whom the actions have been brought are, by reason of the segregation complained of, deprived of the equal protection of the laws guaranteed by the Fourteenth Amendment. . . .

39

SAVING NATURE

Although occasionally writers such as Henry David Thoreau celebrated the beauty and power of nature, modern environmentalism began only late in the nineteenth century, as cities and industry grew so rapidly that they flattened and contaminated nature even as railroads increased access to it. In 1872 Congress created the first national park, Yellowstone, and twenty years later, after prodding by a new environmental organization, the Sierra Club, Congress enabled the president to set up wilderness areas. Theodore Roosevelt promoted more rational uses of scarce timber and mining resources after 1900. Franklin D. Roosevelt initiated important conservation projects, including the Tennessee Valley Authority and the Civilian Conservation Corps, during the Depression.

Environmentalism as a mass movement arose chiefly in the 1960s as people began to worry about not only the despoliation of wilderness but also the pollution of air, drinking water, and food and the wholesale annihilation of plant and animal species. In part this was because of a series of horror stories: polluted rivers spontaneously catching fire, poisons detected in human tissues and mothers' milk, acid rain destroying lakes and streams, massive coastal oil spills, air too "smoggy" to breathe safely. But the writings of scientists and naturalists, from Paul Erlich's *The Population Bomb* to Barry Commoner's *The Closing Circle*, played a part as well.

No book was more important in creating modern environmental consciousness than Rachel Carson's *Silent Spring*. Carson was mainly concerned about DDT, a chemical used in World War II to kill malaria-bearing mosquitoes and then by farmers against agricultural pests. Carson's book addressed, for virtually the first time, the dangers of heavy use of pesticides such as DDT, noting that DDT caused cancer and leukemia in eagles, trout, and other animals, including undoubtedly humans. DDT had also practically wiped out bird populations in some areas. Hence "springs" were now "silent" where birds had sung. Carson indicted consumers for using toxic products. More controversially, she indicted businesses for carelessly manufacturing and heavily advertising such products.

Congress responded to Carson and others with the Clean Air, Clean Water, and Endangered Species Acts and by establishing the Environmental Protection Agency. And these measures mostly worked. By the mid-1990s, even though species and woodlands still vanished and cancer rates remained high, levels of DDT and some other cancer-causing compounds were down sharply, as were soot, carbon monoxide, and sulfur dioxide emissions. Energy usage grew only a fifth as fast as the overall economy. America's water supply was the cleanest in the industrial world.

Rachel Carson was born in Springdale, Pennsylvania, in 1907. Showing an early interest in nature, she studied biology at Pennsylvania College for Women and various graduate schools, and in 1936 joined the U.S. Bureau of Fisheries, where she remained until 1952. Carson's first three books, about life in and around the seas, were brilliant fusions of scientific accuracy and elegant prose. One, *The Sea Around Us*, became a bestseller and was translated into thirty languages. *Silent Spring*, her last book, was also a bestseller but prompted bitter criticism, especially from large-scale producers and users who argued that pesticides increased productivity and therefore living standards. No one, though, refuted her facts and case histories. Carson died in Silver Spring, Maryland, in 1964.

Questions to Consider. Why did Carson call the 1950s "the age of poisons"? Was her proposal to label consumer pesticides with a skull and crossbones practical? Why did she emphasize household products so much, including gardening materials? What was happening in American society in the 1950s that might have prompted this focus on the household and home? What specific measures did Carson propose to protect society from agricultural chemicals? Which of these measures would be most likely to arouse resistance?

Silent Spring (1962)

RACHEL CARSON

So thoroughly has the age of poisons become established that anyone may walk into a store and, without questions being asked, buy substances of far greater death-dealing power than the medicinal drug for which he may be required to sign a "poison book" in the pharmacy next door. A few minutes'

From Rachel Carson, *Silent Spring* (Boston: Houghton Mifflin Company, 1962), 173–184. Copyright 1962 by Rachel L. Carson, renewed 1990 by Roger Christie. Reprinted by permission of Houghton Mifflin Company. All rights reserved.

research in any supermarket is enough to alarm the most stouthearted customer—provided, that is, he has even a rudimentary knowledge of the chemicals presented for his choice.

If a huge skull and crossbones were suspended above the insecticide department the customer might at least enter it with the respect normally accorded death-dealing materials. But instead the display is homey and cheerful, and, with the pickles and olives across the aisle and the bath and laundry soaps adjoining, the rows upon rows of insecticides are displayed. Within easy reach of a child's exploring hand are chemicals in *glass* containers. If dropped to the floor by a child or careless adult everyone nearby could be splashed with the same chemical that has sent spraymen using it into convulsions. These hazards of course follow the purchaser right into his home. A can of a mothproofing material containing DDD [dichloro-diphenyl-dichloroethane], for example, carries in very fine print the warning that its contents are under pressure and that it may burst if exposed to heat or open flame. A common insecticide for household use, including assorted uses in the kitchen, is chlordane. Yet the Food and Drug Administration's chief pharmacologist has declared the hazard of living in a house sprayed with chlordane to be "very great." Other household preparations contain the even more toxic dieldrin.

Use of poisons in the kitchen is made both attractive and easy. Kitchen shelf paper, white or tinted to match one's color scheme, may be impregnated with insecticide, not merely on one but on both sides. Manufacturers offer us do-it-yourself booklets on how to kill bugs. With push-button ease, one may send a fog of dieldrin into the most inaccessible nooks and crannies of cabinets, corners, and baseboards.

If we are troubled by mosquitoes, chiggers, or other insect pests on our persons we have a choice of innumerable lotions, creams, and sprays for application to clothing or skin. Although we are warned that some of these will dissolve varnish, paint, and synthetic fabrics, we are presumably to infer that the human skin is impervious to chemicals. To make certain that we shall at all times be prepared to repel insects, an exclusive New York store advertises a pocket-sized insecticide dispenser, suitable for the purse or for beach, golf, or fishing gear.

Gardening is now firmly linked with the super poisons. Every hardware store, garden-supply shop, and supermarket has rows of insecticides for every conceivable horticultural situation. Those who fail to make wide use of this array of lethal sprays and dusts are by implication remiss, for almost every newspaper's garden page and the majority of the gardening magazines take their use for granted.

So extensively are even the rapidly lethal organic phosphorus insecticides applied to lawns and ornamental plants that in 1960 the Florida State Board of Health found it necessary to forbid the commercial use of pesticides in residential areas by anyone who had not first obtained a permit and

Rachel Carson. (Alfred Eisenstaedt/LIFE Magazine, © Time Warner, Inc.)

met certain requirements. A number of deaths from parathion had occurred in Florida before this regulation was adopted.

Little is done, however, to warn the gardener or homeowner that he is handling extremely dangerous materials. On the contrary, a constant stream of new gadgets makes it easier to use poisons on lawn and garden—and increase the gardener's contact with them. One may get a jar-type attachment for the garden hose, for example, by which such extremely dangerous chemicals as chlordane or dieldrin are applied as one waters the lawn. Such a device is not only a hazard to the person using the hose; it is also a public menace. The *New York Times* found it necessary to issue a warning on its garden page to the effect that unless special protective devices were installed poisons might get into the water supply by back siphonage. Considering the number of such devices that are in use, and the scarcity of warnings such as this, do we need to wonder why our public waters are contaminated?

As an example of what may happen to the gardener himself, we might look at the case of a physician—an enthusiastic sparetime gardener—who began using DDT and then malathion on his shrubs and lawn, making regular weekly applications. Sometimes he applied the chemicals with a hand spray, sometimes with an attachment to his hose. In doing so, his skin and clothing were often soaked with spray. After about a year of this sort of thing, he suddenly collapsed and was hospitalized. Examination of a biopsy specimen of fat showed an accumulation of 23 parts per million of DDT. There was extensive nerve damage, which his physicians regarded as permanent. As time went on he lost weight, suffered extreme fatigue, and experienced a peculiar muscular weakness, a characteristic effect of malathion. All of these persisting effects were severe enough to make it difficult for the physician to carry on his practice. . . .

Among the general population with no known gross exposures to insecticides it may be assumed that much of the DDT stored in fat deposits has entered the body in food. To test this assumption, a scientific team from the United States Public Health Service sampled restaurant and institutional meals. *Every meal sampled contained DDT.* From this the investigators concluded, reasonably enough, that "few if any foods can be relied upon to be entirely free of DDT."

The quantities in such meals may be enormous. In a separate Public Health Service study, analysis of prison meals disclosed such items as stewed dried fruit containing 69.6 parts per million and bread containing 100.9 parts per million of DDT!

In the diet of the average home, meats and any products derived from animal fats contain the heaviest residues of chlorinated hydrocarbons. This is because these chemicals are soluble in fat. Residues on fruits and vegetables tend to be somewhat less. These are little affected by washing—the only remedy is to remove and discard all outside leaves of such vegetables as lettuce or cabbage, to peel fruit and to use no skins or outer covering whatever. Cooking does not destroy residues.

Milk is one of the few foods in which no pesticide residues are permitted by Food and Drug Administration regulations. In actual fact, however, residues turn up whenever a check is made. They are heaviest in butter and other manufactured dairy products. A check of 461 samples of such products in 1960 showed that a third contained residues, a situation which the Food and Drug Administration characterized as " far from encouraging." . . .

The fact that every meal we eat carries its loads of chlorinated hydrocarbons is the inevitable consequence of the almost universal spraying or dusting of agricultural crops with these poisons. If the farmer scrupulously follows the instructions on the labels, his use of agricultural chemicals will produce no residues larger than are permitted by the Food and Drug Administration. Leaving aside for the moment the question whether these legal residues are as "safe" as they are represented to be, there remains the well-known fact that farmers very frequently exceed the prescribed dosages, use the chemical too close to the time of harvest, use several insecticides where one would do, and in other ways display the common human failure to read the fine print.

Even the chemical industry recognizes the frequent misuse of insecticides and the need for education of farmers. One of its leading trade journals recently declared that "many users do not seem to understand that they may exceed insecticide tolerances if they use higher dosages than recommended. And haphazard use of insecticides on many crops may be based on farmers' whims."

The files of the Food and Drug Administration contain records of a disturbing number of such violations. A few examples will serve to illustrate the disregard of directions: a lettuce farmer who applied not one but eight different insecticides to his crop within a short time of harvest, a shipper who had used the deadly parathion on celery in an amount five times the recommended maximum, growers using endrin—most toxic of all the chlorinated hydrocarbons—on lettuce although no residue was allowable, spinach sprayed with DDT a week before harvest.

There are also cases of chance or accidental contamination. Large lots of green coffee in burlap bags have become contaminated while being transported by vessels also carrying a cargo of insecticides. Packaged foods in warehouses are subjected to repeated aerosol treatments with DDT, lindane, and other insecticides, which may penetrate the packaging materials and occur in measurable quantities on the contained foods. The longer the food remains in storage, the greater the danger of contamination.

To the question "But doesn't the government protect us from such things?" the answer is, "Only to a limited extent." The activities of the Food and Drug Administration in the field of consumer protection against pesticides are severely limited by two facts. The first is that it has jurisdiction only over foods shipped in interstate commerce; foods grown and marketed within a state are entirely outside its sphere of authority, no matter what the violation. The second and critically limiting fact is the small number of inspectors on its staff—fewer than 600 men for all its varied work. According to a Food and Drug official, only an infinitesimal part of the crop products moving in interstate commerce—far less than 1 per cent—can be checked with existing facilities, and this is not enough to have statistical significance. As for food produced and sold within a state, the situation is even worse, for most states have woefully inadequate laws in this field. . . .

What is the solution? The first necessity is the elimination of tolerances on the chlorinated hydrocarbons, the organic phosphorus group, and other highly toxic chemicals. It will immediately be objected that this will place an intolerable burden on the farmer. But if, as is now the presumable goal, it is possible to use chemicals in such a way that they leave a residue of only 7 parts per million (the tolerance for DDT), or of 1 part per million (the tolerance for parathion), or even of only 0.1 part per million as is required for dieldrin on a great variety of fruits and vegetables, then why is it not possible, with only a little more care, to prevent the occurrence of any residues at all? This, in fact, is what is required for some chemicals such as heptachlor, endrin, and dieldrin on certain crops. If it is considered practical in these instances, why not for all?

But this is not a complete or final solution, for a zero tolerance on paper is of little value. At present, as we have seen, more than 99 per cent of the interstate food shipments slip by without inspection. A vigilant and aggressive Food and Drug Administration, with a greatly increased force of inspectors, is another urgent need.

This system, however—deliberately poisoning our food, then policing the result—is too reminiscent of Lewis Carroll's White Knight who thought of "a plan to dye one's whiskers green, and always use so large a fan that they could not be seen." The ultimate answer is to use less toxic chemicals so that the public hazard from their misuse is greatly reduced. Such chemicals already exist: the pyrethrins, rotenone, ryania, and others derived from plant substances. Synthetic substitutes for the pyrethrins have recently been developed [so that an otherwise critical shortage can be averted]. Public education as to the nature of the chemicals offered for sale is sadly needed. The average purchaser is completely bewildered by the array of available insecticides, fungicides, and weed killers, and has no way of knowing which are the deadly ones, which reasonably safe. . . .

Until a large-scale conversion to these methods has been made, we shall have little relief from a situation that, by any common-sense standards, is intolerable. As matters stand now, we are in little better position than the guests of the Borgias.

40

Nonviolence and Protest

When the Supreme Court ordered public schools desegregated in 1954, the country's leading civil rights organizations—the NAACP, CORE, and the National Urban League—were all situated in the North. They drew their strength mainly from teachers, journalists, lawyers, students, businesspeople, and other persons who made up the tiny black middle class, and challenged racial oppression mostly through lawsuits and political lobbying. The initiatives of these organizations might affect Southern blacks and change the lives of black rural and urban workers, who made up most of the black population, because most blacks still lived in the South and did manual labor. But the organizations themselves were not based on this Southern black majority and so were unable to involve these African-Americans in the civil rights struggle or to mount direct challenges to racial injustice in the section of the country where it mattered most.

By the late 1950s the situation was changing. In part this resulted from efforts to implement the Brown decision, particularly in New Orleans, Louisiana, and Little Rock, Arkansas. There militant whites met black students with violence, prompting not only federal intervention but black demonstrations in support of desegregation. Southern NAACP chapters now grew rapidly, giving that organization a regional strength it had not enjoyed before. Even more important were the direct actions against segregated public facilities led by the Reverend Martin Luther King, Jr., and the civil rights group he founded in 1957, the Southern Christian Leadership Conference (SCLC). The first of these actions was precipitated by an incident in Montgomery, Alabama, in December 1955, when a woman named Rosa Parks refused to move to a seat at the back of the bus, where bus regulations required blacks to sit. When Parks was arrested, Montgomery blacks, acting under King's general leadership, began a boycott of the bus system that involved unprecedented mass meetings in local black churches and lasted until the city finally desegregated its public transportation a year later. This success spurred similar actions elsewhere against the racial caste system and propelled King and the SCLC to the forefront of civil rights protest.

In the early 1960s the Congress of Racial Equality sent "freedom riders" on bus trips into the South to find out whether interstate bus facilities were integrated. A new group, the Student Nonviolent Coordinating Committee (SNCC), organized sit-ins in segregated cafes, stand-ins at segregated theaters, and swim-ins at segregated beaches. Then in early 1963, King and the SCLC organized boycotts and marches in the industrial city of Birmingham, Alabama, during which thousands of black men, women, and children were beaten, shot at, attacked by dogs, sprayed with hoses, and imprisoned. Among the imprisoned was King. The Birmingham protests ended after important city business and civic leaders pledged to begin the process of local desegregation.

In June 1963 President John F. Kennedy asked for congressional action to bar segregation in public accommodations. In August of that summer, over 250,000 people gathered in Washington to demonstrate in support of this initiative and on behalf of civil and voting rights for African-Americans. The keynote speaker to this immense throng, collected at the foot of the Lincoln Memorial in the largest and possibly the last multiracial gathering of its type, was Martin Luther King, Jr., the movement's greatest orator and its most inspiring and distinguished leader. His speech, "I Have a Dream," was soon a part of the American language and consciousness.

Questions to Consider. What was King asking in his speech? What different groups did he seem to have in mind as he delivered it? Which groups, hearing or reading King's words, would have been most responsive to his message? Which groups, hearing or reading his words, would have been most unresponsive or hostile? Why was King careful to mention Stone Mountain and Lookout Mountain as well as the Rockies? Why did he end by invoking religious as well as racial tolerance even though the civil rights struggle was against race-based injustice? Did he seem aware that the civil rights movement might move into a new period of bitterness, confrontation, and violence? Are King's words still moving today?

I Have a Dream (1963)

MARTIN LUTHER KING, JR.

Five score years ago, a great American, in whose symbolic shadow we stand, signed the Emancipation Proclamation. This momentous decree came as a great beacon light of hope to millions of Negro slaves who had been seared in the flames of withering injustice. It came as a joyous daybreak to end the long night of captivity.

But one hundred years later, we must face the tragic fact that the Negro is still not free. One hundred years later, the life of the Negro is still sadly crippled by the manacles of segregation and the chains of discrimination. One hundred years later, the Negro lives on a lonely island of poverty in the midst of a vast ocean of material prosperity. One hundred years later, the Negro is still languishing in the corners of American society and finds himself an exile in his own land. So we have come here today to dramatize an appalling condition. . . .

We have also come to this hallowed spot to remind America of the fierce urgency of *now*. This is not time to engage in the luxury of cooling off or to take the tranquilizing drug of gradualism. *Now* is the time to make real the promises of democracy. *Now* is the time to rise from the dark and desolate valley of segregation to the sunlit path of racial justice. *Now* is the time to open the doors of opportunity to all of God's children. *Now* is the time to lift our nation from the quicksands of racial injustice to the solid rock of brotherhood.

It would be fatal for the nation to overlook the urgency of the moment and to underestimate the determination of the Negro. This sweltering summer of the Negro's legitimate discontent will not pass until there is an invigorating autumn of freedom and equality. Nineteen sixty-three is not an end, but a beginning. Those who hope that the Negro needed to blow off steam and will now be content will have a rude awakening if the nation returns to business as usual. There will be neither rest nor tranquillity in America until the Negro is granted his citizenship rights. The whirlwinds of revolt will continue to shake the foundations of our nation until the bright day of justice emerges.

But there is something that I must say to my people who stand on the warm threshold which leads into the palace of justice. In the process of gaining our rightful place we must not be guilty of wrongful deeds. Let us not seek to satisfy our thirst for freedom by drinking from the cup of bitterness and hatred. We must forever conduct our struggle on the high plane of dig-

Reprinted by arrangement with The Heirs to the Estate of Martin Luther King, Jr., c/o Writers House, Inc., as agent for the proprietor. Copyright 1963 by Martin Luther King, Jr. Copyright renewed 1991 by Coretta Scott King.

"I have a dream." Dr. Martin Luther King, Jr., spoke to over two hundred thousand people gathered at the Lincoln Memorial in August 1963. (Corbis-Bettmann)

nity and discipline. We must not allow our creative protest to degenerate into physical violence. Again and again we must rise to the majestic heights of meeting physical force with soul force.

The marvelous new militancy which has engulfed the Negro community must not lead us to a distrust of all white people, for many of our white brothers, as evidenced by their presence here today, have come to realize that their freedom is inextricably bound to our freedom. We cannot walk alone.

And as we walk, we must make the pledge that we shall march ahead. We cannot turn back. There are those who are asking the devotees of civil rights, "When will you be satisfied?"

We can never be satisfied as long as the Negro is the victim of the unspeakable horrors of police brutality.

We can never be satisfied as long as our bodies, heavy with fatigue of travel, cannot gain lodging in the motels of the highways and the cities.

We cannot be satisfied as long as the Negro's basic mobility is from a smaller ghetto to a larger one.

We can never be satisfied as long as a Negro in Mississippi cannot vote and a Negro in New York believes he has nothing for which to vote.

No, no, we are not satisfied, and we will not be satisfied until justice rolls down like waters and righteousness like a mighty stream. . . .

Go back to Mississippi, go back to Alabama, go back to South Carolina, go back to Georgia, go back to Louisiana, go back to the slums and ghettos of our Northern cities, knowing that somehow this situation can and will be changed. Let us not wallow in the valley of despair.

I say to you today, my friends, that in spite of the difficulties and frustrations of the moment I still have a dream. It is a dream deeply rooted in the American dream.

I have a dream that one day this nation will rise up and live out the true meaning of its creed: "We hold these truths to be self-evident; that all men are created equal."

I have a dream that one day on the red hills of Georgia the sons of former slaves and the sons of former slaveowners will be able to sit down together at the table of brotherhood.

I have a dream that one day even the state of Mississippi, a desert state sweltering with the heat of injustice and oppression, will be transformed into an oasis of freedom and justice.

I have a dream that my four little children will one day live in a nation where they will not be judged by the color of their skin but by the content of their character.

I have a dream today.

I have a dream that one day the state of Alabama, whose governor's lips are presently dripping with the words of interposition and nullification, will be transformed into a situation where little black boys and black girls will be able to join hands with little white boys and girls and walk together as sisters and brothers.

I have a dream today.

I have a dream that one day every valley shall be exalted, every hill and mountain shall be made low, the rough places will be made plain, and the crooked places will be made straight, and the glory of the Lord shall be revealed, and all flesh shall see it together.

This is our hope. This is the faith with which I return to the South. With this faith we will be able to hew out of the mountain of despair a stone of hope. With this faith we will be able to transform the jangling discords of our nation into a beautiful symphony of brotherhood.

With this faith we will be able to work together, to pray together, to struggle together, to go to jail together, to stand up for freedom together, knowing that we will be free one day.

This will be the day when all of God's children will be able to sing with new meaning, "My country 'tis of thee, sweet land of liberty, of thee I sing. Land where my father died, land of the Pilgrims' pride, from every mountainside, let freedom ring."

And if America is to be a great nation, this must become true. So let freedom ring from the prodigious hilltops of New Hampshire. Let freedom ring from the mighty mountains of New York. Let freedom ring from the heightening Alleghenies of Pennsylvania!

Let freedom ring from the snowcapped Rockies of Colorado! Let freedom ring from the curvaceous peaks of California! But not only that; let freedom ring from Stone Mountain of Georgia! Let freedom ring from Lookout Mountain of Tennessee!

Let freedom ring from every hill and molehill of Mississippi. From every mountainside, let freedom ring.

When we let freedom ring, when we let it ring from every village and every hamlet, from every state and every city, we will be able to speed up that day when all of God's children, black men and white men, Jews and Gentiles, Protestants and Catholics, will be able to join hands and sing in the words of the old Negro spiritual, "Free at last! Free at last! Thank God Almighty, we are free at last!"

41

Women's Liberation

After its bright triumph of the early 1920s, interest in the movement for women's rights lagged, then gathered new steam in the 1950s. This resurgence resulted partly from a trend in the workforce: 27 percent of adult women worked outside the home in 1940, 33 percent in 1960, and 50 percent in 1980. With so many women in the workforce, they gradually made their concerns heard: equal pay for equal work, managerial positions in heretofore all-male administrations, elimination of sexual and physical harassment. Working wives, it turned out, often strained traditional male-dominant marriages, and both the divorce rate and the need for new child-care arrangements increased. Also, married or not, working women saw their lives focusing less exclusively on children and domesticity. They therefore looked increasingly to modern birth control devices and to abortion. (The Supreme Court declared abortion legal in 1973.) From 1960 to 1980, the birth rate decreased 50 percent.

But if these trends provided the underpinnings for the modern women's movement, true feminism—the struggle for women's liberation—came only with the addition of "consciousness raising" to these socioeconomic tendencies. Here, too, there was a crucial underlying trend: many more women were college-educated than ever before. In 1940 approximately 15 percent of American women had completed at least one year of college, and women earned about one-fourth of all bachelor's degrees given by U.S. colleges. By 1960, about 20 percent of all women had gone to college, and women earned one-third of all bachelor's degrees. By 1980, the percentage of women attending college had increased to 40 percent and women earned nearly half of all U.S. bachelor's degrees.

In part, Betty Friedan was addressing these millions of educated but underemployed women in her pathbreaking *The Feminine Mystique,* published in 1963 and excerpted below. Friedan attacked the mass media for brainwashing women into models of domesticity. The National Organization for Women (NOW), created in 1966 with Friedan's support, pressed for eliminating all discriminatory legal sexual distinctions. A half-century after the suffrage amendment, politics witnessed major gains for women. They became governors in numerous states, including Texas, one of the three largest. Women senators were elected from several states, including Florida, another of the three largest. Mayors in many of the nation's largest cities, including Chicago and Houston, were women. They held three cabinet positions under Jimmy Carter and one each under Reagan and Bush. Two women were appointed Supreme Court justices, and one ran as a Democratic party vice-presidential candidate. Women were commonplace in the American military force sent to the Persian Gulf in 1991, although not initially in official combat roles.

Betty Friedan was born in 1921 in Illinois and attended Smith College and the University of California at Berkeley. In the early 1960s Friedan was a wife and mother who, having lost her job as a newspaper reporter, was contributing to popular magazines. Noticing that editors frequently cut her references to women's careers in favor of more material on homemaking, she began to analyze the housewife fantasy and to interview housewives themselves. The result was *The Feminine Mystique* (1963), an instant best seller that catapulted its author to the forefront of the women's movement and earned her countless offers to lecture and teach. Friedan was the founding president of the National Organization for Women from 1966 to 1970 and also helped found the National Women's Political Caucus and the National Association to Repeal Abortion Laws. None of it was easy. "A lot of people," she recalled, "treated me like a leper."

Questions to Consider. Betty Friedan argued in *The Feminine Mystique* that American women suffered from a "problem that has no name." What was that problem? Was she the first to discover it? What were her methods of investigating and reporting it? Why did it have no name? Did Friedan name it? Would all American women have responded to Friedan's arguments? What kinds of women would have been most likely to respond? How revolutionary was her message? What social or political measures would be required to deal effectively with this problem?

The Feminine Mystique (1963)

BETTY FRIEDAN

The suburban housewife—she was the dream image of the young American women and the envy, it was said, of women all over the world. The Ameri-

Excerpted from *The Feminine Mystique* by Betty Friedan. Copyright © 1963 by Betty Friedan and renewed 1991 by Betty Friedan. Reprinted by permission of W. W. Norton & Company, Inc.

A balding Jock Semple of the Boston Athletic Association accosts Karen Switzer of Syracuse in an effort to enforce the BAA's rule barring women from running in the Boston Marathon, 1967. In the late 1960s there were still few opportunities for women to participate in serious sports at any level, a situation that changed significantly only with the passage of federal antidiscrimination legislation. (Corbis-Bettmann)

can housewife—freed by science and labor-saving appliances from the drudgery, the dangers of childbirth and the illnesses of her grandmother. She was healthy, beautiful, educated, concerned only about her husband, her children, her home. She had found true feminine fulfillment. As a housewife and mother, she was respected as a full and equal partner to man in his world. She was free to choose automobiles, clothes, appliances, supermarkets; she had everything that women ever dreamed of.

In the fifteen years after World War II, this mystique of feminine fulfillment became the cherished and self-perpetuating core of contemporary American culture. Millions of women lived their lives in the image of those pretty pictures of the American suburban housewife, kissing their husbands goodbye in front of the picture window, depositing their stationwagonsful of children at school, and smiling as they ran the new electric waxer over the spotless kitchen floor. They baked their own bread, sewed their own and their children's clothes, kept their new washing machines and dryers running all day. They changed the sheets on the beds twice a week instead of once, took the rug-hooking class in adult education, and pitied their poor frustrated mothers, who had dreamed of having a career. Their only dream was to be perfect wives and mothers; their highest ambition to have five children and a beautiful house, their only fight to get and keep their husbands. They had no thought for the unfeminine problems of the world outside the home; they wanted the men to make the major decisions. They gloried in their role as women, and wrote proudly on the census blank: "Occupation: housewife."

For over fifteen years, the words written for women, and the words women used when they talked to each other, while their husbands sat on the other side of the room and talked shop or politics or septic tanks, were about problems with their children, or how to keep their husbands happy, or improve their children's school, or cook chicken or make slipcovers. Nobody argued whether women were inferior or superior to men; they were simply different. Words like *emancipation* and *career* sounded strange and embarrassing; no one had used them for years. . . .

But on an April morning in 1959, I heard a mother of four, having coffee with four other mothers in a suburban development fifteen miles from New York, say in a tone of quiet desperation, "the problem." And the others knew, without words, that she was not talking about a problem with her husband, or her children, or her home. Suddenly they realized they all shared the same problem, the problem that has no name. They began, hesitantly, to talk about it. Later, after they had picked up their children at nursery school and taken them home to nap, two of the women cried, in sheer relief, just to know they were not alone. . . .

Just what was this problem that has no name? What were the words women used when they tried to express it? Sometimes a woman would say "I feel empty somehow . . . incomplete." Or she would say, "I feel as if I don't exist." Sometimes she blotted out the feeling with a tranquilizer. Sometimes she thought the problem was with her husband, or her children, or that what she really needed was to redecorate her house, or move to a better neighborhood, or have an affair, or another baby. Sometimes, she went to a doctor with symptoms she could hardly describe: "A tired feeling . . . I get so angry with the children it scares me . . . I feel like crying without any reason." (A Cleveland doctor called it "the housewife's syndrome.") A number of women told me about great bleeding blisters that break out on their hands and arms. "I call it the housewife's blight," said a family doctor in Pennsylvania. "I see it so often lately in these young women with four, five and six children who bury themselves in their dishpans. But it isn't caused by detergent and it isn't cured by cortisone." . . .

In 1960, the problem that has no name burst like a boil through the image of the happy American housewife. In the television commercials the pretty housewives still beamed over their foaming dishpans and *Time's* cover story on "The Suburban Wife, an American Phenomenon" protested: "Having too good a time . . . to believe that they should be unhappy." But the actual unhappiness of the American housewife was suddenly being reported—from the *New York Times* and *Newsweek* to *Good Housekeeping* and CBS Television ("The Trapped Housewife"), although almost everybody who talked about it found some superficial reason to dismiss it. . . .

Of the growing thousands of women currently getting private psychiatric help in the United States, the married ones were reported dissatisfied with their marriages, the unmarried ones suffering from anxiety and, finally, depression. Strangely, a number of psychiatrists stated that, in their experience, unmarried women patients were happier than married ones. So the door of all those pretty suburban houses opened a crack to permit a glimpse of uncounted thousands of American housewives who suffered alone from a problem that suddenly everyone was talking about, and beginning to take for granted, as one of those unreal problems in American life that can never be solved—like the hydrogen bomb. . . .

I do not accept the answer that there is no problem because American women have luxuries that women in other times and lands never dreamed of; part of the strange newness of the problem is that it cannot be understood in terms of the age-old material problems of man: poverty, sickness, hunger, cold. The women who suffer this problem have a hunger that food cannot fill. . . .

Are the women who finished college, the women who once had dreams beyond housewifery, the ones who suffer the most? According to the experts they are, but . . . housewives of all educational levels suffer the same feeling of desperation.

The fact is that no one today is muttering angrily about "women's rights," even though more and more women have gone to college. In a recent study of all the classes that have graduated from Barnard College, a significant minority of earlier graduates blamed their education for making them want "rights," later classes blamed their education for giving them career dreams, but recent graduates blamed the college for making them feel it was not enough simply to be a housewife and mother; they did not want to feel guilty if they did not read books or take part in community activities. But if education is not the cause of the problem, the fact that education somehow festers in these women may be a clue.

If the secret of feminine fulfillment is having children, never have so many women, with the freedom to choose, had so many children, in so few years, so willingly. If the answer is love, never have women searched for love with such determination. And yet there is a growing suspicion that the problem may not be sexual, though it must somehow be related to sex. I have heard from many doctors evidence of new sexual problems between man and wife—sexual hunger in wives so great their husbands cannot satisfy it. . . .

Can the problem that has no name be somehow related to the domestic routine of the housewife? When a woman tries to put the problem into words, she often merely describes the daily life she leads. What is there in this recital of comfortable domestic detail that could possibly cause such a feeling of desperation? Is she trapped simply by the enormous demands of her role as modern housewife: wife, mistress, mother, nurse, consumer, cook, chauffeur; expert on interior decoration, child care, appliance repair, furniture refinishing, nutrition, and education? . . .

If I am right, the problem that has no name stirring in the minds of so many American women today is not a matter of loss of femininity or too much education, or the demands of domesticity. It is far more important than anyone recognizes. It is the key to these other new and old problems which have been torturing women and their husbands and children, and puzzling their doctors and educators for years. It may well be the key to our future as a nation and a culture. We can no longer ignore that voice within women that says: "I want something more than my husband and my children and my home."

42

Backlash and Riot

The 1954 Supreme Court decision in *Brown* v. *The Board of Education of Topeka* and the 1955 Montgomery bus boycott marked the beginning of the modern civil rights movement, an enterprise that in the 1950s engaged the efforts of both blacks and whites. Within a few short years of these important victories, however, the character of the movement changed. Predominantly black civil rights organizations, such as the National Association for the Advancement of Colored People (NAACP) and the Southern Christian Leadership Conference (SCLS), had initially welcomed the support and participation of whites. But in the early 1960s, when civil rights activists sought to secure voting rights, a savage white backlash ensued that fueled the anger of young African-Americans. Whites, they believed, should get out of the movement.

Martin Luther King's "I Have a Dream" speech, made in 1963 before the largest crowd ever assembled in the cause of civil rights, was a stunning moment of interracial harmony. But the March on Washington marked the beginning of the end of peaceful multiracial protest. Massive, fiercely contested voter registration drives were underway in the South. Black protest leadership passed to groups such as the Black Muslims, a sect that preached black pride and separatism and condemned whites as "devils," and the Black Panthers, who espoused a blend of black nationalism and revolutionary Communism.

More ominously, urban violence now erupted in the North. The horrifying riot in the Watts ghetto of Los Angeles in 1965 lasted four days, killed 34 people, destroyed 750 buildings and 200 businesses, and resulted in 3,900 arrests. In the summer of 1967 ghetto riots exploded in 127 American cities, including Detroit, where 43 people died and fire gutted 14 square miles, and Newark, the scene of 26 deaths and 1,500 injuries. Another 168 cities experienced ghetto riots following the assassination of Martin Luther King, Jr., in April 1968, leaving another 46 people dead and $40 million worth of damage.

In 1968 President Lyndon B. Johnson appointed a commission to study urban rioting and how to prevent it. Chaired by Illinois governor Otto Kerner, the commission produced a major study of ghetto behavior and conditions and their causes and consequences. The Kerner Commission called "white racism" the single most important factor in triggering urban violence and made sweeping federal policy recommendations to keep the United States from becoming two nations, black and white, separate and unequal. The report influenced the passage of the Fair Housing Act of 1968 and the Supreme Court's approval of forced busing as a way to combat de facto school segregation. It also led universities to admit more students of color, if need be through affirmative action guidelines that would allow more minority admissions.

Questions to Consider. The Kerner Commission report focused on underlying conditions as well as violent behavior. Why might its authors have taken this approach? Some critics accused the Commission of excusing violent behavior by placing such stress on the conditions that produced it rather than on the bad behavior itself. Was this a valid criticism? Other critics argued that it was pointless to blame racist attitudes for ghetto conditions and therefore ghetto violence because government policies could not really change attitudes and so the report seemed doomed to failure. Was this a valid criticism? Lastly, some critics said the report neglected important factors promoting urban violence, including the unhealthy consequences of an uncontrolled gun culture, an uncontrolled drug culture, and an uncontrolled mass commercial culture. Should the Commission have addressed these issues?

Report of the Commission on Civil Disorders (1968)

Why did it happen?

In addressing this question we shift our focus from the local to the national scene, from the particular events of the summer of 1967 to the factors within the society at large which have brought about the sudden violent mood of so many urban Negroes.

The record before this Commission reveals that the causes of recent racial disorders are imbedded in a massive tangle of issues and circumstances—social, economic, political, and psychological—which arise out of the historical pattern of Negro-white relations in America.

From *Report of the National Advisory Commission on Civil Disorders* (Government Printing Office, Washington, D.C., 1968), 203–208.

These factors are both complex and interacting; they vary significantly in their effect from city to city and from year to year; and the consequences of one disorder, generating new grievances and new demands, become the causes of the next. It is this which creates the "thicket of tension, conflicting evidence and extreme opinions" cited by the President.

Despite these complexities, certain fundamental matters are clear. Of these, the most fundamental is the racial attitude and behavior of white Americans toward black Americans. Race prejudice has shaped our history decisively in the past; it now threatens to do so again. White racism is essentially responsible for the explosive mixture which has been accumulating in our cities since the end of World War II. At the base of this mixture are three of the most bitter fruits of white racial attitudes:

Pervasive discrimination and segregation. The first is surely the continuing exclusion of great numbers of Negroes from the benefits of economic progress through discrimination in employment and education, and their enforced confinement in segregated housing and schools. The corrosive and degrading effects of this condition and the attitudes that underlie it are the source of the deepest bitterness and at the center of the problem of racial disorder.

Black migration and white exodus. The second is the massive and growing concentration of impoverished Negroes in our major cities resulting from Negro migration from the rural South, rapid population growth and the continuing movement of the white middle-class to the suburbs. The consequence is a greatly increased burden on the already depleted resources of cities, creating a growing crisis of deteriorating facilities and services and unmet human needs.

Black ghettos. Third, in the teeming racial ghettos, segregation and poverty have intersected to destroy opportunity and hope and to enforce failure. The ghettos too often mean men and women without jobs, families without men, and schools where children are processed instead of educated, until they return to the street—to crime, to narcotics, to dependency on welfare, and to bitterness and resentment against society in general and white society in particular.

These three forces have converged on the inner city in recent years and on the people who inhabit it. At the same time, most whites and many Negroes outside the ghetto have prospered to a degree unparalleled in the history of civilization. Through television—the universal appliance in the ghetto—and the other media of mass communications, this affluence has been endlessly flaunted before the eyes of the Negro poor and the jobless ghetto youth.

As Americans, most Negro citizens carry within themselves two basic aspirations of our society. They seek to share in both the material resources of our system and its intangible benefits—dignity, respect and acceptance. Outside the ghetto many have succeeded in achieving a decent standard of life, and in developing the inner resources which give life meaning and direction. Within the ghetto, however, it is rare that either aspiration is achieved.

Yet these facts alone—fundamental as they are—cannot be said to have caused the disorders. Other and more immediate factors help explain why these events happened now.

Recently, three powerful ingredients have begun to catalyze the mixture.

Frustrated hopes. The expectations aroused by the great judicial and legislative victories of the civil rights movement have led to frustration, hostility and cynicism in the face of the persistent gap between promise and fulfillment. The dramatic struggle for equal rights in the South has sensitized Northern Negroes to the economic inequalities reflected in the deprivations of ghetto life.

Legitimation of violence. A climate that tends toward the approval and encouragement of violence as a form of protest has been created by white terrorism directed against nonviolent protest, including instances of abuse and even murder of some civil rights workers in the South; by the open defiance of law and federal authority by state and local officials resisting desegregation; and by some protest groups engaging in civil disobedience who turn their backs on nonviolence, go beyond the Constitutionally protected rights of petition and free assembly, and resort to violence to attempt to compel alteration of laws and policies with which they disagree. This condition has been reinforced by a general erosion of respect for authority in American society and reduced effectiveness of social standards and community restraints on violence and crime. This in turn has largely resulted from rapid urbanization and the dramatic reduction in the average age of the total population.

Powerlessness. Finally, many Negroes have come to believe that they are being exploited politically and economically by the white "power structure." Negroes, like people in poverty everywhere, in fact lack the channels of communication, influence and appeal that traditionally have been available to ethnic minorities within the city and which enabled them—unburdened by color—to scale the walls of the white ghettos in an earlier era. The frustrations of powerlessness have led some to the conviction that there is no effective alternative to violence as a means of expression and redress, as a way of "moving the system." More generally, the result is alienation and hostility toward the institutions of law and government and the white society which controls them. This is reflected in the reach toward racial consciousness and solidarity reflected in the slogan "Black Power."

These facts have combined to inspire a new mood among Negroes, particularly among the young. Self-esteem and enhanced racial pride are replacing apathy and submission to "the system." Moreover, Negro youth, who make up over half of the ghetto population, share the growing sense of alienation felt by many white youth in our country. Thus, their role in recent civil disorders reflects not only a shared sense of deprivation and victimization by white society but also the rising incidence of disruptive conduct by a segment of American youth throughout the society.

Incitement and encouragement of violence. These conditions have created a volatile mixture of attitudes and beliefs which needs only a spark to ignite mass violence. Strident appeals to violence, first heard from white racists, were echoed and reinforced last summer in the inflammatory rhetoric of black racists and militants. Throughout the year, extremists crisscrossed the country preaching a doctrine of black power and violence. Their rhetoric was widely reported in the mass media; it was echoed by local "militants" and organizations; it became the ugly background noise of the violent summer.

We cannot measure with any precision the influence of these organizations and individuals in the ghetto, but we think it clear that the intolerable and unconscionable encouragement of violence heightened tensions, created a mood of acceptance and an expectation of violence, and thus contributed to the eruption of the disorders last summer.

The Police. It is the convergence of all these factors that makes the role of the police so difficult and so significant. Almost invariably the incident that ignites disorder arises from police action. Harlem, Watts, Newark and Detroit—all the major outbursts of recent years—were precipitated by routine arrests of Negroes for minor offenses by white police.

But the police are not merely the spark. In discharge of their obligation to maintain order and insure public safety in the disruptive conditions of ghetto life, they are inevitably involved in sharper and more frequent conflicts with ghetto residents than with the residents of other areas. Thus, to many Negroes police have come to symbolize white power, white racism and white repression. And the fact is that many police do reflect and express these white attitudes. The atmosphere of hostility and cynicism is reinforced by a widespread perception among Negroes of the existence of police brutality and corruption, and of a "double standard" of justice and protection—one for Negroes and one for whites.

43

Life and Choice

Except for a brief "baby boom" period after 1945, the number of children born to the average American woman has steadily decreased since the early nineteenth century. She had seven children on average in the early 1800s, four in the late 1800s, three in the early 1900s, two in the late 1900s. In the nineteenth century, the chief methods for limiting births were primitive contraception, abstinence, and, especially, abortion. In the early twentieth century, however, abortion became illegal in most states, and abstinence in marriage was less acceptable to husbands and wives. Improved contraception and delays in first marriages therefore became increasingly important birth-limiting measures. The falling birthrate since 1960 has come chiefly from a dramatic improvement in contraceptive techniques, especially contraceptive sterilization, the pill, the intrauterine device, and the vaginal sponge. Less important but still significant has been a rise in abortion rates, most notably in the five years that followed the historic 1973 Supreme Court decision in *Roe* v. *Wade,* which ruled restrictive state abortion laws unconstitutional.

Roe v. *Wade* reflected major changes in American society. These included advances in birth control technology, a desire to limit family size, and, especially, increased attention to the rights of women. One of these rights, according to modern feminists, is "reproductive freedom," of which abortion on demand was a crucial part. *Roe* v. *Wade* also typified a notable long-term shift in how the Supreme Court has viewed Constitutional "rights"—or at least the question of which rights are the truly vital ones. In theory, all rights in the Constitution are of equal value, but over the years the Court, reflecting changes in social values, has always cherished some rights as more important than others. In the nation's early days, private property was given special consideration; later this came to include the rights of businesses and liberty of contract. Then, in the 1930s and 1940s, economic rights lost pride of place to the rights enumerated in the First Amendment. In recent years the right to vote and to attend racially integrated schools has been judged to be of fundamental importance. With the *Roe* v. *Wade* decision, so has the right to privacy.[1]

Justice Harry Blackmun's decision, which invalidated the statutes of thirty states that forbade abortions except to save the mother's life, sparked bitter controversy. "Prolife" forces, most affiliated with religious denominations and uncompromisingly opposed to abortion, denounced the ruling. They called for a Constitutional amendment defining human life as beginning at conception, picketed abortion clinics, and successfully urged Congress to curtail most Medicaid funds for abortions. Meanwhile, "prochoice" advocates organized in support of the right of a woman (rather than the state) to choose whether or not to have an abortion. They also supported doctors' rights to perform abortions and poor women's rights to obtain them. By the 1980s, a political candidate's position on abortion could make or break a campaign, just as a Supreme Court nominee's position on *Roe* v. *Wade* could make or break a Court nomination.

Harry Blackmun, author of the *Roe* v. *Wade* decision, was born in Illinois in 1908. He grew up in the Minneapolis-St. Paul area and then headed east to attend Harvard College and Harvard Law School. Blackmun returned to Minneapolis to open a private practice before moving to Rochester, Minnesota, as legal counsel for the world-famous Mayo Clinic. A hard-working, serious-minded, moderate Republican, he was first appointed to the federal judiciary by President Dwight Eisenhower in 1959. Blackmun, a boyhood friend of Chief Justice Warren Burger, was promoted to the Supreme Court in 1970 after the Senate had rejected Richard Nixon's first two nominations to fill a recent vacancy. Although Blackmun was initially perceived as Burger's "Minnesota twin," the *Roe* v. *Wade* ruling (from which Justices Byron White and William Rehnquist dissented) marked the beginning of his drift away from the conservative Burger wing of the Court toward the more liberal wing associated with Justice William Brennan.

Questions to Consider. On what two Constitutional grounds did the appellant seek to overturn restrictive Texas abortion laws? Of the three reasons commonly given to justify restricting abortions since the nineteenth century, which did Blackmun consider most important? Where in the Constitution did he find grounds for the right to privacy claimed by the appellant? Did Blackmun consider a woman's right to privacy a guarantee of an absolute right to abortion? The State of Texas (the appellee) argued that states could restrict abortion because the state has a "compelling interest" in protecting the right of an unborn fetus under the

1. In *Rust* v. *Sullivan* (1991) the Supreme Court decided that medical personnel in family planning clinics receiving federal funds may not mention abortion or abortion facilities to clients.

provisions of the Fourteenth Amendment. How did Blackmun deal with this argument? Why did he call Texas's position "one theory of life"? Why did Blackmun discuss "trimesters" and "viability" at such length? If medical technology were to shift the point of viability from the third to the second trimester, would that undercut the force of *Roe* v. *Wade*?

Roe v. *Wade* (1973)

HARRY BLACKMUN

The principal thrust of appellant's attack on the Texas statutes is that they improperly invade a right, said to be possessed by the pregnant woman, to choose to terminate her pregnancy. Appellant would discover this right in the concept of personal "liberty" embodied in the Fourteenth Amendment's Due Process Clause; or in personal, marital, familial, and sexual privacy said to be protected by the Bill of Rights.

It perhaps is not generally appreciated that the restrictive criminal abortion laws in effect in a majority of States today are of relatively recent vintage. Those laws, generally proscribing abortion or its attempt at any time during pregnancy except when necessary to preserve the pregnant woman's life, are not of ancient or even of common law origin. Instead, they derive from statutory changes effected, for the most part, in the latter half of the nineteenth century. . . .

Three reasons have been advanced to explain historically the enactment of criminal abortion laws in the nineteenth century and to justify their continued existence.

It has been argued occasionally that these laws were the product of a Victorian social concern to discourage illicit sexual conduct. Texas, however, does not advance this justification in the present case, and it appears that no court or commentator has taken the argument seriously. . . .

A second reason is concerned with abortion as a medical procedure. When most criminal abortion laws were first enacted, the procedure was a hazardous one for the woman. . . . Modern medical techniques have altered this situation. Appellants refer to medical data indicating that abortion in early pregnancy, that is, prior to the end of first trimester, although not without its risk, is now relatively safe. . . . The State retains a definite interest in protecting the woman's own health and safety when an abortion is proposed at a late stage of pregnancy.

The third reason is the State's interest—some phrase it in terms of duty—in protecting prenatal life. Some of the argument for this justification rests

From *Roe* v. *Wade*, 410 U.S. 113 (1973).

on the theory that a new human life is present from the moment of conception. The State's interest and general obligation to protect life then extends, it is argued, to prenatal life. Only when the life of the pregnant mother herself is at stake, balanced against the life she carries within her, should the interest of the embryo or fetus not prevail. Logically, of course, a legitimate State interest in this area need not stand or fall on acceptance of the belief that life begins at conception or at some other point prior to live birth. In assessing the State's interest, recognition may be given to the less rigid claim that as long as at least *potential* life is involved, the State may assert interests beyond the protection of the pregnant woman alone. . . .

The Constitution does not explicitly mention any right of privacy. In a line of decisions, however, going back perhaps as far as *Union Pacific R. Co.* v. *Botsford* (1891), the Court has recognized that a right of personal privacy, or a guarantee of certain areas or zones of privacy, does exist under the Constitution. . . . These decisions make it clear that only personal rights that can be deemed "fundamental" or "implicit in the concept of ordered liberty," are included in this guarantee of personal privacy. They also make it clear that the right has some extension to activities relating to marriage, procreation, contraception. . . .[1]

This right of privacy, whether it be founded in the Fourteenth Amendment's concept of personal liberty and restrictions upon state action, as we feel it is, or, as the District Court determined, in the Ninth Amendment's reservation of rights to the people, is broad enough to encompass a woman's decision whether or not to terminate her pregnancy. The detriment that the State would impose upon the pregnant woman by denying this choice altogether is apparent. Specific and direct harm medically diagnosable even in early pregnancy may be involved. Maternity, or additional offspring, may force upon the woman a distressful life and future. Psychological harm may be imminent. Mental and physical health may be taxed by child care. There is also the distress, for all concerned, associated with the unwanted child, and there is the problem of bringing a child into a family already unable, psychologically and otherwise, to care for it. In other cases, as in this one, the additional difficulties and continuing stigma of unwed motherhood may be involved. All these are factors the woman and her responsible physician necessarily will consider in consultation. . . .

On the basis of elements such as these, appellants argue that the woman's right is absolute and that she is entitled to terminate her pregnancy at whatever time, in whatever way, and for whatever reason she alone chooses. With this we do not agree. Appellant's arguments that Texas either has no valid interest at all in regulating the abortion decision, or no interest strong enough to support any limitation upon the woman's sole determination, is unpersuasive. The Court's decisions recognizing a right of privacy also acknowledge that some state regulation in areas protected by that right is

1. References to prior court decisons have been omitted.

appropriate. As noted above, a State may properly assert important interests in safeguarding health, in maintaining medical standards, and in protecting potential life. At some point in pregnancy, these respective interests become sufficiently compelling to sustain regulation of the factors that govern the abortion decision. The privacy right involved, therefore, cannot be said to be absolute. In fact, it is not clear to us that the claim . . . that one has an unlimited right to do with one's body as one pleases bears a close relationship to the right of privacy previously articulated in the Court's decisions. The Court has refused to recognize an unlimited right of this kind in the past.

We therefore conclude that the right of personal privacy includes the abortion decision, but that this right is not unqualified and must be considered against state interests in regulation. . . .

Appellee [the state of Texas] argues that the State's determination to recognize and protect prenatal life from and after conception constitutes a compelling state interest. We do not agree fully. . . .

The Constitution does not define "person" in so many words. Section 1 of the Fourteenth Amendment contains three references to "person." The first, in defining "citizens," speaks of "persons born or naturalized in the United States." The word also appears both in the Due Process Clause and in the Equal Protection Clause. "Person" is used in other places in the Constitution. . . . But in nearly all these instances, the use of the word is such that it has application only postnatally. None indicates, with any assurance, that it has any possible prenatal application. All this, together with our observation, that throughout the major portion of the nineteenth century prevailing legal abortion practices were far freer than they are today, persuades us that the word "person," as used in the Fourteenth Amendment, does not include the unborn. . . .

Texas urges that, apart from the Fourteenth Amendment, life begins at conception and is present throughout pregnancy, and that, therefore, the State has a compelling interest in protecting that life from and after conception. We need not resolve the difficult question of when life begins. When those trained in the respective disciplines of medicine, philosophy, and theology are unable to arrive at any consensus, the judiciary, at this point in the development of man's knowledge, is not in a position to speculate as to the answer.

In view of all this, we do not agree that, by adopting one theory of life, Texas may override the rights of the pregnant woman that are at stake. We repeat, however, that the State does have an important and legitimate interest in preserving and protecting the health of the pregnant woman, whether she be a resident of the State or a nonresident who seeks medical consultation and treatment there, and that it has still *another* important and legitimate interest in protecting the potentiality of human life. These interests are separate and distinct. Each grows in substantiality as the woman approaches term and, at a point during pregnancy, each becomes "compelling."

With respect to the State's important and legitimate interest in the health of the mother, the "compelling" point, in the light of present medical knowledge, is at approximately the end of the first trimester. This is so because of the now established medical fact, referred to above . . . that until the end of the first trimester mortality in abortion is less than mortality in normal childbirth. It follows that, from and after this point, a State may regulate the abortion procedure to the extent that the regulation reasonably relates to the preservation and protection of maternal health. Examples of permissible state regulation in this area are requirements as to the qualifications of the person who is to perform the abortion; as to the licensure of that person; as to the facility in which the procedure is to be performed, that is, whether it must be a hospital or may be a clinic or some other place of less-than-hospital status; as to the licensing of the facility; and the like.

This means, on the other hand, that, for the period of pregnancy prior to this "compelling" point, the attending physician, in consultation with his patient, is free to determine, without regulation by the State, that in his medical judgment the patient's pregnancy should be terminated. If that decision is reached, the judgment may be effectuated by an abortion free of interference by the State.

With respect to the State's important and legitimate interest in potential life, the "compelling" point is at viability. This is so because the fetus then presumably has the capability of meaningful life outside the mother's womb. State regulation protective of fetal life after viability thus has both logical and biological justifications. If the State is interested in protecting fetal life after viability, it may go so far as to proscribe abortion during that period except when it is necessary to preserve the life or health of the mother.

Measured against these standards, the Texas Penal Code, in restricting legal abortions to those "procured or attempted by medical advice for the purpose of saving the life of the mother," sweeps too broadly.

To summarize and to repeat:

A state criminal abortion statute of the current Texas type, that excepts from criminality only a *life saving* procedure on behalf of the mother, without regard to pregnancy stage and without recognition of the other interests involved, is violative of the Due Process Clause of the Fourteenth Amendment.

(a) For the stage prior to approximately the end of the first trimester, the abortion decision and its effectuation must be left to the medical judgment of the pregnant woman's attending physician.

(b) For the stage subsequent to approximately the end of the first trimester, the State, in promoting its interest in the health of the mother, may, if it chooses, regulate the abortion procedure in ways that are reasonably related to maternal health.

(c) For the stage subsequent to viability the State, in promoting its interest in the potentiality of human life, may, if it chooses, regulate, and even proscribe, abortion except where it is necessary, in appropriate medical judgment, for the preservation of the life or health of the mother.

Watergate

On June 17, 1972, five men were arrested for rifling the files and tapping the telephones of the Democratic National Committee in the Watergate office building in Washington, D.C. Thus was born the Watergate affair that transfixed the nation for the next two years. All five burglars, it turned out, were former agents of the Central Intelligence Agency (CIA). Two of the men, James McCord and G. Gordon Liddy, were currently working for the Committee to Re-elect the President (CRP, or, popularly, CREEP), an independent organization supporting President Richard Nixon's bid for reelection. McCord and Liddy had connections with another former CIA agent, E. Howard Hunt, who, like Liddy, now served as a White House aide. The other burglars were Cubans who had been associated with the Bay of Pigs operation in Cuba.

After the trial and conviction of the five burglars, McCord broke silence by indicating, first, that the head of CRP himself, none other than former Attorney General John N. Mitchell, had approved the break-in and, second, that White House agents had paid "hush money" to the burglars. Newspaper reporters, the Federal Bureau of Investigation, and a special Senate committee on campaign practices opened investigations and soon learned that CRP had used extortionist tactics to raise an illegal slush fund from corporations for the 1972 presidential campaign, and that CRP had used this fund to pay for burglaries, wiretaps, forgeries, phony demonstrations, and other "dirty tricks" to discredit and punish Nixon critics.

By the summer of 1973 it was clear that President Nixon's closest aides, including advisers H. R. Haldeman and John D. Ehrlichman and counsel John W. Dean, had tried to interfere with the Watergate investigations and were withholding valuable evidence, notably tapes of White House conversations during the period under question. When the Senate committee, wondering who (including President Nixon) knew what, requested access to the tapes, Nixon pleaded executive privilege and refused to release them; and when Archibald Cox, a special Watergate prosecutor whom Nixon had appointed, asked for the tapes, the president ordered Cox's dismissal, even though several Justice Department officials resigned in protest.

During the next few months more than thirty former Nixon advisers were indicted for federal crimes, including Dean, Ehrlichman, Haldeman, Mitchell, and former Secretary of Commerce and CRP finance chairman Maurice Stans. The House Judiciary Committee began preparing articles of impeachment against the president. On August 4, 1974, the Supreme Court ordered Nixon to release the tapes. Investigators, hoping to unearth the "smoking pistol" (direct evidence, if it existed, that the president himself had authorized the cover-up), were eager to examine them.

The tapes did indeed provide such evidence. According to a June 1972 conversation, Nixon knew of the Watergate break-in forty-eight hours after it happened. He also withheld evidence, authorized bribes, and used the FBI and the CIA to thwart congressional investigators. A September 1972 tape showed Nixon's intent, in the aftermath of Watergate, to use the FBI and the Justice Department against the administration's enemies. In March 1973, in response to legal counsel John Dean's concern about washing money—"the sort of thing Mafia people can do"—for paying blackmail, Nixon replied that the money could be obtained. The Watergate scandal came gradually to cover a wide array of wrongdoing: favors in exchange for campaign contributions, misuse of public funds, the deceiving of Congress about the secret bombing of Indochina, and illegal surveillance and espionage of political opponents and journalists. On August 9 Richard Nixon announced his resignation of the presidency.

The House Judiciary Committee ultimately triggered Nixon's resignation by voting to recommend to the full House of Representatives that Nixon be impeached. The vote was by a 2–1 margin. Many Republicans joined the Democratic majority in support of impeachment, although some did not, including future Senate majority leader Trent Lott of Mississippi. Representative Barbara Jordan (D-Texas) provided a powerful summary statement, excerpted below, of the Committee's case against Nixon.

Barbara Jordan was born in Houston, Texas, in 1936 to a Baptist warehouse clerk and his wife. With Texas still segregated, Jordan attended Texas Southern University, an all-black college, then headed to Boston University Law School, where in 1959 she was one of two black women—and one of two women—in a graduating class of 128. Jordan returned to Houston to practice law, became active in the Democratic party, decided not to marry so that she could devote herself to politics, and in 1966 became the first woman ever elected to the Texas Senate and its first African-American since 1883. She entered Congress in 1972, gained national acclaim as a member of the Judiciary Committee, then resigned, partly for reasons of health, in 1978 to teach at the University of Texas.

Questions to Consider. Why did Jordan develop her case by quoting from the men who drafted the Constitution and ratified it? Who seems to have been her main audience as she developed these points? What criticism might she have been anticipating and trying to deflect? Why did she spend so much time on explaining the criteria for impeachment? Did she strengthen her case by quoting from Madison, Joseph Story, and others? How serious do her charges sound? Were there, in fact, sufficient grounds for bringing impeachment charges against Nixon? What actions might Nixon have taken that would have made the case against him even stronger?

Statement on Impeachment (1974)

BARBARA JORDAN

Earlier today we heard the beginning of the Preamble to the Constitution of the United States. "We, the people." It is a very eloquent beginning. But when that document was completed, on the seventeenth of September in 1787, I was not included in that "We, the people." I felt somehow for many years that George Washington and Alexander Hamilton just left me out by mistake. But through the process of amendment, interpretation, and court decision I have finally been included in "We, the people."

Today, I am an inquisitor. I believe hyperbole would not be fictional and would not overstate the solemnness that I feel right now. My faith in the Constitution is whole, it is complete, it is total. I am not going to sit here and be an idle spectator to the diminution, the subversion, the destruction of the Constitution.

"Who can so properly be the inquisitors for the nation as the representatives of the nation themselves?" (*Federalist*, no. 65.) The subject of its jurisdiction are those offenses which proceed from the misconduct of public men. That is what we are talking about. In other words, the jurisdiction comes from the abuse of violation of some public trust. It is wrong. I suggest, it is a misreading of the Constitution for any member here to assert that for a member to vote for an article of impeachment means that that member must be convinced that the president should be removed from office. The

From *The New York Times*, July 23, 1974. Reprinted by permission.

A Robert Pryor cartoon showing Nixon "caught in a web of tapes." Nixon, with his heavy beard, long nose, and narrow shoulders, was a cartoonist's delight throughout his long career. ("Nixon Caught in a Web of Tapes," by Robert Pryor. Courtesy of John Locke Studios, Inc.)

Constitution doesn't say that. The powers relating to impeachment are an essential check in the hands of this body, the legislature, against and upon the encroachment of the executive. In establishing the division between the two branches of the legislature, the House and the Senate, assigning to the one the right to accuse and to the other the right to judge, the framers of this Constitution were very astute. They did not make the accusers and the judges the same person.

We know the nature of impeachment. We have been talking about it awhile now. "It is chiefly designed for the president and his high ministers" to somehow be called into account. It is designed to "bridle" the executive if he engages in excesses. "It is designed as a method of national inquest into the conduct of public men." (Hamilton, *Federalist,* no. 65.) The framers confined in the Congress the power if need be, to remove the president in order to strike a delicate balance between a president swollen with power and grown tyrannical, and preservation of the independence of the executive. The nature of impeachment is a narrowly channeled exception to the separation-of-powers maxim; the federal convention of 1787 said that. It limited impeachment to high crimes and misdemeanors and discounted and opposed the term "maladministration." It is to be used only for great misdemeanors" so it was said in the North Carolina ratification convention. . . .

The drawing of political lines goes to the motivation behind impeachment; but impeachment must proceed within the confines of the constitutional term "high crimes and misdemeanors."

Of the impeachment process, it was Woodrow Wilson who said that "nothing short of the grossest offenses against the plain law of the land will suffice to give them speed and effectiveness. Indignation so great as to overgrow party interest may secure a conviction; but nothing else can."

Common sense would be revolted if we engaged upon this process for petty reasons. Congress has a lot to do. Appropriations, tax reform, health insurance, campaign finance reform, housing, environmental protection, energy sufficiency, mass transportation. Pettiness cannot be allowed to stand in the face of such overwhelming problems. So today we are not being petty. We are trying to be big because the task we have before us is a big one.

This morning, in a discussion of the evidence, we were told that the evidence which purports to support the allegations of misuse of the CIA by the president is thin. We are told that evidence is insufficient. What that recital of the evidence this morning did not include is what the president did know on June 23, 1972. The president did know that it was Republican money, that it was money from the Committee for the Re-Election of the President, which was found in the possession of one of the burglars arrested on June 17.

What the president did know on June 23 was the prior activities of E. Howard Hunt, which included his participation in the break-in of Daniel Ellsberg's psychiatrist, which included Howard Hunt's participation in the Dita Beard ITT affair, which included Howard Hunt's fabrication of cables designed to discredit the Kennedy administration. . . .

At this point I would like to juxtapose a few of the impeachment criteria with some of the president's actions.

Impeachment criteria: James Madison, from the Virginia ratification convention. "If the president be connected in any suspicious manner with any person and there be grounds to believe that he will shelter him, he may be impeached."

We have heard time and time again that the evidence reflects payment to the defendants of money. The president had knowledge that these funds were being paid and that these were funds collected for the 1972 presidential campaign.

We know that the president met with Mr. Henry Petersen twenty-seven times to discuss matters related to Watergate and immediately thereafter met with the very persons who were implicated in the information Mr.

Petersen was receiving and transmitting to the president. The words are "if the president be connected in any suspicious manner with any person and there be grounds to believe that he will shelter that person, he may be impeached."

Justice Story: "Impeachment is intended for occasional and extraordinary cases where a superior power acting for the whole people is put into operation to protect their rights and rescue their liberties from violations."

We know about the Huston plan. We know about the break-in of the psychiatrist's office. We know that there was absolute complete direction in August 1971 when the president instructed Ehrlichman to "do whatever is necessary." This instruction led to a surreptitious entry into Dr. Fielding's office.

"Protect their rights." "Rescue their liberties from violation."

The South Carolina ratification convention impeachment criteria: those are impeachable "who behave amiss or betray their public trust."

Beginning shortly after the Watergate break-in and continuing to the present time, the president has engaged in a series of public statements and actions designed to thwart the lawful investigation by government prosecutors. Moreover, the president has made public announcements and assertions bearing on the Watergate case which the evidence will show he knew to be false.

These assertions, false assertions, impeachable, those who misbehave. Those who "behave amiss or betray their public trust."

James Madison again at the Constitutional Convention: "A president is impeachable if he attempts to subvert the Constitution."

The Constitution charges the president with the task of taking care that the laws be faithfully executed, and yet the president has counseled his aides to commit perjury, willfully disregarded the secrecy of grand jury proceedings, concealed surreptitious entry, attempted to compromise a federal judge while publicly displaying his cooperation with the processes of criminal justice.

"A president is impeachable if he attempts to subvert the Constitution."

If the impeachment provision in the Constitution of the United States will not reach the offenses charged here, then perhaps that eighteenth-century Constitution should be abandoned to a twentieth-century paper shredder. Has the president committed offenses and planned and directed and acquiesced in a course of conduct which the Constitution will not tolerate? That is the question. We know that. We know the question. We should now forthwith proceed to answer the question. It is reason, and not passion, which must guide our deliberations, guide our debate, and guide our decision.

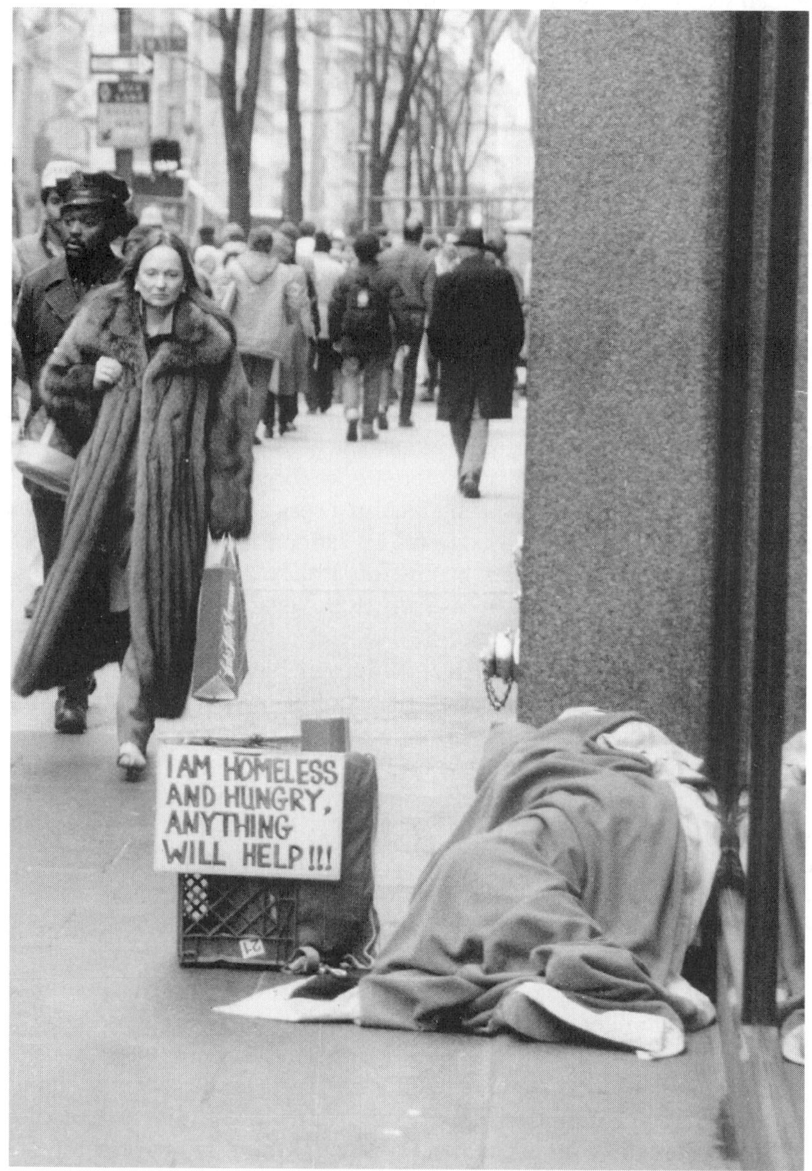

Cityscape. (Wide World Photos, Inc.)

CHAPTER SEVEN

Contemporary Times

45. Enterprise Unleashed

First Inaugural Address (1981)
RONALD REAGAN

46. The Urban Ordeal

Defending Children (1987)
MARIAN WRIGHT EDELMAN

47. Technology and Work

The Work of Nations (1991)
ROBERT B. REICH

48. Blood and Sand

Address on the War with Iraq (1991)
GEORGE BUSH

49. Contract

Contract with America (1994)
NEWT GINGRICH

Reactionary Chic (1995)
LEWIS H. LAPHAM

50. A President Besieged

Report to Congress (1998)
KENNETH STARR

White House Response to the Starr Report (1998)

45

Enterprise Unleashed

Ronald Reagan first made his mark in politics with a televised appeal in 1964 on behalf of conservative Senator Barry Goldwater, the Republican presidential candidate. Reagan argued a position popular with the Sunbelt and the suburbs where Republicans were beginning to show strength—that federal government high taxes, social programs, and regulations were strangling individual freedom and threatening to drag the country "down to the ant heap of totalitarianism." He also showed himself to be a brilliant speaker—relaxed, confident, earnest, and poised, with a warm voice, a gift for turning a phrase, and a knack for seeming simultaneously friendly and determined. The speech failed to rescue Goldwater's foundering campaign, but it did launch Reagan's own political career, which led first to the California governor's mansion and then to the White House.

Reagan's major victory in the presidential election of 1980 can be traced to several sources. The Democratic candidate, incumbent Jimmy Carter, was widely perceived as a weak president, unable to lift the country from a lingering economic slump or to rescue American diplomatic hostages from the clutches of Moslem fundamentalists in Iran. But Reagan was himself a strong candidate, promising repeatedly (as he had on Goldwater's behalf sixteen years before) to cut taxes, deregulate business, balance the federal budget, and increase military spending—in brief, to restore unregulated capitalism and global supremacy, the twin pillars of the American system. That some of these promises appeared contradictory, mutually exclusive, or impossible was no problem, Reagan argued. According to "supply-side economics," which Reagan popularized, the country could accomplish these ends simply by cutting taxes enough to trigger massive investment and rapid growth, thus generating higher tax revenues despite lower tax rates. Reagan's Republican rival, George Bush, dismissed this notion as "voodoo economics." Nevertheless, Reagan's form of voodoo proved enormously popular with the American business community, which aggressively supported and financed his candidacy. President Reagan's inaugural address, excerpted below, signaled his determination to follow through on his campaign promises.

Born in 1914, Ronald Reagan won initial fame in Hollywood, where he worked in films and was president of the Screen Actors' Guild. During the 1950s he appeared on television and did publicity for General Electric Company. A two-term governor of California, he was by 1980 both a seasoned politician and a seasoned actor—photogenic, comfortable before the cameras, and possessing a mellifluous, compelling voice. No president since Franklin D. Roosevelt, with whom Reagan has often compared himself, used the electronic media so effectively or to such political advantage. His critics labeled him "the Teflon president" because he managed for years to escape unscathed from scandal or policy gaffes. But his friends called him "the Great Communicator," perhaps the finest of the century.

Questions to Consider. What was the nature of the "crisis" that Reagan saw in the United States in 1981? How did this crisis manifest itself at the government level? Why did Reagan say "government is the problem"? Did the president propose specific steps to deal with this? What steps did he propose for forcing government to live "within its means"? How, given these principles, was it possible for Reagan to oversee the biggest increase in the federal deficit in American history?

First Inaugural Address (1981)

RONALD REAGAN

These United States are confronted with an economic affliction of great proportions. We suffer from the longest and one of the worst sustained inflations in our national history. It distorts our economic decisions, penalizes thrift, and crushes the struggling young and the fixed-income elderly alike. It threatens to shatter the lives of millions of our people.

Idle industries have cast workers into unemployment, causing human misery and personal indignity. Those who do work are denied a fair return for their labor by a tax system which penalizes successful achievement and keeps us from maintaining full productivity.

But great as our tax burden is, it has not kept pace with public spending. For decades, we have piled deficit upon deficit, mortgaging our future and our children's future for the temporary convenience of the present. To continue this long trend is to guarantee tremendous social, cultural, political, and economic upheavals.

From *The New York Times,* January 21, 1981.

The winning team. President-elect Ronald Reagan and Vice-President-elect George Bush at their first post-election news conference, November 7, 1980, after demolishing the Democratic ticket in the wake of the Iran hostage crisis. (Wide World Photos, Inc.)

You and I as individuals can, by borrowing, live beyond our means, but only for a limited period of time. Why, then, should we think that collectively, as a nation, we are not bound by that same limitation? . . .

In this present crisis, government is not the solution to our problem. Government is the problem.

From time to time, we have been tempted to believe that society has become too complex to be managed by self-rule, that government by an elite group is superior to government for, by, and of the people. But if no one among us is capable of governing himself, then who among us has the capacity to govern someone else?

All of us together, in and out of government, must bear the burden. The solutions we seek must be equitable, with no one group singled out to pay a higher price.

We hear much of special interest groups. Our concern must be for a special interest group that has been too long neglected. It knows no sectional boundaries or ethnic and racial divisions, and it crosses political party lines.

It is made up of men and women who raise our food, patrol our streets, man our mines and our factories, teach our children, keep our homes, and heal us when we are sick—professionals, industrialists, shopkeepers, clerks, cabbies, and truckdrivers. They are, in short, "We the people," this breed called Americans. . . .

So, as we begin, let us take inventory. We are a nation that has a government—not the other way around. And this makes us special among the nations of the earth. Our government has no power except that granted it by the people. It is time to check and reverse the growth of government, which shows signs of having grown beyond the consent of the governed.

It is my intention to curb the size and influence of the federal establishment and to demand recognition of the distinction between the powers granted to the federal government and those reserved to the states or to the people.

All of us need to be reminded that the federal government did not create the states; the states created the federal government.

So there will be no misunderstanding, it is not my intention to do away with government. It is, rather, to make it work—work with us, not over us; to stand by our sides, not ride on our backs. Government can and must provide opportunity, not smother it—foster productivity, not stifle it.

If we look to the answer as to why, for so many years, we achieved so much, prospered as no other people on earth, it was because here, in this land, we unleashed the energy and individual genius of man to a greater extent than has ever been done before. Freedom and the dignity of the individual have been more available and assured here than in any other place on earth. The price for this freedom has been high at times. But we have never been unwilling to pay that price.

It is no coincidence that our present troubles parallel and are proportionate to the intervention and intrusion in our lives that result from unnecessary and excessive growth of government. . . .

So with all the creative energy at our command, let us begin an era of national renewal. Let us renew our determination, our courage, and our strength. And let us renew our faith and our hope. We have every right to dream heroic dreams. . . .

In the days ahead, I will propose removing the roadblocks that have slowed our economy and reduced productivity. Steps will be taken aimed at restoring the balance between the various levels of government. Progress may be slow—measured in inches and feet, not miles—but we will progress. It is time to reawaken this industrial giant, to get government back within its means, and to lighten our punitive tax burden. And these will be our first priorities; on these principles there will be no compromise.

46

THE URBAN ORDEAL

The rise of Reagan conservatism moved serious discussion of the problems of poverty and urban blight to the edges of party politics. That there *were* such problems was apparent. It was difficult to travel in any American city without encountering unprecedented numbers of homeless people, so many that census takers barely counted them, lawyers barely represented them, doctors barely treated them, and public health officers barely coped with their existence. It was also difficult to follow the daily news without being assailed by instances of criminal violence. Large sections of cities became off-limits for many people; at night most sections became off-limits for nearly everyone. Drug dealers carried deadlier weapons than most police officers. School administrators frisked pupils for firearms.

The statistics told their own story: life expectancy among black urban males was falling; real income for urban workers was also falling. Rates of illegitimate birth were rising, as were rates of urban drug addiction and rates of domestic violence, rape, and murder. For a time, Detroit became the murder capital of the world, only to be displaced soon after by Houston—which in turn was overtaken by Washington, D.C. And there were the comparisons. Calcutta, the sprawling Indian city, has long been a byword for nightmarish squalor. In 1990 a group of foreign businessmen maintained that life in Calcutta, though desperate, might be preferable to the misery and viciousness of New York City. An American journalist agreed.

But serious as these problems were, they were largely problems of the poor at a time when the national mood and the national leadership were unsympathetic to reforms. Nevertheless, those who have a will to reform often find a way, usually by changing the terms of debate and organizing from outside. Faced with an unwillingness to debate poverty, reformers in the 1980s talked instead about the needs of children (just as, faced with an unwillingness to debate violence, they talked instead about the ravages of firearms). Thus arose one of the most visible and influential initiatives of the 1980s—the Children's Defense Fund—and the career of Marian Wright Edelman, the woman who led it.

Marian Wright Edelman was born in 1939 in South Carolina. She attended Spelman College and Yale Law School and, in 1963, became a staff attorney for the National Association for the Advancement of Colored People. She was congressional liaison for Martin Luther King's Poor People's Campaign in 1968 and director of the Harvard Center for Law and Education before founding the Children's Defense Fund in Washington, D.C. The purpose of the Fund was to monitor and propose improvements in government policies and programs in child-related areas: child and maternal health, education, child care, child welfare, adolescent pregnancy prevention, youth employment, and family support systems. Called "the 101st senator on children's issues" and "the nation's most effective lobbyist on behalf of children," Edelman, with the Children's Defense Fund, initiated a major long-term campaign in 1983 to prevent teenage pregnancy and provide positive life options for youth. The following excerpt is from her 1987 book, *Families in Peril,* which encapsulated many of the arguments and data that earned the Fund its high reputation for effective advocacy.

Questions to Consider. What single factor, in Marian Wright Edelman's view, best accounted for black family deterioration? Why did she stress the point that both white and black children were suffering from poverty? Do any of her statistics surprise you? Of the six reasons she gave for child poverty generally, which do you find most, and least, persuasive? What is the "highest ideal" that Edelman referred to in her final paragraph?

Defending Children (1987)

MARIAN WRIGHT EDELMAN

A 1985 Children's Defense Fund (CDF) study, *Black and White Children in America: Key Facts,* found that black children have been sliding backward. Black children today are more likely to be born into poverty, lack early prenatal care, have a single mother or unemployed parent, be unemployed as teenagers, and not go to college after high school graduation than they were in 1980. . . .

We also found that:

Reprinted by permission of the publisher from *Families in Peril: An Agenda for Social Change* by Marian Wright Edelman. Cambridge, Mass.: Harvard University Press, Copyright © 1987 by the President and Fellows of Harvard College.

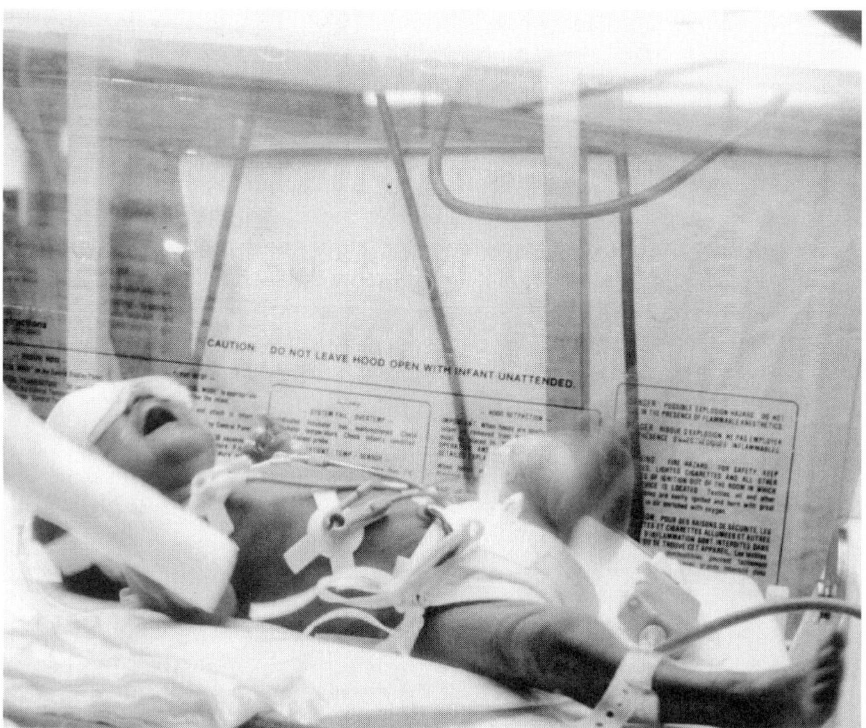

An innocent victim. A "crack baby," addicted to cocaine because the mother was an addict. Addictive illegal drugs were a plague throughout urban America. "Crack" cocaine, easily affordable and quickly addictive, was particularly deadly. (© 1990 John Chiasson/Gamma-Liaison, Inc.)

- Only four out of every ten black children, compared to eight out of every ten white children live in two-parent families.
- Births to unmarried teenagers occur five times more often among blacks than whites, although birth rates for black teens, married and unmarried, have been *declining,* while the birth rate among white unmarried teens has been *increasing* in recent years.
- In 1983, 58 percent of all births to black women were out of wedlock. Among black women under the age of twenty, the proportion was over 86 percent. For thirty years these out-of-wedlock ratios have increased inexorably. They have now reached levels that essentially guarantee the poverty of many black children for the unforeseeable future.

Since the main reason that black children live with only a mother is that most unmarried pregnant black women do not marry before giving birth, what has become of the fathers? They remain single. The pattern is quite clear. . . .

One crucial question is: When did the rate of marriage formation drop among young black males? In the 1970s it paralleled the decline of employment prospects of young black males, which resulted in only 29.8 percent of black teens and 61 percent of black twenty- to twenty-four-year-old men being employed by 1978. From 1978 to 1985 things got a bit worse for both black teens and males in their twenties.

Why did this economic disaster for black men occur? It is difficult to say precisely, but I think that the other factors which contributed included the softening of the labor market generally in the 1970s, poor education, continuing discrimination, and a reciprocal sense of defeatism among some inner-city and rural men. There is no question but that the number of Americans who wanted to work and could not find jobs was larger in 1980 than it had been in 1970. The economy absorbed unprecedented numbers of baby-boomers, women, and immigrants; in the process it left behind the same people who have always been at the end of the American line. . . .

The American family crisis is not just a black family crisis. Both public and private sector neglect and anti-family policy have contributed to a downward spiral for families and children, black and white. Those who suffer the most are of course the poor. Although the data on poverty, family dissolution, and teenage pregnancy are grimmer for blacks than for whites, the data for whites and for our society as a whole are themselves quite grim. In some respects (education, income of two-parent families, women's earnings, child nutrition, infant mortality) black rates have been improving and narrowing the gap between whites—or were doing so until the budget cuts and near-depression of the early 1980s. In certain other respects the gap has been narrowing because blacks have been standing still while whites are slipping backward. . . .

We must recognize that, if only by dint of their overwhelmingly majority status, whites make up most of the children and young adults about whom we should be concerned.

Nearly half of all black children in the United States are poor, an appalling figure. But a sixth of white children are poor, and that is also appalling. There are 8.1 million poor *white* children in the U.S., and 4.3 million poor black children—a two to one ratio. Together, more than one out of five American children are poor, including nearly one out of four children under the age of six.

Overall, children in America have become far poorer than other age groups. During the past fifteen years their poverty rates have soared, even as poverty among adults generally has stayed stable. . . .

Poverty is the greatest child killer in the affluent United States of the mid-1980s. More American children die each year from poverty than from traffic fatalities and suicide combined. Over a five-year period, more American children die from poverty than the total number of American battle deaths during the Vietnam War. . . .

Children are poor because our nation has lost its moral bearings. We must work to change the national climate and focus attention on families and children. Recent federal government policy has spawned a new set of beatitudes which measure success not by how many needy pregnant women can be provided cost-effective prenatal care to prevent infant deaths and birth defects, but by how many families can be denied Medicaid and turned away from public health clinics. . . .

Children are poor because their parents cannot find work. Today unemployment is at historically high levels, given the context of well over three years of economic recovery. . . .

Millions of children remain locked in poverty because hard-working parents cannot make enough income to provide for their basic needs. Recent governmental and private sector policies have resulted not only in high unemployment but in low wages for those who are working, increasing poverty and making the struggle of poor families harder. . . .

Poor families struggling to survive on meager wages have faced another burden: skyrocketing federal taxes. In 1979 a family of four with earnings at the poverty line paid less than 2 percent of its income in federal Social Security and income taxes. In 1986 that same family, if still earning (inflation-adjusted) poverty-line wages, has nearly 11 percent of its income taken by the federal government. Tax rates for single-parent families are even higher. . . .

Children are poor because of decreasing government support at a time of increasing need, which has resulted from economic recession, unemployment, low wages, and increased taxes on the poor. The America of the 1980s presents a cruel paradox: while the rich are getting richer and often getting more government help, the poor are getting poorer and receiving less help. The decline in federal assistance for children has made living in poverty a harsher existence for 13 million children, and it has crippled the efforts of their families to struggle back up out of poverty. . . .

Children are poor because of demographic changes and the growth of female-headed families. In 1970 one baby in nine was born to a single mother. In 1983 one baby in five was. If the trends continue, by 1990 one out of five white babies and three out of four black babies will be born into female-headed households. . . .

The United States today has the challenge and opportunity of showing the world a living justice by eradicating child poverty and putting a floor of decency under every American family. To do less is to betray our highest ideal. This task cannot be relegated just to government or to somebody else. Every individual has a responsibility to try to make a difference, to give imaginative flesh to the ideal of justice. We should aim high.

47

Technology and Work

After population growth, cheap land, and bountiful resources, it was technological innovation—the work of creative individuals such as Eli Whitney, Isaac M. Singer, Andrew Carnegie, and Henry Ford—that was the driving force of American industrialization. After World War II, modern industries like petrochemicals, aerospace, and electronics helped power an unprecedented twenty-five years of almost uninterrupted growth in real national income. At every hand, it seemed, technology yielded products of prosperity: plastics and pharmaceuticals, satellites and jetliners, televisions and computers.

By the 1970s, however, doubt had appeared concerning the future and even the benefits of technology. These doubts stemmed in part from the "oil shocks" of 1973 and 1979, when exploding petroleum prices produced not only stagflation—a combination of high unemployment and rising prices—but also concern about whether science could discover usable substitutes for hydrocarbon fuels. Another source of doubt came from fear that technology was destructive as well as creative. Evidenced by a rapidly growing environmental movement, this fear centered chiefly on nuclear-powered electric plants with their radiation dangers and on the petrochemical industry, whose "unnatural" nonbiodegradable products and byproducts polluted the nation's air, water, and soil.

A final source of technological doubt concerned not whether we could find new energy supplies or avoid poisoning ourselves but whether, given continuing stagflation and the success of foreign competitors such as Germany and Japan, the United States was technologically competitive—that is, technological enough. Most scientists and corporate executives argued that in fact we needed more technology, not less, a view that helped fuel the computer revolution of the 1990s.

Robert B. Reich offered a counterpoint to this technological optimism. The optimists believed that the globalization of the marketplace and the accelerated development of "high-tech" industries would mean tremendous economic growth for the United States, a view that the boom of the 1990s largely confirmed. But Reich argued that these developments would benefit mostly the new intelligentsia, a "fortunate fifth" of persons who would earn excellent incomes as (for example) researchers, writers, communications specialists, and design engineers. The majority of "globally vulnerable" workers would not fare well in the global economy, and in fact, Reich predicted, would be left far behind, thereby increasing the gulf between rich and poor in ways that could very well threaten America's social fabric. This prediction, too, has proved largely correct.

Robert Reich was born in Scranton, Pennsylvania, in 1946. Educated at Dartmouth, Oxford, and Yale, he has taught at Harvard and Brandeis Universities, has written several books (*The Next American Frontier, Tales of a New America, The Work of Nations*), and has been a member of the governing board of the "good government" group, Common Cause. Reich served as secretary of labor in the Clinton administration.

Questions to Consider. To what extent is Robert Reich merely using a different vocabulary to describe the old dichotomy between "white collar" and "blue collar" workers? Why, according to Reich, will the relationship between "symbolic analysts" and less sophisticated workers change so dramatically? If events prove Reich to be correct and great disparities in wealth result, what does he recommend to "close the gap"? Is his reasoning persuasive?

The Work of Nations (1991)

ROBERT B. REICH

Regardless of the profitability or market share of a nation's corporations, the economic success of a nation (or, more accurately, the region of the global economy denominated by the nation's political borders) must be judged ultimately by how well its citizens are able to live and whether these standards of living can be sustained and improved upon in the future. . . .

Increasingly, one's capacity to command both tangible and intangible wealth is determined by the value that the global economy places on one's skills and insights. The ubiquitous and irrepressible law of supply and demand no longer respects national borders. In this new world economy, symbolic analysts hold a dominant position. American symbolic analysts are especially advantaged. The quality of the nation's universities is unsur-

From *The Work of Nations* by Robert Reich. Copyright © 1991 by Robert B. Reich. Reprinted by permission of Alfred A. Knopf, Inc.

Robert Reich. Robert Reich, soon to be named Secretary of Labor, with President-elect Bill Clinton and Vice-President-elect Al Gore, December 1992. (Wide World Photos)

passed; its best primary and secondary schools are among the finest in the world; no other country provides the same quality of on-the-job training within entire regions specializing in one or another kind of symbolic analysis. In this Americans can take pride.

For the two other major categories of worker, however, the law of supply and demand does not bode well. Routine producers, confronted with an immense and rapidly growing pool of unskilled and semiskilled laborers worldwide, find their incomes slipping and their jobs disappearing. In-person servers, while largely sheltered from such direct competition, suffer the indirect effects and find themselves in an increasingly precarious position. A shrinking labor pool within America's borders may ease their plight somewhat in the future, but competition from workers who otherwise would have entered into routine production, from immigrants, and from labor-saving machinery may offset much of the gain. Primarily as a result of these trends, the earnings of Americans (as well as those of citizens of many other nations) have begun to diverge. Hence the challenge: to improve the living standards of the majority of Americans now occupying the two latter categories, who are losing ground in the global economy.

The problem is far from insoluble. In fact, the range of potential solutions is well understood. Finding the political will to implement them poses a considerably greater challenge.

One response is to offset the polarizing tendencies of the new global economy through a truly progressive income tax, coupled with the closure of gaping tax loopholes.

Today, the ideal of tax progressivity seems faintly quaint in the United States, although several other industrialized nations continue to regard it as a viable means for moderating income inequities. By 1990, America's income-tax rate on its wealthiest citizens was the lowest of any industrialized nation. A more progressive income tax is no panacea for widening income disparities rooted in the emerging worldwide division of labor, of course, but it would at least ameliorate the trend. The contrary strategy—featuring a low marginal tax on the highest incomes and a growing reliance on Social Security payroll taxes, sales taxes, user fees, property taxes, and lotteries—moves us in exactly the opposite direction.

A second response to the widening gap is to guard against class rigidities by ensuring that any reasonably talented American child can become a symbolic analyst—regardless of family income or race. Here we see the upside of the globalized economy. Unlike America's old hierarchical and somewhat isolated economy, whose white-collar jobs were necessarily limited in proportion to the number of blue-collar jobs beneath them, the global economy imposes no particular limit upon the number of Americans who can sell symbolic-analytic services worldwide. In principle, all of America's routine production workers could become symbolic analysts and let their old jobs drift overseas to developing nations. The worldwide demand for symbolic analysis is growing so briskly that even under these circumstances real wages would still move steadily upward. . . .

Even under these most optimistic circumstances it is doubtful that there would be radical growth in the number of Americans who became research scientists, design engineers, management consultants, advertising and marketing specialists, film producers, directors, editors and publishers, software engineers, writers, architects, or—even if the world really needed them—investment bankers and lawyers. So other responses are also needed. One is to increase the number of Americans who could apply symbolic analysis to production and in-person services. There is ample evidence, for example, that access to computerized information can enrich production jobs by enabling workers to alter the flow of materials and components in ways that generate new efficiencies. Production workers empowered by computers thus have broader responsibilities and more control over how production is organized. They cease to be "routine" workers—becoming, in effect, symbolic analysts at a level very close to the production process. . . .

This abbreviated catalogue of ways to improve the plight of America's globally vulnerable citizens is not intended as a definitive guide, but rather to suggest the realms of policy in which such solutions are apt to be found. I do not want to minimize the difficulty of designing and executing such remedies effectively, but only to show that they are neither mysterious nor beyond our grasp. The fundamental difficulty is not in imagining or implementing solutions. The greatest challenge comes in summoning the political determination to embark upon them. Good education, training, health care, and public infrastructure—available to all Americans—will be costly.

The reader may appropriately object that "more money" is no solution. Clearly it is not the whole solution. *Methods* of educating, training, providing health care, and building and maintaining infrastructure can surely be improved upon. But while money may not be sufficient, it is certainly a necessary prerequisite, and the facile assumption that money already has been dedicated generously to these ends is false, as I will show in more detail in the next chapter.

If there are to be additional expenditures, who is to pay? Most working Americans, already under a heavy tax load, cannot afford to shoulder the added financial burden of higher levels of public spending. It would have to be borne instead by the one group of Americans whose earnings have been increasing—our symbolic analysts. Of course, symbolic analysts would also bear the cost of any changes in the tax code designed to redistribute income and thus to reduce the polarizing domestic effects of a globalized economy.

Thus a central question concerns the extent to which America's fortunate citizens—especially symbolic analysts, who, with about half the nation's income, constitute the greatest part of the most fortunate fifth of the population—are willing to bear these burdens. But herein lies a paradox: As the economic fates of Americans diverge, the top may be losing the long-held sense of connectedness with the bottom fifth, or even the bottom four-fifths, that would motivate such generosity.

Ironically, as the rest of the nation grows more economically dependent than ever on the fortunate fifth, the fortunate fifth is becoming less and less dependent on them. The economic interdependence that Tocqueville observed in nineteenth-century America is slipping away. Increasingly, the fortunate fifth are selling their expertise on the global market and are able to maintain and enhance their standard of living and that of their children even as that of other Americans declines. No longer does their well-being depend exclusively or primarily on the productivity, purchasing power, or wage restraint exercised by the other four-fifths of the population. The American executive software engineer, linked to his worldwide web by computer, modem, and facsimile machine, is apt to be more dependent on design engineers in Kuala Lumpur, fabricators in Taiwan, bankers in Tokyo and Bonn, and sales and marketing specialists in Paris and Milan than on routine production workers in a factory on the other side of town.

Yet without the support of the fortunate fifth, it will be almost impossible to muster the resources, and the political will, necessary for change. . . .

The direction we are heading is reasonably clear. If the future could be predicted on the basis of trends already underway, laissez-faire cosmopolitanism would become America's dominant economic and social philosophy. Left to unfold on its own, the worldwide division of labor not only will create vast disparities of wealth within nations but may also reduce the willingness of global winners to do anything to reverse this trend toward inequality—either within the nation or without. Symbolic analysts, who hold most of the cards in this game, could be confident of "victory." But what of the losers?

We are presented with a rare historical moment in which the threat of worldwide conflict seems remote and the transformations of economies and technology are blurring the lines between nations. The modern nation-state, some two hundred years old, is no longer what it once was: Vanishing is a nationalism founded upon the practical necessities of economic interdependence within borders and security against foreigners outside. There is thus an opportunity for us, as for every society, to redefine who we are, why we have joined together, and what we owe each other and the other inhabitants of the world. The choice is ours to make. We are no more slaves to present trends than to vestiges of the past. We can, if we choose, assert that our mutual obligations as citizens extend beyond our economic usefulness to one another, and act accordingly.

48

BLOOD AND SAND

After World War II, the Middle East, with its vast oil reserves, was of strategic importance to both the United States and the Soviet Union. The presence there of Israel, a state with strong political and military ties to the United States virtually since Israel's founding in 1948, has made the area doubly important to American policy makers. As a consequence, every modern U.S. president has expended enormous financial and political resources to maintain American influence in the Middle East. There have been some successes from the standpoint of the American government. In 1953 President Dwight Eisenhower used the Central Intelligence Agency to replace an unfriendly government with a friendly one in oil-rich Iran; in 1958 he deployed the Sixth Fleet to maintain a friendly government in Lebanon. In 1978 Jimmy Carter helped bring about the so-called Camp David Accords between Israel and Egypt, the Arab world's most populous state.

But the United States has also experienced many failures in the region, not least in the very places where initial policies succeeded. In the late 1970s, for example, Islamic partisans seized control of Iran and its oil fields, taking fifty-two American hostages in the process. President Carter, unable to respond effectively, plummeted in public opinion polls and lost the 1980 election to Ronald Reagan partly because of his handling of the Iran crisis. President Reagan himself then came to grief when Israeli and Syrian invasions of Lebanon shattered that country's unity in 1982. Concerned about Syrian and Soviet influence, Reagan sent U.S. Marines to Beirut, the Lebanese capital, as part of a peacekeeping force, only to see more than two hundred of them killed in a terrorist attack. Just three months later, even though the president had called the American presence "essential," he ordered the force's withdrawal.

On August 2, 1990, Iraq, which had concluded a long and inconclusive war with Iran, invaded Kuwait, an oil-rich sheikdom abutting Iraq in the Persian Gulf not far from Kuwait's border with the desert kingdom of Saudi Arabia, the largest oil producer in the world. President George Bush immediately branded the Iraqi president, Saddam

Hussein, a "bloody tyrant" and vowed that this brutal aggression "will not stand." During the following weeks the United States sent 250,000 troops to Saudi Arabia to protect it from Iraqi invasion and persuaded several European and Arab countries (including the dictator of Syria, a long-time U.S. foe) to send forces to join the Americans. The United States also obtained the backing of the United Nations Security Council for economic sanctions against Iraq, with a deadline of January 15, 1991, for Iraqi withdrawal from Kuwait. In November (after the congressional elections) another 200,000 American troops put still bigger teeth in the multinational force facing Iraqi soldiers across the borders of Kuwait.

In early January—after a historic debate that lasted several days and was broadcast live from gavel to gavel—the Senate and the House of Representatives voted to support President Bush's request for what everyone agreed was tantamount to a declaration of war: an endorsement of the U.N. resolution threatening military action if Iraq did not leave Kuwait by January 15. Saddam Hussein, however, made no move. On January 16, Bush ordered a full-scale air assault, including a dazzling array of electronic weaponry, against military targets in Kuwait and Iraq. That evening he delivered the following television address to explain and defend his decision.

Born in Massachusetts in 1924, George Bush was the son of Prescott Bush, a Wall Street banker and U.S. senator. He attended private schools and, after service with the navy in World War II, took a degree in economics at Yale, where he also played baseball. Bush then moved to Texas, where he made money in the oil business. He lost a race on the Republican ticket for the U.S. Senate before, in 1966, winning election to Congress from Houston. During the Nixon years, Bush served as U.N. ambassador and chairman of the Republican National Committee; under Gerald R. Ford he was chief of the Liaison Office in China and director of the Central Intelligence Agency. Defeated by Ronald Reagan for the 1980 Republican presidential nomination, Bush agreed to run as Reagan's vice-presidential nominee. This was the ticket that trounced Jimmy Carter in 1980 and mauled Walter Mondale in 1984. With a record of party loyalty and Reagan's popularity behind him, Bush easily won the nomination for president in 1988 and, with Dan Quayle on the bottom of the ticket, thrashed Democrat Michael Dukakis to keep the White House in Republican hands. Four years later, Bush himself lost the presidency to Democrat Bill Clinton.

Questions to Consider. President Bush gave several reasons for taking action against Iraq. Which of them seems to have been most important? What reasons did he give for taking military action rather than waiting for the economic sanctions possibly to produce results?

Which reasons seem to have mattered most to him? What kind of war did the president seem to anticipate? What did he mean when he said this war would not be "another Vietnam"? What did he mean by "the new world order"?

Address on the War with Iraq (1991)

GEORGE BUSH

Just two hours ago, allied air forces began an attack on military targets in Iraq and Kuwait. These attacks continue as I speak. Ground forces are not engaged.

This conflict started Aug. 2, when the dictator of Iraq invaded a small and helpless neighbor. Kuwait, a member of the Arab League and a member of the United Nations, was crushed, its people brutalized. Five months ago, Saddam Hussein started this cruel war against Kuwait; tonight, the battle has been joined.

This military action, taken in accord with United Nations resolutions and with the consent of the United States Congress, follows months of constant and virtually endless diplomatic activity on the part of the United Nations, the United States and many, many other countries.

Arab leaders sought what became known as an Arab solution, only to conclude that Saddam Hussein was unwilling to leave Kuwait. Others traveled to Baghdad in a variety of efforts to restore peace and justice. Our Secretary of State, James Baker, held an historic meeting in Geneva, only to be totally rebuffed.

This past weekend, in a last-ditch effort, the Secretary General of the United Nations went to the Middle East with peace in his heart—his second such mission. And he came back from Baghdad with no progress at all in getting Saddam Hussein to withdraw from Kuwait.

Now, the twenty-eight countries with forces in the gulf area have exhausted all reasonable efforts to reach a peaceful resolution, and have no choice but to drive Saddam from Kuwait by force. We will not fail.

As I report to you, air attacks are under way against military targets in Iraq. We are determined to knock out Saddam Hussein's nuclear bomb potential. We will also destroy his chemical weapons facilities. Much of Saddam's artillery and tanks will be destroyed. Our operations are designed to best protect the lives of all the coalition forces by targeting Saddam's vast military arsenal.

From *The New York Times,* January 17, 1991.

Aftermath of the war with Iraq. This tank was abandoned by Iraqis in their retreat. But to the cow who came looking for food it meant nothing. In the background an oil well burns out of control. (Abbas/Magnum Photos, Inc.)

Initial reports from General [Norman] Schwartzkopf are that our operations are proceeding according to plan. Our objectives are clear: Saddam Hussein's forces will leave Kuwait. The legitimate government of Kuwait will be restored to its rightful place, and Kuwait will once again be free.

Iraq will eventually comply with all relevant United Nations resolutions, and then, when peace is restored, it is our hope that Iraq will live as a peaceful and cooperative member of the family of nations, thus enhancing the security and stability of the Gulf.

Some may ask, why act now? Why not wait? The answer is clear. The world could wait no longer. Sanctions, though having some effect, showed no signs of accomplishing their objective. Sanctions were tried for well over five months, and we and our allies concluded that sanctions alone would not force Saddam from Kuwait.

While the world waited, Saddam Hussein systematically raped, pillaged and plundered a tiny nation no threat to his own. He subjected the people of Kuwait to unspeakable atrocities, and among those maimed and murdered, innocent children.

While the world waited, Saddam sought to add to the chemical weapons arsenal he now possesses, an infinitely more dangerous weapon of mass destruction—a nuclear weapon. And while the world waited, while the world talked peace and withdrawal, Saddam Hussein dug in and moved massive forces into Kuwait.

While the world waited, while Saddam stalled, more damage was being done to the fragile economies of the Third World, emerging democracies of Eastern Europe, to the entire world, including to our own economy.

The United States, together with the United Nations, exhausted every means at our disposal to bring this crisis to a peaceful end. However, Saddam clearly felt that by stalling and threatening and defying the United Nations, he could weaken the forces arrayed against him.

While the world waited, Saddam Hussein met every overture of peace with open contempt. While the world prayed for peace, Saddam prepared for war.

I had hoped that when the United States Congress, in historic debate, took its resolute action, Saddam would realize he could not prevail, and would move out of Kuwait in accord with the United Nations resolutions. He did not do that. Instead, he remained intransigent, certain that time was on his side.

Saddam was warned over and over again to comply with the will of the United Nations, leave Kuwait or be driven out. Saddam has arrogantly rejected all warnings. Instead he tried to make this a dispute between Iraq and the United States of America.

Well he failed. Tonight twenty-eight nations—countries from five continents, Europe and Asia, Africa and the Arab League—have forces in the Gulf area standing shoulder to shoulder against Saddam Hussein. These countries had hoped the use of force could be avoided. Regrettably, we now believe that only force will make him leave.

Prior to ordering our forces into battle, I instructed our military commanders to take every necessary step to prevail as quickly as possible, and with the greatest degree of protection possible for American and Allied service men and women. I've told the American people before that this will not be another Vietnam, and I repeat this here tonight. Our troops will have the best possible support in the entire world, and they will not be asked to fight with one hand tied behind their back. I'm hopeful that this fighting will not go on for long and that casualties will be held to an absolute minimum.

This is an historic moment. We have in this past year made great progress in ending the long era of conflict and cold war. We have before us the opportunity to forge for ourselves and for future generations a new world order, a world where the rule of law, not the law of the jungle, governs the conduct of nations.

When we are successful, and we will be, we have a real chance at this new world order, an order in which a credible United Nations can use its peacekeeping role to fulfill the promise and vision of the U.N.'s founders. We have no argument with the people of Iraq. Indeed, for the innocents caught in this conflict, I pray for their safety.

Our goal is not the conquest of Iraq. It is the liberation of Kuwait. It is my hope that somehow the Iraqi people can, even now, convince their dictator that he must lay down his arms, leave Kuwait and let Iraq itself rejoin the family of peace-loving nations.

Thomas Paine wrote many years ago: "These are the times that try men's souls." Those well-known words are so very true today. But even as planes of the multinational forces attack Iraq, I prefer to think of peace, not war. I am convinced not only that we will prevail, but that out of the horror of combat will come the recognition that no nation can stand against a world united. No nation will be permitted to brutally assault its neighbor. . . .

And let me say to everyone listening or watching tonight: When the troops we've sent in finish their work, I'm determined to bring them home as soon as possible. Tonight, as our forces fight, they and their families are in our prayers.

May God bless each and every one of them, and the coalition forces at our side in the Gulf, and may He continue to bless our nation, the United States of America.

CONTRACT

A striking feature of American politics since the election of Dwight Eisenhower in 1952 is that although the Republicans have won the presidency twice as often as the Democrats and thus have largely controlled both the executive and (through appointments) the judicial branches, they seemed unable to gain control of Congress. Even when they briefly controlled the Senate in the 1950s and 1980s, they remained the minority in the House of Representatives—a Democratic stronghold for over forty years.

The elections of 1994 abruptly changed all this. Midway through Democrat Bill Clinton's first term, the Republican party triumphed in congressional races throughout the country. When the dust settled, the Republicans had solid control of the Senate for the third time since 1952, a control strengthened in succeeding months when two Democrats switched parties. In the House the shift was even more dramatic; the Republicans gained over eighty seats, giving them, for the first time since World War II, a powerful majority. And although a Democrat still occupied the White House, many observers expected the presidency to revert to Republican domination in the near future.

The post-1994 Republicans were not only numerically strong. To a remarkable degree, they were also united. In the fall of 1994, some 367 Republican candidates for the House of Representatives publicly supported the "Contract with America," a bold set of procedural reforms and conservative policy initiatives devised mainly by Georgia Republican Newt Gingrich. Most of these candidates were elected. What was telling about the 1994 congressional elections, in fact, was that while Democratic incumbents were falling right and left, not one Republican incumbent lost. The Contract, reproduced below, thus became a major political document, and Gingrich became Speaker of the House, dedicated to passing as much of the Contract as he could as quickly as possible. For at least the first few months of their Washington reign, the Republicans enjoyed considerable success.

Voter analysis shows that Republicans won in 1994 because they enjoyed exceptional support among certain groups: young voters, especially young males; white Southerners, especially white male

Southerners; and male voters everywhere, especially white males. The South thus completed a shift toward the Republican party that had begun with Barry Goldwater's campaign in 1964. Most of the new Republican congressional leaders were Southerners, and the national party leadership was Southern to an unprecedented degree. But the antiwelfare, anti–affirmative action, anti–illegal immigrant, antiunion, antiregulatory, anti–high tax, probusiness, and promilitary positions of the Republicans were clearly compelling to a great many American voters in addition to white male Southerners. Furthermore, two special interest groups appeared to have been influential: the National Rifle Association, which campaigned aggressively against Democrats who had supported a ban on assault rifles and a waiting period for buying handguns; and the loosely confederated antiabortion movement, which opposed prochoice, mostly Democratic candidates.

Republicans raised and spent lots of money. The average House candidate in 1994 spent $200,000; successful first-time Republican candidates spent $675,000. Fifteen of the top twenty fundraisers among successful first-year candidates were Republicans, who spent on average over $1 million per race. Many Republican newcomers to the House used their own funds for campaigning, sometimes to the tune of $250,000 or more. This pattern, and the fact that the "Contract with America" did not address key issues of campaign financing and special interest lobbying, helped fuel the skepticism of some observers, including Lewis Lapham, editor of *Harper's Magazine,* whose essay on the Contract and the Gingrich insurgency is excerpted below.

Born in 1943 in Pennsylvania, Newt Gingrich is the adopted son of an Army soldier. Gingrich attended Emory University, received graduate degrees in history from Tulane, and taught American history at West Georgia College before winning a House seat as a Republican in 1978. He cultivated a combative style, assailing Democrats in Washington for ethical lapses and big-spending liberalism. He also took advantage of television coverage of the House chamber to deliver partisan attacks from the floor, including verbal assaults on Democratic House Speakers Jim Wright and Tip O'Neill. Gingrich was elected Republican Whip in 1984 largely on the basis of his influence over younger Republicans and his reputation as a fire-breathing conservative who hated to compromise. He also raised major political money, attracting $2 million (including $410,000 from insurance, medical, securities, and legal interests) in 1993–1994 alone. Gingrich resigned as Speaker in December 1998 and announced that he would not seek reelection to the House.

Lewis H. Lapham was born in 1935 to a San Francisco banking family and attended Hotchkiss School and Yale University. A newspaper reporter from 1957 to 1962 and a magazine writer during the 1960s, Lapham became managing editor of *Harper's* in 1971 and editor in 1975. The author of several books on class, status, and power in contemporary America, he is a member of the Council on Foreign Relations.

Questions to Consider. Of the eight recommendations of the "Contract with America" pertaining to the operations of the House of Representatives itself, which one strikes you as most important? Would implementation of the four recommendations on committee organization and work have increased or decreased the internal power of the House leadership and of the committees themselves? Of the ten national policy recommendations in the Contract, which might have had the greatest impact? Was there a common thread tying these recommendations together?

What did Lewis Lapham see as the main features of the Contract and of Gingrich Republicanism? What appeared to bother Lapham most, corruption or hypocrisy? Was Lapham persuasive in arguing that the militant conservatives of the 1990s actually resembled the countercultural activists of the 1960s? Was he right in saying that the conservatives already control most of America? What did Lapham mean when he said that the Republicans offered everyone except the "propertied classes" mainly prisons and sermons? Do you agree?

Contract with America (1994)

NEWT GINGRICH

As Republican Members of the House of Representatives and as citizens seeking to join that body we propose not just to change its policies, but even more important, to restore the bonds of trust between the people and their elected representatives. That is why, in this era of official evasion and posturing, we offer instead a detailed agenda for national renewal, a written commitment with no fine print.

This year's election offers the chance, after four decades of one-party control, to bring to the House a new majority that will transform the way Congress works. That historic change would be the end of government that is too big, too intrusive, and too easy with the public's money. It can be the beginning of a Congress that respects the values and shares the faith of the American family.

From *Contract with America* by Newt Gingrich. Copyright © 1994 by Republican National Committee, Reprinted by permission of Times Books, a division of Random House, Inc.

Newt Gingrich, whose biting attacks on Democrats and the federal government led the Republicans to congressional power in the 1990s. In 1998 Gingrich himself resigned as Speaker of the House and from Congress, in part because of public disillusionment with his brand of vituperative partisanship. (John Harrington/Black Star)

Like Lincoln, our first Republican president, we intend to act "with firmness in the right, as God gives us to see the right." To restore accountability to Congress. To end its cycle of scandal and disgrace. To make us all proud again of the way free people govern themselves.

On the first day of the 104th Congress, the new Republican majority will immediately pass the following major reforms, aimed at restoring the faith and trust of the American people in their government:

First, require all laws that apply to the rest of the country also apply equally to the Congress;

Second, select a major independent auditing firm to conduct a comprehensive audit of Congress for waste, fraud, or abuse;

Third, cut the number of House committees, and cut committee staff by one-third;

Fourth, limit the terms of all committee chairs;

Fifth, ban the casting of proxy votes in committee;

Sixth, require committee meetings to be open to the public;

Seventh, require a three-fifths majority vote to pass a tax increase;

Eighth, guarantee an honest accounting of our federal budget by implementing zero baseline budgeting.

Thereafter, within the first hundred days of the 104th Congress, we shall bring to the House Floor the following bills, each to be given full and open debate, each to be given a clear and fair vote, and each to be immediately available this day for public inspection and scrutiny.

The Fiscal Responsibility Act

• A balanced budget/tax limitation amendment and a legislative line-item veto to restore fiscal responsibility to an out-of-control Congress, requiring them to live under the same budget constraints as families and businesses.

The Taking Back Our Streets Act

• An anti-crime package including stronger truth in sentencing, "good faith" exclusionary rule exemptions, effective death penalty provisions, and cuts in social spending from this summer's crime bill to fund prison construction and additional law enforcement to keep people secure in their neighborhoods and kids safe in their schools.

The Personal Responsibility Act

• Discourage illegitimacy and teen pregnancy by prohibiting welfare to minor mothers and denying increased AFDC for additional children while on welfare, cut spending for welfare programs, and enact a tough two-years-and-out provision with work requirements to promote individual responsibility.

The Family Reinforcement Act

• Child support enforcement, tax incentives for adoption, strengthening rights of parents in their children's education, stronger child pornography laws, and an elderly dependent care tax credit to reinforce the central role of families in American society.

The American Dream Restoration Act

• A $500-per-child tax credit, begin repeal of the marriage tax penalty, and creation of American Dream Savings Accounts to provide middle-class tax relief.

The National Security Restoration Act

• No U.S. troops under UN command and restoration of the essential parts of our national security funding to strengthen our national defense and maintain our credibility around the world.

The Senior Citizens Fairness Act

• Raise the Social Security earnings limit, which currently forces seniors out of the workforce, repeal the 1993 tax hikes on Social Security benefits, and provide tax incentives for private long-term care insurance to let older Americans keep more of what they have earned over the years.

The Job Creation and Wage Enhancement Act

• Small business incentives, capital gains cut and indexation, neutral cost recovery, risk assessment/cost-benefit analysis, strengthening of the Regulatory Flexibility Act and unfunded mandate reform to create jobs and raise worker wages.

The Common Sense Legal Reforms Act

• "Loser pays" laws, reasonable limits on punitive damages, and reform of product liability laws to stem the endless tide of litigation.

The Citizen Legislature Act

• A first-ever vote on term limits to replace career politicians with citizen legislators.

Further, we will instruct the House Budget Committee to report to the floor and we will work to enact additional budget savings, beyond the budget cuts specifically included in the legislation described above, to ensure that the federal budget deficit will be less than it would have been without the enactment of these bills.

Respecting the judgment of our fellow citizens as we seek their mandate for reform, we hereby pledge our names to this *Contract with America.*

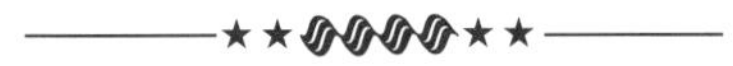

Reactionary Chic (1995)

LEWIS H. LAPHAM

The 104th Congress assembled in Washington on January 4 amid a dark murmur of sworn oaths about rescuing the captive spirit of American success from the dungeons of big government, and as I listened to the right-wing radio broadcasters sending their furious signals from their newly installed transmitters in the basement of the Capitol, I was struck by the resemblance between this season's Republican revolution and the old countercultural rebellion of thirty years ago. Once again the partisans of a romantic anti-politics intended a guerrilla raid on the wicked cities of death and time. Although nobody described the mission in precisely those words, the exuberant cheers welcoming Newt Gingrich to the Speaker's chair in the House of Representatives (loud cries of "Newt!" "Newt!" "Newt!") swelled with high purpose and zealous intent, the applause rising to the pitch of enthusiasm appropriate to the arrival of a hero or a saint. Here at last was the purifying wind from the South, the politician who had been touring the country both before and after the November election preaching the gospel of revolt, sacker of shibboleths and government spending programs come to lead the American people out of the deserts of the welfare state.

Under the circumstances and given the fierce expectations gathered on the Republican side of the aisle, Gingrich's inaugural address as Speaker of the House was surprisingly and uncharacteristically mild. Pronouncing the occasion "historic," he put aside for the moment his familiar persona as arrogant bully and humbly introduced himself as an adopted child and a common man. . . .

Like so much else about the Republican risorgimento, the political passion was attached to a preferred image rather than a plain or ambiguous fact, not to the Gingrich who had just delivered a conciliatory speech but to the Gingrich renowned for being nasty and brutish and short—the militant Gingrich blessed with a boll weevil's appetite for destruction who had ordered a skull of *Tyrannosaurus rex* as an ornament for his new office in the Longworth building.

It was the scornful Gingrich who had come to stand during his sixteen years in Congress as the shared symbol of resentment binding together the several parties of the disaffected right—the Catholic conservatives with the Jewish neoconservatives, the libertarians with the authoritarians, Pat Robertson's Christian Coalition with the disciples of David Duke. Clearly a man for

Copyright © 1995 by *Harper's Magazine*. All rights reserved. Reproduced from the March issue by special permission.

all grievances, Gingrich summed up (in his person as well as in his lectures on the decline and fall of American civilization) the whole of the conservative objection that since the dawn of the Reagan revolution in the early 1980s has comprised the course of required reading at the Heritage Foundation and the American Enterprise Institute. Over the last fifteen years I probably have read two or three thousand variations of the complaint—editorials in the *Wall Street Journal,* articles in *Commentary* and *The New Criterion,* the speeches of William Bennett and the columns of George Will, the soliloquies of Rush Limbaugh, the books in the line of frowning succession, from Allan Bloom's *The Closing of the American Mind* through George Gilder's *Wealth and Poverty,* Dinesh D'Souza's *Illiberal Education,* and Charles Murray's *Losing Ground,* etc.—but when I delete the repetitions and piece together what remains of a coherent narrative, the entire sum of the great suburban remonstrance fits within the span of a short fairy tale. As follows:

Once upon a time, before the awful misfortunes of the 1960s, America was a theme park constructed by nonunion labor along the lines of the Garden of Eden. But then something terrible happened, and a plague of guitarists descended upon the land. Spawned by the sexual confusions of the amoral news media, spores of Marxist ideology blew around in the wind, multiplied the powers of government, and impregnated the English departments at the Ivy League universities, which then gave birth to the monster of deconstruction that devoured the arts of learning. Pretty soon the trout began to die in Wyoming, and the next thing that anybody knew the nation's elementary schools had been debased, too many favors were being granted to women and blacks, federal bureaucrats were smothering capitalist entrepreneurs with the pillows of government regulation, prime-time television was broadcasting continuous footage from Sodom and Gomorrah, and the noble edifice of Western civilization had collapsed into the rubble of feminist prose.

The story somehow made more sense when set against the operatic backdrop of the Cold War, possibly because the familiar stage design recalled to mind the first act of *The Nutcracker Suite* when the toy soldier does battle with the army of horrific mice. The evil Soviet empire furnished the book and lyrics for the election campaigns of both Presidents Reagan and Bush, and for a few years it was possible to imagine that the fungus blighting the apple trees in the American orchard had something to do with the weather on the totalitarian steppe. The sudden tearing down of the Berlin Wall took everybody by surprise—the director of the CIA as well as the editors at *National Review*—and the tellers of the tale found themselves in pressing need of other antagonists to take the place of the grim but harmless ogre. The departure of the Russian trolls prompted a casting call for prospective bogeymen and likely villains. The Japanese couldn't play the part because they were lending the United States too much money; the Colombian drug lords were too few and too well connected in Miami; Manuel Noriega and Saddam Hussein failed the audition; the Arab oil cartel was broke; and the Chinese were busy making shirts for Ralph Lauren.

In the absence of enemies abroad, the protectors of the American dream began looking for inward signs of moral weakness rather than outward shows of military force; instead of examining the dossiers of foreign tyrants, they searched the local newspapers for flaws in the American character, and the surveillance satellites overhead Leipzig and Sevastopol were reassigned stations over metropolitan Detroit and the back lots of Hollywood studios. Within a matter of months the authorities rounded up as suspects a motley crowd of specific individuals and general categories of subversive behavior and opinion—black male adolescents as well as leftist English professors, multiculturalists of all descriptions, the liberal news media, the 1960s, the government in Washington, welfare mothers, homosexuals, drug criminals, performance artists, illegal immigrants. Some enemies of the state were easier to identify than others, but in all instances the tellers of the tale relied on images seen in dreams or on the network news rather than on the lessons of their own experience.

Believing themselves under assault from what they took to be the hostile forces of history, the heirs and servants of American oligarchy chose to cast themselves as rebels against "the system," as revolutionary idealists at odds with a world they never made. The pose was as lucicrous as it was familiar. Here were the people who owned most of what was worth owning in the country (the banks and business corporations as well as the television networks and most of the members of Congress) pretending that they were victims of a conspiracy raised against them by the institutions that they themselves controlled. What was even more extraordinary was the general likeness between their own revolutionary pretensions and the posturing of the 1960s counterculture that they so often and so loudly denounced. Although I had made occasional notes over a number of years about the similarities between the two camps of *soi-disant* revolutionaries, it wasn't until last October 19, during the course of a publisher's lunch at the Harvard Club in New York, that I fully appreciated the extent to which the reactionary chic of the 1990s mimics the set of 1960s attitudes memoralized by Tom Wolfe in the phrase "radical chic."

Sponsored by the Manhattan Institute (a think tank that funds rightist political theory) and meant to welcome the arrival of a new work of neoconservative doctrine (*Dictatorship of Virtue,* by Richard Bernstein), the lunch attracted a crowd of fifty individuals who for the most part were affiliated with publications and charitable foundations (among them *Forbes, Commentary,* and the John M. Olin Foundation) known for their allegiance to the miracle of finance capitalism. The intellectual tide last fall was running strongly in favor of more prisons and higher interest rates, and the mood in the dining room was smiling and complacent. The Democrats clearly were on their way to defeat in the November elections . . .

Listening to Bernstein talk about "the tyranny of the left" crushing the universities under the iron heel of "moralistic liberalism," I understood that I was revisiting a make-believe time and place not unlike the one that used to be known as the Age of Aquarius. . . . Thirty years ago it was "the conservative establishment" that was at fault, a conspiracy largely composed of university professors, government bureaucrats, and network television executives who couldn't play guitar and trembled at the sound of Dylan's harmonica. Now it is "the liberal establishment" that is at fault, a conspiracy largely composed of university professors, government bureaucrats, and network televison executives who can't quote freely from *The Federalist* and tremble before the wisdom of Alvin Toffler and Arianna Huffington. . . .

But to whom do they then direct their protests, and what names do they put on their placards and cast like stones into the teeth of time? How do they organize the sullen draft of their hastily recruited enemies into coherent legions and simple slogans?

As so often in moments of rhetorical crisis, it was the belligerent Gingrich who answered the questions with the phrase "discredited liberal establishment," which connoted both the absence of virtue and the presence of a monolith not unlike the old Soviet Union. Understood as a conspiracy of dunces, the "discredited liberal establishment" could be held responsible for all the mistakes that had been made with the planning of the American Eden. It was the "discredited liberal establishment" that opened the Pandora's box out of which sprang the three evil spirits that wrecked the economic and spiritual environment. As follows:

THE WELFARE STATE

To hear the story told on the fairways of the nation's better golf courses, the American welfare state is a foreign country that resembles Rwanda or Chiapas. Although administered as a protectorate by the U.S. government and supplied with an ungodly sum of money, the metaphysical terrain is so harsh, and the moral climate so poor, that we can never rescue the place, and we would all be better off if we just withdrew our army of Harvard sociologists and let the local rulers sign a treaty with the Baptist Church. If the line of argument is familiar, it is because it so closely parallels the argument advanced by the radical Sixties left in opposition to the Vietnam War. Why continue to underwrite an expensive and futile expedition doomed to certain failure?

The blurring of the distinctions between crime and race and moral behavior plays to the prejudice of an audience eager to believe the worst that can be said of people whom they would rather not know, and to the extent that the word "poor" can be made to serve as a synonym for "black," the big-city slums become alien nations on the wrong side of the cultural and economic frontiers. Gingrich is especially skillful at conveying his point in the unspoken subtext, and during last year's election campaign he often summarized the nation's troubles in a single sentence made to the measure of the six o'clock news: "It is impossible to maintain civilization with twelve-year-olds having babies, fifteen-year-olds killing each other, seventeen-year-olds dying of AIDS, and eighteen-year-olds receiving diplomas they cannot read."

What he had in mind (and what his audiences knew he had in mind) was the desolation of Harlem or East Los Angeles. . . .

Murray and Hernstein's book *The Bell Curve* argues that the excessive number of crimes committed by black people, as well as their poverty and lack of employment, can be attributed, more or less directly, to their low I.Q. ratings. The pseudoscientific speculaton adds a few more brush strokes to the standard portrait of black people as synonyms for catastrophe. The image deletes the greater part of the black presence in the country—the rise of the black middle class over the last thirty years, the successes achieved under the rules of affirmative action, the real ratios between impoverished white and black people (two white to one black), the dramatis personae appearing in television situation comedies, the complexion of the United States Army—but it is an image that serves the plotlines of a bedtime story about the wages of sin.[1] As conditions in the slums deteriorate, which they inevitably must as a consequence of their designation as enemy countries, the slums come to look just the way they are supposed to look in the suburban imagination. The burned-out buildings and the number of dead in the streets support the notion that crimes allied with poverty can be classified as individual moral problems rather than a common political problem. At long last and with a clear conscience, the governing and possessing classes can comfort themselves with the thought that poor people deserve what they get, that their misery is nobody's fault but their own. The bleak prospect confirms the Republican faith in prisons and serves as an excuse for imposing de facto martial law on a citizenry construed as a dangerous rabble. Even the sunniest neoconservative optimisms carry the threat of stern punishment, and the tone of the intolerant scold that appears in the speeches of Gingrich and Bennett (as well as in those of Irving Kristol, Charles Krauthammer, and Michael Novak) has been most succinctly expressed by *Washington Times* columnist Cal Thomas: "If we will not be constrained from within by the power of God, we must be constrained from without by the power of the State, acting as God's agent."

THE LIBERAL NEWS MEDIA

Among the partisans of the populist and suburban right, no article of faith is more devoutly held than the one about the feral cynicism of the metropolitan

1. In the proposal submitted to prospective publishers of *The Bell Curve,* Murray didn't mince words about the bigotry that he meant to confirm and sustain. "[There are] a huge number of well-meaning whites who fear that they are closet racists, and this book tells them they are not. It's going to make them feel better about things they already think but do not know how to say." *[Lapham's footnote]*

news media. Although nobody at the mall ever can remember seeing a journalist who didn't look like the boy or girl next door, the crowd sitting around the tables in the food court likes to think that the news comes to them from sallow-faced leftists who cut up the wholesome American moral fabric into patches of socialist propaganda and strips of pornographic film.

The supposition bears comparison to Jane Fonda's belief in the innocence of Ho Chi Minh. The manufacture and sale of the nation's news is the work of very large, very rich, and very timid corporations—the Washington Post Co., Fox Broadcasting, and Turner Network Television. The managers of the commercial television networks, like the publishers of large and prosperous newspapers, define news as anything that turns a profit, no matter how indecent the photograph or how inane the speeches, and they seldom take chances with any line of thought that fails to agree with what their audiences wish to see and hear.

The *Wall Street Journal,* probably the most widely read newspaper in the country, heavily favors the conservative side on any and all questions of public policy, and both the *Washington Post* and the *New York Times* fortify their op-ed pages with columnists who strongly defend the established order—William Safire and A. M. Rosenthal in the *Times,* Charles Krauthammer, George Will, and Richard Harwood in the *Post.* The vast bulk of the nation's talk-radio shows (commanding roughly 80 percent of the audience) reflect a conservative bias, and so do all but one or two of the television talk shows that deal with political topics on PBS, CNN, and CNBC. . . .

As proof of the absurdity implicit in the complaint about the liberal news media, I can think of no better demonstration than the one offered by Rush Limbaugh to the C-Span cameras in mid-December of last year at the Radisson Hotel in Baltimore. Ripe with self-congratulation and glistening under the lights like a Las Vegas lounge comic, Limbaugh appeared as the principal banquet speaker before an audience of newly elected Republican congressmen attending a three-day conference organized by the Heritage Foundation and meant to acquaint them with their tasks as saviors of the Republic. Eager and young and as freshly scrubbed as a cohort of college fraternity pledges, they laughed on cue at Limbaugh's sniggering jokes about President Clinton, condoms, and mushy-headed liberals. Limbaugh told them that in Washington they would find themselves surrounded on all sides by enemies, by newspaper columists and anchorpersons as treacherous as Cokie Roberts, who would cajole them with flattery and then betray them for the price of a cheap headline. "You are going to be hated," Limbaugh said. "Remember that you are targets. Remain hostile."

After twelve years of the administrations of Presidents Reagan and Bush, and two years of the neo-Republican presidency of Bill Clinton, the notion of Washington as a city somehow hostile to political conservatives of any kind was as preposterous as Limbaugh's posing as a victim of liberal tyranny and persecution. . . .

THE MARBLE RUIN OF AMERICAN CIVILIZATION

The last of the dearly beloved tales told around the campfires of the reactionary right is the one about the once sacred temples of American art and political philosophy turned into pornographic movie theaters by the same crew of guitarists and literary critics that poisoned the pure streams of Republican economic thought. The story has so many variants and inflections that it is hard to fix the precise tone of indignation (sometimes choleric, sometimes wistful or smug), but it invariably entails the assigning of subversive motives to the universities, the Hollywood movie companies, the popular-music business, the publishing industry, the Broadway stage, and the aforesaid liberal news media. Although the bad news sometimes takes grandiose forms—Irving Kristol informing the guests at conservative banquets that rock and roll music presents a greater threat to Western civilization than world Communism—for the most part it comes down to a complaint about a cheapened sense of aesthetics and school curricula debased by trendy (i.e., leftist) political alloys. Instead of reading Chaucer, students read the works of minor African poets; instead of going to see Shakespeare's plays, they gape at the sins of the flesh paraded through the courtyard of *Melrose Place.*

Again, as with so many of the other excited announcements emanating from the press offices of the right, the facts of the matter have been suborned by the preferred image. The mournful defenders of classical learning and Renaissance humanism ignore the point that the United States makes business its culture and its culture a business. Art is what sells, and education is what draws a paying crowd. . . . Children learn by example as well as by precept, and they have only to look at Times Square and Disneyland, or consider the triumphs of Roseanne or Ronald Perlman, to know that society bestows its rewards on the talent for figuring a market, not on a knowledge of Thucydides.

Nor is the popular culture by any means as immoral as it is dreamed of in the philosophy of the academic deans on the neoconservative and Christian right. As measured by its lists of best-selling books and long-running Broadway plays, as well as by its successful television comedies, sporting events, and popular songs, the American cultural enterprise (in 1995 as in 1895) is as irremediably conservative as it is relentlessly sentimental. During any Sunday's playing of the Top 40, the rap songs and heavy-metal rhythms show up at the bottom of the list, but as the countdown proceeds upward toward a kindly and forgiving providence, the music turns increasingly sweet and melodic. The lyrics almost always affirm the wisdom of a Rod McKuen poem or a speech by Peggy Noonan—love will last forever; our love will never die; you are the only one; my love for you is like a thousand points of light. . . .

The joke about the marble ruin is that American civilization never was much of a match for Periclean Greece. When the tellers of the sad Republican tale agree to take questions on the subject (reluctantly and usually in a hurry to leave the lecture hall), it turns out that the lost culture for which they grieve is the culture best expressed by the sensibility of the 1950s, the musical comedies of Rodgers and Hammerstein, the history of the world as told by Disney and Time Life, the list of great books that everybody owns but nobody has read.

Hoisted up by the cranes of populist bombast to the platforms of great expectation, the newly enskied 104th Congress confronts an ancient problem in socioeconomics—how does a wealthy and increasingly nervous plutocracy preserve its privileges while at the same time maintaining its reputation as an oppressed minority and a noble cause? . . .

What they have in hand is a dissenting rhetoric best suited to cries from the wilderness, a feeling for nostalgia, a faith in the claptrap futurism of Alvin and Heidi Toffler, the dubious economic theory inherited from the early days of the Reagan revolution, and an instinct for repression. Although convenient to pop quizzes and the nightly television news, the syllabus of glib answers bears comparison to the secrets of the universe packaged for sale in the supermarket press, and it isn't likely to prepare the class for the midterm examination. The electorate last fall was saying something about its fear and uneasiness, about jobs being sent overseas and the future (their own and that of their children) beginning to look like the receding objects seen through the wrong end of a telescope. For the last ten or fifteen years, the parties of the right have managed to convert the emotions rooted in economic anxiety into the politics of cultural anxiety, substituting the questions of moral conduct and deportment (the marble ruin, the heathen poor) for the more intractable ones about the division of the national spoils.

But the act is getting harder to perform, and the audience in the first ten rows has begun to figure out the trick with the coins and the scarves. Let the interest rate continue to rise, and who will applaud the futurist cant ("Parallel Transformations!" "Paradigms!" "Quality Management!") so dear to the heart of Speaker Gingrich? Let the chimera of a balanced budget drift off into the haze of what Washington calls "the out years," and people might begin to notice the difference between the big print and the small print in the Contract With America.

The paragraphs in large print postulate a return to an imaginary time and place in which the work of government could be performed by a volunteer fire department—a few hardy fellows cleaning up the village green after a winter storm, a benign judge adjudicating the occasional land dispute or divorce proceeding, a friendly county official awarding the rights of way for five hundred miles of railroad track in Kansas. The provisions in small print grant the propertied classes the freedom to acquire more property—a freedom expressed, among other ways, in the form of capital-gains tax breaks in the amount of $25 billion a year—and for everybody else, more police and more sermons.

50

A President Besieged

Rumors surfaced during the 1992 Democratic presidential primary that Governor Bill Clinton of Arkansas had had frequent sexual liaisons. At least two women made public accusations. One said he tried to coerce her into sexual relations, indicating possible harassment. During the primary, Clinton, a married man with a daughter, denied the first woman's charges, although after he won both the primary and the presidency, he admitted to a sexual relationship. The second woman, Paula Jones, filed a civil suit that, after the Supreme Court unexpectedly ruled that sitting presidents could be sued in civil court, persisted until a judge dismissed it for lack of evidence in Clinton's second term. The woman's lawyers quickly began mounting an appeal.

A larger problem arose for the president, however. In January 1994, Attorney General Janet Reno responded to pressure from congressional conservatives by asking a three-judge panel to appoint an independent counsel to investigate whether Clinton had a role in questionable Arkansas land dealings in the early 1980s. When Republicans criticized the initial counsel for not being aggressive enough, the judges replaced him, over Reno's objections, with Kenneth Starr, a former judge with close ties to the conservative Southern Republicans who came to power in Congress after the elections of 1994.

The position of independent counsel, or investigator, created by congressional statute to investigate the actions of President Richard Nixon during the Watergate crisis twenty years before, had been used occasionally since then to investigate top officials, including Ronald Reagan over illegal arms shipments to Iran and Nicaragua. But the position had never been used to inquire into what officials did before they became Constitutional officers. The Starr inquiry into "Whitewater," as the Arkansas land affair was called, changed that, making previous behavior fair game. Moreover, Starr aggressively investigated matters not bearing directly on Whitewater, including whether a White House aide really committed suicide; whether Clinton's wife, Hillary, profited from insider information on a commodities trade;

whether White House travel employees were inappropriately dismissed; how FBI files turned up at the White House; and, especially, whether Clinton had sex with a young White House intern, Monica Lewinsky. On this last point, Starr obtained evidence by secretly recording conversations between Lewinsky and a friend. The president, after first denying having sex with Lewinsky, eventually acknowledged that he had.

In 1998 Starr submitted a report to Congress that summarized his key findings. The report consisted mainly of details about Clinton's sexual relations with his intern, together with a list of actions that, in Starr's view, were grounds for impeachment. The concluding section of the Starr report appears below, along with the statement issued by President Clinton's legal counsel that summarizes the White House perspective on the investigation. There were two intriguing constants throughout the Starr investigation. First, the public, although critical of Clinton's personal behavior, consistently approved his performance as president by wide margins. The standing of Hillary Rodham Clinton, whom Clinton married in 1978 and who played a vital role in his political successes, was even higher. Secondly, the president's popularity ratings were consistently higher than those of Kenneth Starr himself, who became one of the most disliked individuals in public life. Interestingly, several of Clinton's bitterest Republican critics, threatened with public exposure, admitted to extramarital sexual dalliances of their own. One of these was Representative Henry Hyde of Illinois, chair of the House Judiciary Committee that would decide whether to recommend impeachment. Hyde's committee did recommend impeachment, and the full House, on a party-line vote, impeached the president. The Senate then voted not to convict.

Kenneth Starr was born in Vernon, Texas, in 1946, the son of a fundamentalist Church of Christ minister. Starr attended Harding College, a Church of Christ institution, and George Washington University. He received a law degree from Duke in 1973, clerked for Chief Justice Warren Burger, and joined the Justice Department in the first Reagan administration. At Justice, Starr supported organized prayer in schools and opposed busing to achieve racial balance. In 1983 Reagan named Starr to the U.S. Court of Appeals, the youngest person ever appointed. Judge Starr opposed affirmative action but supported making flag-burning unconstitutional and requiring parental notification for abortions for minors. In 1989 Starr resigned from the bench to become George Bush's solicitor general. He practiced law privately from Clinton's election until his appointment as independent investigator.

William Jefferson (Bill) Clinton was born in Hope, Arkansas, in 1946. He attended Georgetown and Oxford Universities and took a law degree from Yale in 1973. Returning to Arkansas in 1973 to teach and practice law, Clinton was elected attorney general in 1977 and to the governorship on four occasions, serving as governor for twelve years. A political moderate, Clinton was instrumental in establishing the Democratic Leadership Council as a centrist force in the Democratic party. He hewed to a generally moderate line in winning the presidential elections of 1992 and 1996 and in serving as president. He successfully fought for liberal trade policies over the objections of organized labor, for example, and signed legislation that dramatically curtailed federal welfare subsidies. His reputation as a liberal came chiefly from his opposition to Republican efforts to cut aid to education, cut environmental regulations, and cut taxes in the teeth of a shaky social security system. A significant part of his second term was virtually consumed by the Lewinsky affair, which Democratic critics believed was by Republican design.

Questions to Consider. Why did Starr's report to Congress deal exclusively with the Lewinsky affair, even though most of the investigative work since 1994 focused on other issues? Which acts listed by Starr as potentially impeachable seem the most significant to you? Which acts seem least important? Democrats argued that lying under oath about sex was not the same as using the machinery of government to try to subvert the political process, as Richard Nixon had done. How persuasive was this argument? How valid does Clinton's legal rejoinder to Starr seem? Was this line of defense the most appropriate one the president could have taken?

Report to Congress (1998)

KENNETH STARR

As required by Section 595(c) of Title 28 of the United States Code, the Office of the Independent Counsel ("OIC" or "Office") hereby submits substantial and credible information that President William Jefferson Clinton committed acts that may constitute grounds for an impeachment.

The information reveals that President Clinton:

- lied under oath at a civil deposition while he was a defendant in a sexual harassment lawsuit;
- lied under oath to a grand jury;
- attempted to influence the testimony of a potential witness [Monica Lewinsky] who had direct knowledge of facts that would reveal the falsity of his deposition testimony;
- attempted to obstruct justice by facilitating a witness's [Monica Lewinsky] plan to refuse to comply with a subpoena;

The blunderbuss of impeachment overshooting its target. As suggested by this Tony Auth cartoon of September 23, 1998, the combination of Bill Clinton and the impeachment process brought a glee to American caricaturists that they had not enjoyed since the heyday of Richard Nixon, their all-time favorite target, and they exploited it to the fullest. (Auth © 1998 The Philadelphia Inquirer. Reprinted with permission of UNIVERSAL PRESS SYNDICATE. All rights reserved.)

- attempted to obstruct justice by encouraging a witness [Monica Lewinsky] to file an affidavit that the President knew would be false, and then by making use of that false affidavit at his own deposition;
- lied to potential grand jury witnesses, knowing that they would repeat those lies before the grand jury; and
- engaged in a pattern of conduct that was inconsistent with his constitutional duty to faithfully execute the laws.

The evidence shows that these acts, and others, were part of a pattern that began as an effort to prevent the disclosure of information about the President's relationship with a former White House intern and employee, Monica S. Lewinsky, and continued as an effort to prevent the information from being disclosed in an ongoing criminal investigation.

From *The New York Times,* September 12, 1998.

White House Response to the Starr Report (1998)

CONCLUSION

It has come down to this.

After four years, scores of FBI agents, hundreds of subpoenas, thousands of documents, and tens of millions of dollars. After hiring lawyers, accountants, IRS agents, outside consultants, law professors, personal counsel, ethics advisers, and a professional public relations expert. After impaneling grand juries and leasing office space in three jurisdictions, and investigating virtually every aspect of the President's business, financial, political, official and, ultimately, personal life, the Office of Independent Counsel has presented to the House a Referral that no prosecutor would present to any jury.

The President has admitted he had an improper relationship with Ms. Lewinsky. He has apologized. The wrongfulness of that relationship is not in dispute. And yet that relationship is the relentless focus of virtually every page of the OIC's Referral.

In 445 pages, the Referral mentions Whitewater, the failed land deal which originated its investigation, twice. It never once mentions other issues it has been investigating for years—matters concerning the firing of employees of the White House travel office and the controversy surrounding the FBI files. By contrast, the issue of sex is mentioned more than 500 times, in the most graphic, salacious and gratuitous manner.

The Office of Independent Counsel is asking the House of Representatives to undertake its most solemn and consequential process short of declaring war; to remove a duly, freely and fairly elected President of the United States because he had—as he had admitted—an improper, illicit relationship outside of his marriage. Having such a relationship is wrong. Trying to keep such a relationship private, while understandable, is wrong. But such acts do not even approach the Constitutional test of impeachment—"treason, bribery, or other high crimes and misdemeanors."

The founders were wise to set such a high standard, and were wise to vest this awesome authority in the hands of the most democratic and accountable branch of our Government, and not in the hands of unaccountable prosecutors.

We have sought in this Initial Response to begin the process of rebutting the OIC's charges against the President—charges legal experts have said would not even be brought against a private citizen. The President did not commit perjury. He did not obstruct justice. He did not tamper with witnesses. And he did not abuse the power of the office of the Presidency.

From *The New York Times*, September 13, 1998.